PAUL HARVA

Paul Harvard ha
musical director
winning product.
Theatre.

He is a hugely experienced trainer of actors. Currently he is
the Course Leader for the BA Acting at the London College
of Music. Prior to working at LCM he lectured at many of the
other leading drama schools in the UK – notably the Urdang
Academy where he was Head of Musical Theatre for four
years and Rose Bruford where he was Head of Third Year. He
has also taught at Arts Educational, the Drama Centre,
Guildford School of Acting, Trinity Laban, Italia Conti and
Webber Douglas.

Paul is the author of *Acting Through Song: Techniques and
Exercises for Musical-Theatre Actors*, also published by Nick
Hern Books. Paul's approaches to acting through song are
now recognised internationally and he regularly travels abroad
to deliver masterclasses and lectures based on his book.

THE GOOD AUDITION GUIDES

AUDITION SONGS
by Paul Harvard

CONTEMPORARY DUOLOGUES
edited by Trilby James

CLASSICAL MONOLOGUES
edited by Marina Caldarone

CONTEMPORARY MONOLOGUES
edited by Trilby James

CONTEMPORARY MONOLOGUES FOR TEENAGERS
edited by Trilby James

SHAKESPEARE MONOLOGUES
edited by Luke Dixon

SHAKESPEARE MONOLOGUES FOR YOUNG PEOPLE
edited by Luke Dixon

The Good Audition Guides

AUDITION SONGS
FOR WOMEN

PAUL HARVARD

NICK HERN BOOKS
London
www.nickhernbooks.co.uk

A NICK HERN BOOK

The Good Audition Guides:
Audition Songs for Women
First published in Great Britain in 2020
by Nick Hern Books Limited
The Glasshouse, 49a Goldhawk Road, London W12 8QP

Designed and typeset by Nick Hern Books, London
Printed and bound by Ashford Colour Press, Gosport,
Hampshire

A CIP catalogue record for this book
is available from the British Library

ISBN 978 1 84842 457 9

MIX
Paper from
responsible sources
FSC
www.fsc.org FSC® C011748

Contents

Part One: The Knowledge

About This Book   11

The Terminology   23

The Exercises   33

The Audition   65

Part Two: The Songs

Soprano/Mezzosoprano

CLASSICAL MUSICAL THEATRE (1925–65)

'Can't Help Lovin' Dat Man'
    from *Show Boat*   90

'Dear Friend'
    from *She Loves Me*   95

'I Have Confidence'
    from *The Sound of Music*   101

'Many a New Day'
    from *Oklahoma!*   106

'Mister Snow'
    from *Carousel*   110

'Much More'
    from *The Fantasticks*   114

'My Lord and Master'
    from *The King and I*   119

CONTEMPORARY MUSICAL–THEATRE BALLADS (Post-1965)

'Home'
    from *Beauty and the Beast*   124

'How Could I Ever Know'
    from *The Secret Garden*   130

6

'Your Daddy's Son'
   from *Ragtime*   136

'Not a Day Goes By'
   from *Merrily We Roll Along*   141

'Patterns'
   from *Baby*   147

'When I Look at You'
   from *The Scarlet Pimpernel*   152

'If I Could'
   from *The Hired Man*   158

'Take Me to the World'
   from *Evening Primrose*   164

CONTEMPORARY MUSICAL-THEATRE UP-TEMPO (Post-1965)

'Crossword Puzzle'
   from *Starting Here, Starting Now*   169

'The Glamorous Life'
   from *A Little Night Music*   174

'Greenfinch and Linnett Bird'
   from *Sweeney Todd*   181

'No Man Left for Me'
   from *The Will Rogers Follies*   186

'So Many People'
   from *Saturday Night*   191

COMEDY/CHARACTER SONGS

'I Need a Fling'
   from *Lend Me a Tenor*   196

'The Girl in 14G'   200

'Glitter and be Gay'
   from *Candide*   205

'I Know Things Now'
   from *Into the Woods*   210

'Miss Byrd'
    from *Closer Than Ever*   215

Alto

CLASSICAL MUSICAL THEATRE (1925–65)

'Aldonza'
    from *Man of La Mancha*   222

'The Boy Next Door'
    from *Meet Me in St. Louis*   229

'Far from the Home I Love'
    from *Fiddler on the Roof*   233

'I Get a Kick Out of You'
    from *Anything Goes*   238

'Just You Wait'
    from *My Fair Lady*   243

CONTEMPORARY MUSICAL-THEATRE BALLADS (Post-1965)

'Breathe'
    from *In the Heights*   248

'I'm Here'
    from *The Color Purple*   254

'Lying There'
    from *Edges*   261

'Now That I've Seen Her'
    from *Miss Saigon*   267

'Out of Love'
    from *Adventures in Love*   273

'Wait a Bit'
    from *Just So*   278

'Where is the Warmth?'
    from *The Baker's Wife*   284

'Woman'
    from *The Pirate Queen*   290

8

CONTEMPORARY MUSICAL–THEATRE UP–TEMPO (Post-1965)

'Astonishing'
from *Little Women*　296

'Everything Else'
from *Next to Normal*　302

'Just One Step'
from *Songs for a New World*　307

'The Life I Never Led'
from *Sister Act*　313

'Pulled'
from *The Addams Family*　318

'The Spark of Creation'
from *Children of Eden*　323

'Waiting for Life'
from *Once on This Island*　329

COMEDY/CHARACTER SONGS

'Accident Prone'　334

'In Short'
from *Edges*　340

'Moments in the Woods'
from *Into the Woods*　346

'Notice Me, Horton'
from *Seussical*　354

'Times Like This'
from *Lucky Stiff*　359

PART ONE:
THE KNOWLEDGE

About This Book

WHO IS IT FOR?

If you need to sing in an audition, then this book is for you. It is an easy-to-use, accessible resource that will help you discover the perfect song choice – no matter what your audition needs. You might be applying for a vocational musical-theatre course, or a place on a performing-arts degree. If so, this book will help you find a first-rate, distinctive song that shows off your voice and reveals your full potential. Or you might have an audition for an acting programme. If singing is not your first skill, you will want to find a song that sits comfortably in your range – *that you feel confident with* – but that also highlights your strengths as an actor. The songs you need are identified inside. The book can assist you if you are auditioning for a school production, or for a youth drama group – enabling you to find the song you need to land the role you want. Finally, this book is an invaluable tool if you are already in vocational training, or are a professional actor. It will help you broaden your understanding of the musical-theatre repertoire so you can continuously develop your portfolio of songs, and is a great resource when you need to find the right material for a last-minute casting.

WHAT IS INSIDE?

The book explores fifty songs that have been carefully selected because they work particularly well in audition. For each song there is a detailed, bespoke self-rehearsal guide. These guides contain the sort of information you would receive from sessions with a vocal coach and a director – providing you with the professional expertise and technical advice you need to deliver a high-quality performance. Each guide is like a singing lesson and an acting class rolled into one.

The self-rehearsal guides begin by describing what are commonly known as the given circumstances of the song (see p. 23). They outline how it fits into the narrative arc of the musical, summarise what has happened previously, and provide key information about character and setting. The lyric of the song is then analysed as a piece of dramatic text, helping you develop a clear understanding of the writer's intentions. Potential objectives and actions (see pp. 25–26) are discussed to open up possibilities for the sort of acting choices you might play. The pivotal dramatic moments of the song, called events, are pinpointed where appropriate – and acting tips are provided to help you shape your overall performance.

Alongside the investigation of the acting content, the self-rehearsal guides explore how to tackle the songs from both a musical and vocal perspective. A recommended recording of the song is suggested for you to listen to that can help you learn the music accurately and understand the correct vocal style. This is particularly useful if you don't have access to a singing teacher who can help you learn the music. The vocal range and original key signature of the song are identified, and your choice of accent is discussed. At times, cuts are also suggested, as you will need to shorten some songs for audition. Finally, the guides offer advice on how to deliver the songs vocally and musically. For those looking to deliver a more advanced-level performance, perhaps for a drama-school audition or a professional casting, the technical set-ups and vocal delivery required for the song are examined. These provide an overview of the musculature you should use to ensure your vocal performance is healthy, repeatable, dynamic and stylistically accurate. The technical language in this book is heavily reliant on the work of Jo Estill, the American voice specialist, who died in 2010. The Estill method is a very useful system because it is anatomically specific. It allows you to understand, feel and recreate the precise muscular patterning needed to achieve the different sounds used in musical theatre. In particular, this book frequently references Estill's work on voice qualities (see pp. 28–31), such as Twang and Belt. Advice is also given on musical decisions, such as dynamics and phrasing.

At the end of each guide you will find directions to a suggested website where you can purchase the correct sheet music for the song, as, for copyright reasons, the music and lyrics can't be included in this book.

ADDITIONAL SUPPORT

To support the specific detail of the self-rehearsal guides, at the beginning of the book there are three extended chapters that contain overarching advice that will help you to prepare, rehearse and perform any of the songs. The first chapter provides definitions for the acting, singing and musical terminology you will encounter in the book. The second contains a series of easy-to-follow acting and singing exercises that will help you to improve your vocal delivery, and to produce a truthful and spontaneous performance of the lyric. The final chapter provides advice about audition technique. It deals with issues like making a good impression when entering the room, communicating musical instructions to the pianist, singing to a panel, and responding to redirection.

CHOOSING A SONG THAT SUITS YOUR VOCAL RANGE

The first factor you need to consider when choosing a song for any audition is: 'Does it suit my vocal range?' The song material in this book is divided into two sections: Soprano/Mezzosoprano and Alto. The first section is generally for women with higher voices, the second for those who mainly have a deeper sound. These terms – Soprano, Mezzosoprano and Alto – categorise a singer not only by their pitch range, but also reflect where their voice has the best timbre, where it sits most comfortably and resonantly. Modern vocal training allows all singers to expand their upper ranges through exercise. So as an alto, for example, you may find you are able to sing higher than some mezzosopranos – but are still classed as an alto because your voice sounds best in a lower register.

Because of these anomalies, you may find that, if you are an alto, some of the songs on the Soprano/Mezzosoprano list may also work for you. Equally, if you usually sing soprano, you might find songs on the Alto list that you can use. Therefore, to aid you with your decision-making, each song has its precise vocal range outlined in the self-rehearsal guide. If you don't know your own vocal range, it is worth asking a friend or teacher who plays the piano to check this with you. Typical vocal ranges for the three voice types are as follows:

Soprano: C4 to C6
(middle C to two octaves above middle C)

Mezzosoprano: A3 to A5
(the A below middle C to the A an octave-and-a-half above middle C)

Alto: F3 to F5
(the F below middle C to the F an octave-and-a-half above middle C)

TRANSPOSING SONGS

Sometimes actors consider transposing a song into a lower key if it is too high for them. Whilst many sheet-music websites – which sell the music you will need for your audition – offer this facility, it is not something to be recommended. An experienced audition panel – who will know the repertoire well – are able to tell if you are not singing your song in its usual key. If you change the key signature of a song so you don't have to sing the high G, they will assume it is because you can't. You may as well enter the audition with a placard saying: 'I can't sing above an F♯!' Therefore you are well-advised to choose a song you can deliver in the original key – which is indicated in the self-rehearsal guides – in the vast majority of circumstances.

A final point to consider when thinking about range is ensuring that your chosen piece doesn't stretch you to breaking point. For a song to be advisable you need to be able hit the top note when you are nervous, feeling a bit off-colour, and at nine o'clock in the morning. Don't select a song if you can only deliver the big belt when you are feeling on top form, have your fingers crossed, and the wind is blowing from the south-west!

CHOOSING A SONG THAT SUITS YOUR CASTING TYPE

Whilst it is essential to choose a song that sits within your vocal range, it is also highly advantageous to pick material that reflects your 'casting type'. This term refers to the type of characters that you would most likely be cast as professionally – because they are of a similar age, physicality, personality and life experience to yourself. Traditionally your casting type would also have been defined by ethnicity, but with the advent of 'colour-blind' or 'non-traditional' casting, many contemporary productions commendably choose to ignore the ethnicity of the actors in stories in which race is not germane. An increasing number of productions are also casting 'gender-blind', and although this is to be much encouraged in other circumstances, songs written for men have not been included in this book due to the technical difficulties presented by differences in the male/female vocal range. However, if you are particularly interested in singing a song originally written for the male voice, you can find some great material in the companion book *Audition Songs for Men*.

Reflecting your casting type in your song choice is particularly important in professional castings, as it allows the audition panel to sense whether you might be suitable for a particular role. If you are auditioning for *Les Misérables*, do they see you as a Cosette or an Éponine? If you have a casting for *Grease*, are you right for Sandy or for Rizzo? Of course, if you are applying for a place at a drama school, you will not be auditioning for a specific role, but these questions are still valid. If you choose a song that suits your casting type it will give you the best opportunity to show the tutors your potential, and reveal that you have an understanding of yourself as a developing actor.

To help you decide which of the songs in this book might suit you best, look at the 'Choose this song if' section at the top of each self-rehearsal guide, which provides an overview of the character and helps you to understand quickly if it may work for you.

UNDERSTANDING YOUR CASTING

When I teach in drama schools, I often lead Professional Development classes for students who are preparing to enter the industry. A question I am regularly asked by final-year students is: 'What is my casting?' In helping them to answer this query I encourage them to look at the roles they have performed before, particularly those they felt they did well in, and to try and identify any commonalities they notice about those characters. If you have played parts before then try this task for yourself: you may find it gives you a clearer comprehension of your casting type.

If you have not had much previous performance experience, another way to gain an insight into your likely casting is to consider how you relate to some of the archetypes we see in plays and films. Are you the romantic lead, the villain, or the sidekick? Would you play the soldier or the solicitor? The chimney sweep or the aristocrat? You should also consider whether you look your age, or could be cast as someone younger or older. Decide if you have a modern, contemporary appearance that would work for musicals like *Spring Awakening* or *Hamilton*, or whether your style and demeanour is more suitable for period pieces like *Carousel* or *My Fair Lady*. You may be right for both – depending on how you choose to behave, dress and style your hair. These are all factors in understanding what type of material may suit you.

But perhaps the best way to understand your casting type is to ask some close friends, whose opinions you trust, how you come across in day-to-day life. Choose people who you think will not only be honest, but also sensitive. It can be challenging to hear how you come across to others, particularly if the answers are not entirely flattering and were not what you were expecting. Get them to answer the following questions about you, and encourage them to be as frank as possible:

- How old do you look? (Get them to express this in range of five years, for example: 15 to 20, or 33 to 38).

- If they were to choose five adjectives to describe the way you come across, what would they be? (For example: inquisitive, shy, flirtatious, flamboyant, confrontational.)

- If they were to name three professions you could convincingly play, what would they be? (For example: a fashion model, an estate agent, a doctor.)

After this exercise you should have a much clearer understanding of your casting type – or what is sometimes called your 'unique selling point' (USP) – and therefore a better sense of what songs might work for you.

CHOOSING A SONG THAT IS THE APPROPRIATE MUSICAL STYLE

If you are auditioning for a particular production, it is beneficial to select material that has a similar style to the show you are trying out for. This helps the panel determine whether you can sing and act in an appropriate manner for that particular score. To aid your understanding of which composers and lyricists wrote in a similar stylistic vein, outlined below are some of the major sub-genres of musical theatre featured in this book, their characteristics, and the composers and lyricists who wrote in that particular style. To aid you, the sub-genre of musical theatre that each song belongs to is indicated in the self-rehearsal guides.

Note: If you are auditioning for a drama school, rather than for a production, you will not normally need to restrict yourself to a particular style of musical theatre – unless this is specified in the school's audition requirements. In auditions for vocational courses, you are normally best advised to choose any musical-theatre song that most suits your voice and personality.

MUSICAL COMEDY

When: The era of musical comedy was between approximately 1925 and 1943.

Key Composers/Lyricists: Cole Porter, Irving Berlin, Richard Rodgers and Lorenz Hart, Jerome Kern and Oscar Hammerstein II, Harry Warren, Kurt Weill, and the Gershwin brothers.

Acting Style: Musical comedy had its roots in the bawdy world of vaudeville and burlesque and, as a result, these first American musicals were often little more than a series of popular songs, comic sketches and dances strung together by a tenuous storyline. The frothy, light-hearted writing of this period was symptomatic of the prevailing social circumstances of the time, as it offered audiences of the 1920s and '30s some escape from their memories of the First World War and the harsh realities of the Great Depression. Because it is generally upbeat, to act this material well you need to find real pleasure in the linguistic ingenuity of lyricists like Cole Porter and Lorenz Hart. You should really taste the rhythms and rhymes in your mouth, so the panel can share in the wit and brilliance of the lyrics. Your performance usually needs to be positive, uplifting, and laced with a sense of cheek and fun.

Musical Style: The songs of this period tended to be heavily influenced by jazz, and many of them have gone on to become famous 'standards'. They therefore lend themselves to a jazz singer's interpretative skills, such as the ability to back-phrase, to 'bend' the pitch of notes, and to sing quartertones (a note that lies between two notes on a piano). In the terminology of singing teacher Jo Estill (see pp. 28–31), musical comedy requires a generous usage of the Speech and Twang voice qualities, with some Belt at the end of the big show-stopping numbers. The use of Sob and Cry qualities tends to be limited to the romantic ballads.

BOOK MUSICALS: THE 'GOLDEN AGE'

When: The 'Golden Age' of musical theatre can be defined as being between approximately 1943 and 1965. Some landmark 'book musicals', such as *Show Boat* and *Porgy and Bess*, came before this period, but the landscape of musical theatre is commonly perceived to have been revolutionised with the opening of *Oklahoma!* in 1943.

Key Composers/Lyricists: Richard Rodgers and Oscar Hammerstein II, Alan Jay Lerner and Frederick Loewe, Jerry Bock and Sheldon Harnick, Leonard Bernstein, Jule Styne and Frank Loesser.

Acting Style: Book musicals, which were initially pioneered by lyricist Oscar Hammerstein II, tackled more serious dramatic material than was the case in musical comedy. The songs in book musicals were written to emerge organically out of the scene and to further the plot. In some senses the book musical is the genre's equivalent of psychological realism – Stanislavsky's term for the believable representation of life on the stage. Although you could argue that musicals are not a realistic style of performance – because the characters are singing when they wouldn't do so in life – a key to the dramaturgy of a book musical is that the characters are not *aware* they are singing. In their heads, they are engaging in an ordinary conversation, or are voicing aloud their internal thoughts. The audience just hears these words as sung text, rather than a spoken scene or soliloquy. So when you act this type of song, your aim is to be as truthful and believable as possible, and to perform a series of actions that are psychologically coherent for the character. The acting style is what we might call 'musical realism'.

Musical Style: The vocal set-up required for the work of
Rodgers and Hammerstein, Lerner and Loewe, and Bock and
Harnick is known as 'legit' singing. Legit singing is similar to
a classical set-up; it can require you to be able to sing long
phrases with a legato line and a lowered larynx. In Estill
terms, a legit set-up makes considerable use of Cry and Sob
qualities. In the book musicals penned by these writing teams,
Speech quality is usually confined to the verses and pre-
choruses at the beginning of songs. On the contrary, the
musical style of Bernstein, Styne and Loesser had a strong
connection with jazz and big-band music, so a legit style is
less relevant. Speech, Twang and Belt qualities are more
appropriate for these jazz-based composers, and in the
specific case of Bernstein, Opera quality as well.

CONCEPT MUSICALS

When: Concept musicals were most prevalent in American
and British musical theatre from roughly 1960 to 1990.

Key Composers/Lyricists: John Kander and Fred Ebb, Stephen
Sondheim, and Andrew Lloyd Webber.

Acting Style: From the beginning of the 1960s, musical-theatre
writers began to deconstruct the formula of the integrated
musical play established by Hammerstein – in which the songs
and dances emerged organically out of the plot and furthered
the action. In musicals like Stephen Sondheim's *Company* and
the film version of Kander and Ebb's *Cabaret*, the use of song
was akin to the ideas of German playwright and director
Bertolt Brecht. The songs, rather than moving the story
forward, cut across it and commented upon it. To act songs
from concept musicals, you therefore not only need to
understand and be able to play the character's objectives, you
must have the skills to interpret and communicate the themes
and/or politics of the writing. To do this successfully, concept
musicals often require the use of 'Epic' acting techniques, such
as direct address (see p. 28), narration and the use of a
heightened vocal and physical transformation.

Musical Style: Concept musicals varied greatly in their compositional styles during that thirty-year period, to an extent that it is nearly impossible to define a universal vocal style that would be appropriate. What can be agreed is that Speech quality became ever more vital, as the ability to communicate the themes articulated in the lyric often became more important than the beauty of the singing voice – particularly with the work of Sondheim.

CONTEMPORARY MUSICAL THEATRE

When: From 1965 to the present day.

Key Composers/Lyricists: Andrew Lloyd Webber, Alain Boublil and Claude-Michel Schönberg, Lin-Manuel Miranda, Jason Robert Brown, Andrew Lippa, Jeanine Tesori, Stephen Flaherty and Lynn Ahrens, Stephen Schwartz, Richard Maltby Jr. and David Shire, Alan Menken, Benj Pasek and Justin Paul, William Finn, Elton John, Cy Coleman, and Howard Goodall.

Acting Style: The performance style of contemporary musicals is now very broad. In the 1980s and 1990s there was a trend for productions that became known as 'mega-musicals', shows that were largely sung-through with minimal or no dialogue – and that had lavish production values. But in the last twenty years you will also find shows that are written in traditional book-musical format, like *Wicked* and *In the Heights*, and concept musicals, like *The Last Five Years* and *Spring Awakening*. As such, it is impossible to define a single acting style that is appropriate for contemporary musical theatre – the approach required can only be defined by looking at the form of a particular musical.

Musical Style: From the late 1960s there has been a gradual shift in the musical DNA of Broadway and West End musicals, in that the majority of scores are now influenced by pop or rock music – rather than jazz. (Shows written after 1980 that still use jazz music as their basis, such as Lippa's

The Wild Party and Flaherty and Ahrens's *Ragtime*, tend to be period pieces.) When working on contemporary, pop-based musical-theatre songs, Speech and Twang qualities are the staple set-ups, with Belt used for moments of passion. Cry is also used, though less frequently. Alongside scores where the pop idiom is clear are other musicals that require a different vocal set-up – musicals that have sometimes been classed, a little unkindly perhaps, as 'poperetta'. In musicals like *Les Misérables* and *The Phantom of the Opera*, the musical structures are those of pop songs, but in performance they are often delivered with a vocal set-up that sounds something like classical singing (though rarely what Estill would define as an Opera quality). As a contemporary version of legit singing, this set-up is based around a Speech quality, but is modified to include a lowered larynx, which makes it sound more classical.

The Terminology

ACTING TERMINOLOGY

In order to take best advantage of the advice and exercises in this book, you will need to understand some of the key concepts and terminology relating to performance that are used. Below is a glossary of the most important, beginning with those related to acting.

Given Circumstances

This term, from Russian practitioner Konstantin Stanislavsky, refers to the environmental and societal conditions of a song or scene that influence the actions and behaviour of the character. The given circumstances are derived by answering fundamental questions from the character's perspective, such as: Who am I? Where am I? When is it? What has happened previously?

When working on a full-length production, the answers to these questions are usually ascertained by deriving information through an analysis of the entire script, from historical and social research, and by informed, imaginative choices where no definite answer is possible from the first two approaches. In this book, the elements of the given circumstances that are most important to the delivery of the song are those outlined. On occasion, when the given circumstances of the song as they exist in the musical are unhelpful – or there are none, because the song is from a revue show without a through-narrative – then a set of given circumstances have been invented to make the song easier for you to perform in an audition context.

Objectives

An objective is what the character wants. For example, during 'Climb Ev'ry Mountain' from *The Sound of Music*, the Mother Abbess's objective (what she wants) is: to help Maria find the courage to go out and face her problems. In 'I'd Give My Life for You' from *Miss Saigon*, Kim, whose son Tam is the child of an American GI, is determined that her offspring will be raised in America. Her objective in this song is: to get Tam to understand that she will do whatever it takes to ensure he has a better life.

Units

A unit is a section of dramatic text. Different practitioners divide a text into units in different ways. In my own practice, particularly with song lyrics, I have always found it most useful to start a fresh unit each time the character has a new objective. Here is an example of uniting from the song 'Stay with Me' from *Into the Woods* by Stephen Sondheim:

UNIT 1

What did I clearly say?
Children should listen.

What were you not to do?
Children must see –

And learn.

Why could you not obey?
Children should listen.
What have I been to you?
What would you have me be?
Handsome like a prince?

UNIT 2

Ah, but I am old.
I am ugly.
I embarrass you.

You are ashamed of me.

You are ashamed.
You don't understand.

This song is sung by the mean and controlling Witch to her ward Rapunzel, when she discovers she has been allowing the Prince to visit her in the tower. In the first unit, her objective is: to make Rapunzel fear the consequences of disobeying her. During the second, which starts after the word 'prince', her new objective is: to get Rapunzel to pity her.

Trying to act a lyric in its entirety can sometimes be a daunting challenge, but dividing a song into units in this way – and by knowing what the character is trying to achieve in each section – makes it much easier to perform. As Stanislavsky famously suggested, it is like breaking a cooked turkey into pieces to allow you to consume it piece by piece, rather than trying to eat the whole thing at once.

Actioning

If an objective is what the character wants, then an action is the means they use to get what they want. An action always takes the form of a transitive verb. In the process known as actioning, which was first developed by the American acting teacher Stella Adler, you assign a different transitive verb to each sentence of the text. This system can help you find variety and specificity in your performance, making it more engaging to watch. An action should always help you achieve your objective and should fit into the following format:

I [action] you.

For example, in the title song from *Cabaret*, the objective of Sally Bowles is: to convince the audience to live life to the full. If you were playing Sally, actions you could play on the clientele of the club might include: I uplift you, I entertain you, I inspire you, I amuse you, I thrill you.

When the character is singing onstage alone, the format of actions becomes as follows; if they are singing to themselves:

I [action] myself.

Or if they are singing to a higher power such as Fate:

I [action] Fate.

During the song 'What Makes Me Love Him?' from *The Apple Tree*, Eve's objective is to make sense of her love for Adam. An actress performing this song might use actions such as: I analyse myself, I query myself, I hustle myself, I criticise myself, I mock myself.

Circles of Attention

Your primary function as an actor is as a storyteller. Making good use of what are called 'circles of attention' can help clarify the narrative of your song and ensure your choices make logical sense to the audience or audition panel. This term was originated by Stanislavsky, and refers to the outer limit of where your focus and awareness is placed at any one time. There are three circles of attention. In the first circle, you focus very tightly on yourself. So if you are working in this circle of attention you might be looking at part of your own body, such as your hands, or something extremely close to you, like the floor beneath your feet. When we are remembering something, or dissecting a problem, we often look in the first circle, as our eyes tend to focus on points very close to us. When you are working in the second circle, you are looking at something within the playing space – or in this case, the audition room. If you are looking at the panel, for example, you would be working in the second circle. You are using the third circle when you are looking at something imaginary outside of the space, like the stars or the sky. When using the third circle, you should always see something in your imagination. Human beings often see memories, or picture a future event, in this circle.

Circles of attention are important, in that they enable those watching to infer meaning into what you are doing. When you are on an audition panel, it can be off-putting to watch a singer staring into the middle distance for no particular reason, or whose focus is flitting around nonsensically. Where appropriate, advice on this aspect of performance is given in the self-rehearsal guides.

Acting is Reacting

'Acting is reacting' is one of the most commonly used phrases in contemporary actor-training. As it is central to some of the advice given in this book with regards to acting through song, it merits explanation here.

This idea is centred around the conceit that, in order to perform truthfully, you must act upon genuine internal impulses. These impulses occur when you respond spontaneously to an external stimulus in the moment of acting the song, rather than making a predetermined choice. In many acting methodologies, notably the work of American acting teacher Sanford Meisner, the stimuli for these impulses are usually your fellow actors. When following this key principle of his training, you simply pay attention to their performance and respond. This approach can lead to very truthful, organic work – but must be adapted for audition, where there are rarely other actors to respond to.

Instead, in the audition room, you must generate what director and acting theorist Declan Donnellan calls a 'target'. To describe it somewhat simplistically, a target is a picture that you see in your imagination, and falls into one of four categories. It can be an object that is in the character's field of vision; for example, in the title song from *The Sound of Music*, Maria sings about the beauty of her surroundings, so for the actress playing Maria her targets should include the mountains, the sky, the brook. In the real world, Maria would actually be able to see her surroundings; as an actress you must imagine them. The second kind of target is an image that relates to the character's memory. If I ask you to remember the last film you saw, after a second or two, you will see an image from that film. That is how human memory works – it is always preceded by an image. So when a character remembers something, if you want to act truthfully, you must emulate this process. In 'On My Own' from *Les Misérables*, the actress playing Éponine, like the actress playing Maria, needs to imagine her surroundings – in this case the streets of Paris in the early hours of the morning. But she also needs to see targets from the character's memory, such as times when Marius, for whom she feels unrequited love, was kind to her. The third kind of target is an image that is prompted by the character thinking about the future. Again this reflects life – if I ask you to envision what you will do next weekend, an image will pop into your head. You might see the face of the friend you plan to meet, or the place you intend to visit. The fourth kind of target involves imagining the behaviour of another character. You might see them light a cigarette, begin to cry, or shrug their shoulders. Identifying what you need to see will be crucial for you when preparing the acting performance of your song, as when you begin to see detailed, well-chosen targets, it will provide you with the stimulus you need to respond organically in the moment.

Direct Address

Direct address is a technique that involves you talking straight to the audience or, in this scenario, the audition panel. Rather than pretending that the audience doesn't exist and hiding behind an imaginary 'fourth wall', in direct address the actor makes eye contact with those watching and seeks to change them – by playing their objectives and actions on the spectator. The use of direct address is incredibly useful when delivering certain audition songs – such as comedy numbers, narrative pieces, or a lyric in which the character is seeking answers to a problem – as it can be engaging to watch and can help the panel feel included in the performance.

ESTILL'S SINGING TERMINOLOGY: THE VOICE QUALITIES

The methodology of the late American vocal expert Jo Estill is now predominant in contemporary singing training in the United Kingdom. The methodology she developed has become invaluable because of its specificity – it is a system that allows you to understand, feel and recreate the precise muscular patterning needed to achieve certain identifiable sounds. One of the central tenets of her work is the six 'voice qualities'. A voice quality is a vocal set-up created by manipulating the movable structures of the vocal mechanism into a particular configuration in order to produce a desired, repeatable sound. Although most singing teachers would acknowledge that there are more than six voice qualities, in this book, the six that Estill documented are used as a means to recommend appropriate vocal choices for the songs. A brief outline of some of the main features of the six qualities are given below, along with a recommended example of each that you can listen to. The recordings are all from original cast recordings. In the next chapter there are some exercises that explore the practical application of Estill's ideas if you are interested in utilising some of the more complex technical details in your work.

Note: A detailed analysis of the vocal anatomy is beyond the remit of this book. However, if you want to discover more about the movable structures of the vocal apparatus, and the muscular set-ups of the voice qualities, then these are discussed in detail in *Singing and the Actor* by Gillyanne Kayes.

Cry Quality

Cry quality is a quiet, pure sound, useful for conveying character choices such as innocence, tenderness and thoughtfulness. A clear example of this quality is Kim Crosby singing the opening section of the duet 'No One is Alone' from the original Broadway production of *Into the Woods*. The key components of the set-up are a tilted thyroid cartilage (see p. 37), a raised larynx and thin vocal folds (the two small bands of muscle inside the larynx that vibrate and make contact in order to make sound).

Sob Quality

This quality is very similar to Cry quality in its muscular set-up, the only difference being that, in Sob quality, you have a lowered laryngeal position – which makes the sound darker and more intense. It can be used to communicate moments of sadness, grief and longing. A good example of Sob is Sarah Brightman singing the opening verse of 'Wishing You Were Somehow Here Again' from *The Phantom of the Opera*.

Speech Quality

Speech quality is a fundamental sound of contemporary musical theatre. It is particularly useful when you want to focus the listener on the lyric, rather than the beauty of the voice, as it helps make your singing sound conversational. A clear example of this sound is Judi Dench singing 'Send in the Clowns' from *A Little Night Music*. As its name suggests, Speech is similar, in the way it sounds and is produced, to the manner in which many people talk. Its main features are a neutral laryngeal position, thick vocal folds, and a neutral tongue position.

Twang Quality

Twang quality is a very prevalent sound amongst singers working on contemporary musical theatre, particularly if it is an American show. Often mistakenly classed as purely a nasal sound, Twang can be either nasal or oral, depending on whether the soft palate is in a mid-position or is raised. (The soft palate controls whether sound is directed through your mouth, or through your nose, or through both; see p. 41.) A good example of Twang quality is Idina Menzel singing 'Defying Gravity' from *Wicked*. Some of the key features of the set-up include thin vocal folds, a raised larynx and a high back of the tongue. What differentiates it from Cry quality is that you narrow a fold of mucous membrane inside the pharynx called the aryepiglottic sphincter (or the AES for short). This creates an additional resonator, which gives your sound more edge so that it carries easily across large spaces.

Belt Quality

Described by Estill herself as 'happy yelling', Belt quality is the sung form of a shout. You would rarely belt more than one or two notes in a song, as the quality is normally used to highlight the most passionate and dramatic musical moments. A good example of belt is Jodie Prenger singing the last phrase of 'As Long As He Needs Me' in the West End revival of *Oliver!* The defining features of the quality include thick vocal folds, a high larynx, a tilted cricoid cartilage (which allows you to safely sing high in the voice with thick folds) and an anchored torso (see p. 49).

Opera Quality

A good example of Opera quality being used in a musical is Audra McDonald singing 'Bess, You Is My Woman Now' from the Broadway revival of *Porgy and Bess*. Commonplace in the opera house, the quality is less frequently used in musicals and would only be used for scores where it is stylistically appropriate, such as parts of *Sweeney Todd* and, in some productions, *West Side Story.* Opera is a mixed quality, comprising Speech and Twang qualities, but with thyroid tilt added to sweeten the sound, a lowered larynx to 'cover' the twang resonance, and a strong voice/body connection.

Falsetto Quality

Falsetto quality is very useful for displaying moments of vulnerability, fragility and reflection. A good example of this quality is Julie McKenzie singing the last note of 'Losing My Mind' from the West End production of *Follies.* Falsetto, as defined by Estill, uses an aspirate onset (where some of the breath escapes before the vocal folds vibrate) and vocal folds that are stiff – so they vibrate, but don't meet fully.

MUSICAL TERMINOLOGY

Musical instructions are traditionally written in Italian. The key terms used in the book are translated for you below. If you wish to understand others that may appear on sheet music you purchase, then these can easily and quickly be defined using Google.

- *Colla voce*: literally means 'follow the solo voice'. Wherever this is indicated on your music, it means that you are able to sing in a free manner, and the pianist will follow you.

- *Crescendo*: a gradual increase in volume.

- *Decrescendo*: a gradual decrease in volume.

- *Key signature*: a combination of flats (♭) or sharps (♯) written at the beginning of each stave to indicate the key of a song.

- *Legato*: smooth and connected, without a break between notes.

- *Più mosso*: more quickly (in terms of tempo).

- *Rubato*: literally means 'robbed or stolen' time. At points where this is marked you have freedom to speed up and slow down the tempo at your artistic discretion.

- *Staccato*: short and detached, a note separated from that which follows. Staccato notes are indicated by placing a dot above or below the notehead.

- *Time signature*: an indication of rhythm recorded as two numbers, one on top of the other. The top number denotes the number of beats per bar, with the bottom number defining the note-length of each beat.

The Exercises

SINGING EXERCISES

In the first chapter, we discussed the various factors you must take into consideration when choosing a song. Once you have made a choice, if you are to do yourself justice in the audition, you must then prepare and rehearse that material thoroughly. In order to do this, it is advisable that you spend some time practising with a pianist. However, as this is not always possible, outlined in this chapter are a series of fundamental exercises that you can do on your own, and apply to any number, in order to develop your vocal delivery and improve your acting through song.

For some of the exercises you should work with a backing track to ensure you are working in the correct key. You can access backing tracks for many of these songs online, or you can ask a friend or teacher who plays the piano to record the accompaniment for you.

The technical singing exercises are divided into two categories: Fundamental Exercises, which are suitable for any singer, and Further Exercises, for more advanced material and the more experienced vocalist.

Your Working Copy

To undertake the work in this chapter you will need two copies of the music. The first will be eventually be marked up for the audition pianist (see p. 71). The second will be your own personal working copy – on which you can make notes as you undertake the following exercises.

The following exercises are suitable for all singers.

Marking Your Breath

Your first rehearsal task when you start work on a song should be to decide at which points in the lyric you are going to breathe. You should record these breath-points on your working copy by marking them with small ticks in pencil above the stave. (You shouldn't put breath-marks on the pianist's copy.) It is helpful and important to make these choices *before* you begin any practical work, because, as soon as you start to rehearse a song, your body forms habits. If you make informed choices about where to breathe before you begin practising – and then repeat those choices each time you work on the song – your intended breath-patterns will become part of your muscle memory. This approach will prove to be invaluable, as the last thing the panel want to see in the audition room is you thinking about your breathing. They want to see you acting through song. If you fail to make these decisions before you begin practising, you may find you form bad habits during your early rehearsals – such as breathing in the middle of words or phrases – that can be problematic to rectify and lead to a poor interpretation of the song.

But how do you decide where to breathe? Phrasing your song effectively – and artistically – is an important part of your craft as a singer. In theatre songs, the primary consideration when making choices about phrasing is that the sense of the lyric is communicated – so you should begin by looking at the punctuation. To help make the thought process clear, you should breathe in at the beginning of a new sentence, as it indicates the start of a new thought. Work through your music, marking a breath after each full stop, exclamation mark or question mark. Sometimes, sentences may be too long to sing in one breath and you will need to mark in additional breaths. The composer and lyricist will indicate where these might be necessary in one of the following ways:

1. By using a comma or semicolon.

2. By adding a musical rest in the middle of the sentence.

3. By using a capital letter in the middle of a sentence.

At times you will also need to breathe at these points, at other points it will not be necessary. It is about applying common sense.

Abdominal Release

Once you have marked all of the breath-points, you want to imbed your chosen phrasing into your muscle memory. Before you can do this, it is important to understand a process known as abdominal release. Try the following awareness exercise, which is a technique advocated by singing teacher Janice Chapman called Accent Method breathing:

1. Place your right hand on your abdomen, with your thumb on your navel and the rest of the hand below.

2. Make three short 'z' sounds with an accent on the first sound (i.e. ZZ, zz, zz). With each sound, draw the navel towards the spine till the abdominal wall is pulled in. *Note*: You shouldn't relax the abdominals in between sounds; the abdominal wall should be moving further towards the spine with each sound.

3. After the third 'z' sound, immediately and completely release the abdominal wall so it relaxes over your waistband. This moment of relaxation, where the abdominal wall recoils, is an abdominal release.

An important fact that sometimes confuses untrained singers is this: the abdominal release *is* your in-breath. You don't need to breathe in once you have released; the breath has entered the body, filling your lungs with air. When you release the abdominal wall, the diaphragm flattens and moves downwards. At the same time the intercostal muscles move the ribcage upwards and outwards, increasing the size of the chest cavity. This lowers the internal air pressure in your lungs, causing air from outside the body (which is now of a higher density) to rush in to balance the pressure.

Sirening

Now you have an understanding of abdominal release, you are ready to programme your decisions about breathing into your muscle memory. A good way to do this is by 'sirening' the melody. Sirening – which takes its name from the sound of an ambulance or a fire engine – is a vocal exercise that involves gliding through pitch on an 'ng' sound. When you siren, the sides of your tongue should remain in contact with your upper molars and the soft palate should be lowered. The exercise is as follows:

1. Stand in front of a mirror. This will enable you to monitor the movements of your abdominals in your reflection. Ensure your feet are parallel and directly underneath your hips. Your knees should be soft and your neck long. Place your hand on your abdominal wall as in the previous awareness exercise.

2. Siren through the melody on an 'ng' sound. Use a piano, a backing track or a cast recording to ensure you remain in the right key. When you are sirening, ensure the sound is as quiet as possible. Keep the sides of your tongue against your molars as discussed.

3. Every time you reach one of the breath-points you have marked, release the abdominal wall, as you felt in the awareness exercise. Monitor the movements of the abdominal wall with your hand and in the mirror. When you are managing breath successfully you will feel the abdominal wall moving slowly inwards as you sing. The abdominals will then release forwards at the end of the phrase, to allow the breath to drop in. The longer the phrase, the more you will feel the navel travelling towards the spine. Importantly, you don't need to initiate this inward movement consciously – the body will do it for you. *You should never deliberately pull the abdominals in when you are singing.* Engaging in 'abdominal pumping' only serves to force the air out more quickly. Not only does this mean you run out of breath, it increases the pressure under your vocal folds, which can cause problems such as a constricted (raspy or gravelly) sound, cracking on top notes, and trauma to the vocal folds.

4. Complete the exercise for the entire song.

5. If you are struggling to access your abdominal release whilst standing up, you can try the exercise in alternative positions. You can sit on the edge of a chair with your legs wide apart, your feet planted firmly on the ground, and with a lengthened spine and neck. Working in this position can help you access your release more fully. You can also explore the exercise on all-fours – where the effect of gravity will assist your release – or by leaning your back against the wall with your feet about twenty centimetres away from the wall and your knees slightly bent.

6. Repeat the entire exercise several times until the release feels habitual.

Targeting Breaks in the Voice: the Thyroid Cartilage

Sirening the melody is an excellent initial exercise for working on a new song. Not only does it programme abdominal release into your muscle memory, it also has the same effect on the movements of your larynx (sometimes colloquially referred to as 'the voice box', the larynx is the organ in your neck which houses your vocal folds – the muscles which vibrate when you sing).

When you sing, your larynx changes position in two key ways as you progress through a song. Firstly, as the pitch rises and falls, your larynx moves up and down correspondingly. (If you gently hold your larynx with your fingers and siren on an 'ng' sound from the bottom of your range to the top and down again, you will notice how the larynx moves in relation to the pitch.) The second key laryngeal movement is that of the thyroid cartilage. To locate your thyroid cartilage run your index finger from the centre of your chin slowly down your neck. Stop at the first point of cartilage you encounter. This cartilage, in the centre of the larynx – which is sometimes called the 'Adam's apple' – is the thyroid cartilage. It usually sits in a horizontal position when you are speaking, but when you speak or sing in higher pitches it can tilt in a downward and forwards motion. When in a tilted position, the thyroid cartilage, as it is attached to the vocal folds, causes them to stretch and become thinner. This enables you to access higher pitches, makes your sound quieter and sweeter, and is a factor in helping you access vibrato. (If you hold the thyroid gently between your thumb and index finger and make a whimpering sound like a puppy, you will feel the thyroid tilt.) The movement of the thyroid cartilage from a horizontal to a tilted position is perhaps the most important in singing – and the previous exercise of sirening through the melody can help to make it smooth and controlled.

However, sometimes controlling your thyroid tilt can remain challenging. You may find at certain points of the song you flip from a horizontal to a tilted position – leading to a 'break' in your voice. This can often occur when you jump from a lower note to a higher note. At these moments you may experience a noticeable, and unwanted, shift in your vocal quality – like you are moving from a 'chest voice' to a 'head voice'. These terms are becoming outdated in modern singing training. A more accurate anatomical analysis is that, because of poor thyroid control, you are flipping from singing with thicker vocal folds to thinner vocal folds – or even that your vocal folds stop closing fully as you ascend in pitch and you end up singing in a Falsetto quality. To help finesse these transitions – and eradicate breaks in your voice – try the following exercise. As an example, I have described how you would practise the octave leap at the beginning of the chorus of 'Somewhere Over the Rainbow' from *The Wizard of Oz* – but the exercise would apply for any problematic interval between two notes.

1. Identify the correct pitches for the two notes you are targeting, either by using a piano or by listening to a recording. It is vital that you are practising in the right key.

2. Slide from the bottom note to the top note on a continuous 'ng' sound. (So in this example, you would slide from the note for the syllable 'some' to the note for 'where'.) Do this as quietly as possible, keeping the back of your neck long. Make sure you are not contracting the abdominal wall as you go up in pitch. Repeat this stage several times until you are able to control the slide and there are no sudden shifts in the sound quality.

3. Repeat the slide, but this time, instead of using the 'ng' sound, use the vowel of the bottom note. In this example, as the bottom note is the syllable 'some' you would there be sliding

on an 'uh' vowel. As you do so, keep the tip of the tongue behind your bottom front teeth. Repeat this stage until the slide is smooth and controlled.

4. Repeat stage 3, but now halfway through the slide move from the bottom vowel to the top vowel. In this example, you would therefore slide from an 'uh' vowel (for 'some') to an 'air' vowel (for 'where'), i.e. 'uh-air'. Try to keep the tongue as still as possible as you shift vowels.

5. Now sing the whole phrase with the actual words but still include the slide in the sound, i.e. 'Some-(*slide*)-where over the rainbow'. When you can do this without flipping, you will be successfully tilting your thyroid cartilage.

6. Finally, sing the phrase normally without sounding the slide – but still experience the same sensation you felt when the slide was included.

7. Repeat for all of the problematic intervals in the song.

Managing Breath

When working with new students who have had little prior training, I find that one of their most common concerns is about breath. They often fixate about not having enough breath to sing a long phrase or note. The warning words of their junior-school music teacher – *'Make sure you take a nice big breath'* – are lurking somewhere at the back of their minds. Lack of breath is actually rarely an issue in singing – contemporary research shows that vocal problems are more commonly caused when the singer uses *too much* breath.

The first principle of voice is contact – i.e. the vocal folds must meet for sound to be produced. Make the following sounds on a comfortable pitch and volume: 'oh oh' and 'eh eh'. If you focus on the muscular movements occurring inside of your larynx you will become aware of contact taking place as you make the sounds – this is the vocal folds joining. If you use too much breath pressure it can disrupt this efficient closure of the vocal folds, as the excess breath can blast the vocal folds apart. For example, when you try to sing a high note and you 'crack' – i.e. the sound momentarily cuts outs – this is because the subglottic pressure (the breath pressure created underneath your vocal folds when they close) became too great and the vocal folds were forced apart – so the sound stopped.

A major cause of too much subglottic pressure is what we previously described as 'abdominal pumping'. This is when you deliberately pull in the outer muscles of your abdominal wall. These outer muscles, which you can see if you have a 'six-pack', are called the external obliques.

Many singers erroneously believe that deliberately pulling in the obliques 'supports' their voice and is therefore to be encouraged, but in fact it causes problems. The science of the out-breath works on the premise of positive pressure, meaning that when you sing, the air comes out by itself because the air pressure in your lungs is greater than that in the room. As you sustain longer phrases you will indeed experience the abdominal wall contracting slowly – but this occurs *without you needing to try*. The contraction you feel is the underlying muscle – the transverse abdominis – not the obliques, and is automatic. This process occurs at the moment the balance of pressure changes, i.e. when the air pressure in your lungs becomes lower than the air pressure outside of your body.

Now that this premise is understood, you will find that one of the best ways you can improve the delivery of your song is to learn to avoid driving breath from the abdominal wall. Try and practise the following exercise on a daily basis to avoid overuse of the obliques whilst phonating (making voice):

1. Place your right hand on the abdominal wall and allow the muscles to relax. If you feel that the abdominals are tight then repeat the Accent Method breathing exercise outlined earlier to help you to find a true abdominal release. *Note*: In the Accent Method breathing you deliberately pull the abdominals inwards in order to feel a moment of abdominal release, but you should *not* pull the abdominals inwards at any other point during the rest of this exercise – you are trying to do the exact opposite and keep them relaxed.

2. Once the abdominal wall is released, make the following sounds as you did previously: 'oh oh' and 'eh eh'. Notice the contact in the vocal folds and monitor the abdominal wall,

trying to ensure it remains relaxed and does not kick inwards as you make the sounds. The effort should be in your vocal folds instead. Repeat this stage until you can produce the sounds without any abdominal contraction at all. *Note:* With the next four stages, which become progressively harder, you are aiming for the same physical sensation – the complete relaxation of the abdominal wall.

3. Now make a couple of short 'z' sounds ('zz zz') on a comfortable pitch. Again try to stay completely relaxed in the abdominal wall.

4. Next attempt a sustained 'z' sound of about ten seconds' duration. You will begin to feel the transverse abdominis contract underneath your hand towards the end of the sound, but ensure you don't engage the obliques.

5. Now start on a comfortable note in the lower half of your range and glide upwards and downwards for a few notes on a 'z' sound. Check you don't begin to activate the abdominals as the pitch rises.

6. Finally glide up and down through your full register on a 'z' sound. Go as high as you can whilst keeping the sound quiet and focused. Avoid any contraction in the obliques related to the ascending pitch.

This exercise is excellent for daily training as it helps to break the habit of driving breath when you begin to phonate or ascend in pitch. Personally, I found it had a hugely beneficial effect on my singing. When it was first taught to me, I was already a singer with significant experience, but even so it allowed me to extend my belt register several notes higher in just a few days. My progress had been held back because I was habitually pushing from the abdominals; this exercise helped free me from that poor musculature.

Raising the Soft Palate

As a singing teacher, one of the most common vocal problems I am called on to correct is nasality. A surprising number of singers suffer from a degree of nasality in their voice – even if they are not fully aware of it. This occurs when their vowel sounds are partially coming out through their nose, instead of their mouth, which can make your sound dull. To avoid this unwanted quality you must learn to gain control of the soft palate – a movable fold of muscular fibres and mucous membrane suspended from the back of the roof of the mouth.

As previously mentioned, the function of the soft palate in phonation is to direct sound either through the mouth, the nose, or both. The mouth and the nose are connected by a hole in the roof of the mouth called the 'nasal port'. When the soft palate is raised, it seals off the nasal port and subsequently all sound is directed through the mouth. This is the position you will want most of the time when singing. If you lower the soft palate it will make contact with the back of the tongue, sealing off the oral cavity, and all the sound will come out through the nose. This occurs when you produce what are known as the nasal consonants: 'm' 'n' and 'ng'. (If you hum on an 'm' sound and then hold your nose, the sound will stop – because the soft palate is directing all of the sound through the nose.) When the soft palate is in a mid-position, the sound comes out through both the mouth and the nose. It is when you sing in this set-up that your sound is heard as being nasal. To learn to raise the soft palate – and therefore avoid nasality – you must first become aware of its location and the sensations you feel when it moves. Try the following awareness exercise:

1. Make an 'ee' vowel on a comfortable pitch. Be aware that the tip of your tongue is behind your front teeth, and the sides of the tongue are in contact with your upper molars.

2. Keeping your tongue completely still, move back and forth between an 'ee' sound and an 'ng' sound, i.e. 'EE ng EE ng EE ng'. Every time you make the 'ng' sound you will feel something lowering in the roof of your mouth and making contact with the tongue. This is the soft palate.

Now that you can feel the movement of the soft palate you can begin to eradicate nasality from the song. Explore the following exercise:

1. The letter 'g' springs the soft palate up into a raised position. In a speaking position, practise moving from an extended 'n'

sound (where the soft palate is down) to a vowel proceeded by the letter 'g'. For example: 'nnGee, nnGah, nnGoo'. You should feel a sensation of lifting occur in the roof of the mouth – this is the soft palate. As you do this, rest a hand gently underneath the jaw to monitor that you are only raising the soft palate, rather than also lowering the jaw.

2. Sing through the song, placing the letter 'g' in front of all of the vowels. So for example, 'happy birthday to you' would become 'Gaa-Gee Geerr-Gay Goo Goo'. Again, practise with a hand underneath your chin.

3. Now try singing the song normally, a little slower than usual, focusing on the sensation of keeping the soft palate raised. You can check that you have achieved the correct position by pinching your nose occasionally as you sing. If there is no change in the sound when you pinch your nose then your soft palate is raised. (Avoid doing this on the letters 'm', 'n' and 'ng' as the soft palate will be down and the sound will stop.) If the sound quality changes on any of your vowels when you pinch your nose, then this means that your soft palate is in a mid-position for that word – and your sound is nasal.

4. Once you have worked through the entire song, go back and target any words that were nasal by placing a 'g' sound in front of the vowel you were struggling with. For example, if you identified the word 'walk' as being problematic, then your 'aw' vowel would be nasal. In a speech position practise repeatedly lifting the soft palate on this vowel, i.e. 'nnGaw, nnGaw, nnGaw'. This will help you build a new muscle memory for that particular word. Once you have repeated this stage for all problematic words/vowels, run the song again. With detailed practice the nasality should disappear.

Improving Articulation

In my experience of hosting audition workshops with casting directors, I have found that criticism of a singer's articulation is often a common piece of feedback. The reason for this is, if the panel are struggling to understand the lyric, it is hard for them to engage with the story being told.

Try the following exercise to work on your consonants. You may want to wash your hands before you begin.

1. Open your mouth slightly and rest the tip of your index finger gently between your front teeth. (You should twist your wrist so your fingernail is facing sideways towards the wall, rather than upwards towards the ceiling.)

2. During the exercise you want to avoid biting down on your finger – the aim is to keep the jaw relaxed. To test this, try biting very gently on your finger – then relax the jaw whilst maintaining the contact between your teeth and fingertip. As you relax you will find a feeling of ease and release in the muscles of the jaw; this is the sensation you should seek to sustain throughout the exercise. Once you can you access this lack of tension in the muscles controlling the jaw, move on to the next stage.

3. Keeping your finger between your teeth, slowly and clearly make the following consonant sounds: 'b', 'p', 'd', 't', 'r', 'j' 'ch', and 'k'. It is fine to move the lips but try to keep the jaw relaxed as you did previously.

4. Repeat Stage 3, but this time repeat each consonant in the sequence three times, i.e. 'b, b, b', 'p, p, p', etc. Make each consonant clearly without engaging the jaw.

5. You are now ready to work on the song. Maintaining your finger position, speak slowly through the lyric focusing on producing each consonant clearly.

6. Repeat the previous stage but now sing the song, rather than speak it.

7. Finally take your finger out and sing the song normally. Because your tongue had to work harder when your finger was in place, it will now be more agile when asked to work in its normal position – so you should notice an improvement in the clarity of your articulation.

Note: If you don't want to use your finger for these exercises, an alternative is to purchase a bone prop. These are available online from the vocal specialist Annie Morrison at www.themorrisonboneprop.com.

FURTHER EXERCISES

The following exercises are suitable for advanced vocalists.

Tongue Position

A feature of a well-trained musical-theatre voice is that the vowel sounds of the song are balanced, i.e. the resonance of those vowels is as equal as possible. When you produce different vowels, your tongue changes position. These modifications in position can unintentionally create big changes in the level of resonance – and make your vocal quality uneven. You therefore want to minimise these movements in order to make your sound more balanced. To achieve this, you should aim to keep the middle of the tongue as still as possible whilst singing. Not only will this help you to form vowel sounds with an equal resonance, it can also make your vocal production less effortful.

Try the following awareness exercise:

1. Sing an 'ee' vowel on a comfortable pitch and sustain the note for a few seconds. As you hold the note, become aware of the position of your tongue. You will notice that the tip of your tongue is in contact with your lower front teeth, and the sides of your tongue are touching your upper molars. This is an ideal tongue position for singing.

2. Now try speaking an 'ee' vowel followed by an 'ah'.

3. Repeat this several times. You will notice that the sides of your tongue drop downwards and lose contact with the molars each time you move into the 'ah' vowel.

As you can see from this exercise, habitually, the middle of your tongue can move significantly as you progress from one vowel to another. Aside from the change in resonance, this can be problematic when you try to sing high notes. As discussed previously, when you make higher pitches, your larynx needs to rise. Your tongue is attached to your larynx by a small bone called the hyoid bone. So if you allow the middle of the tongue to drop – as you just noticed when you made the 'ah' vowel – then the larynx will drop with it. This can make it hard to create and sustain higher pitches. Therefore it is doubly important to relearn how to produce your vowel sounds – by keeping the middle of the tongue as still as you can. Try this next exercise:

1. Make an 'ee' vowel on a comfortable pitch. Be aware of the tongue position described in the awareness exercise: the tip of the tongue behind the front teeth, the sides of the tongue in contact with the upper molars.

2. Speak through the following sequence of paired vowels: 'ee-ay', 'ee-ah', 'ee-aw', 'ee-oo'. With each pair, glide slowly from the first vowel to the second – keeping the sides of the tongue as still as possible. You are retraining your muscles to produce each vowel with a reduced movement of the tongue – by using the 'ee' sound as a basis for all of your vowels.

3. Repeat Stage 2, but this time sing, rather than speak, the paired vowels. Do this on a comfortable pitch. It is appropriate to breathe between each pair. Again try to minimise the movement of the tongue.

4. You are now ready to apply this technique to your song. Sing through the entire song on an 'ee' vowel, maintaining the prescribed tongue position. You will likely find the song easier to sing because of the efficient tongue position of the 'ee' vowel.

5. Now sing through the lyric on the vowel sounds, only with the consonants removed. Again focus on minimising the tongue movements.

6. Finally sing through the entire song with the consonants back in – but still keeping the tongue as still as possible. You should notice an improvement in the balance of your vowel sounds, and your voice may feel easier to produce.

Onset

Another great way to improve the delivery of your song is by enhancing your understanding and control of onset. The term 'onset' refers to what happens to your breath and your vocal folds when you begin to phonate. There are three different types of onset:

Aspirate – an aspirate onset occurs when the breath passes through the vocal folds before they begin to vibrate. Try holding your larynx gently with your fingers and make the following sounds: 'hhheee', 'fffaaahh', 'sshhaaww'. If you extend the first consonant you will notice the breath escaping before there is vibration. When singing you must use an aspirate onset every time a phrase starts with a word that begins with a devoiced consonant (i.e. 'f', 'k', 'p', 's', 't', 'ch', 'sh' and 'th' – as in the word 'thing'). Whilst it is therefore required when singing, unnecessary use of this particular onset, for example on a vowel sound, can lead to an undesired breathy tone.

Glottal – a glottal onset occurs when the breath is held momentarily behind the vocal folds, and then released in an explosive manner. Hold your larynx. Slowly make the sounds 'uh oh' – like a child realising they have done something wrong. You will be aware of a build-up of subglottic pressure before each sound. The explosive release, and the strong subsequent vocal-fold closure, is a glottal. Beginning with this onset in a song will help you access a Speech quality. However, if you use glottals too frequently it can be vocally tiring and make it harder to access thyroid tilt and higher pitches.

Simultaneous – a simultaneous onset occurs when the release of breath and the vocal-fold vibration occur at exactly the same time. Hold your larynx one more time and gently speak some extended vowels on a confortable pitch, i.e. 'eeee', 'aahh', 'oooo'. Glide into each sound, avoiding a glottal onset. You will feel under your fingers that the vibration in your larynx starts at the moment you begin to breath out. Simultaneous onsets are a key feature of nearly all singing – but particularly when using a legit or operatic style.

Any good singer uses each of the three onsets. All are important, safe, necessary and healthy, if used correctly. However, it is undoubtedly much easier to sing a majority of songs if you are able to access a simultaneous set-up consistently and avoid unintentional glottal and aspirate onsets. You can and should use the other two onsets at times for stylistic reasons – but if you use a simultaneous onset for the majority of the song your technical delivery will greatly improve.

The following exercise will help you improve your simultaneous onset:

1. Before you work on the onsets in your song, you first need to practise in a speaking position. First explore using an aspirate onset. Speak a series of vowels in a slow, elongated manner, placing an extended 'h' sound in front of each: i.e. 'hhaaahhh', 'hhhey', 'hhheee', 'hhhaw', 'hhhooo', 'hhhair', 'hhhigh'. Focus on making the transition from the 'h' sound into every vowel as smooth as possible. It can be beneficial to make a gliding gesture with your hands as you do this, as physicalising the work can help build greater awareness and control of what is occurring within the larynx.

2. Now try to apply the same feeling of a vocal glide to a simultaneous onset. Work through your vowels again. Start with an aspirate onset first, then repeat the vowel but removing the letter 'h' to give you a simultaneous onset. For example: 'hhaaahhh' then 'aahh', 'hhhey' then 'eeyy'. Try to achieve the same smooth beginning to the sound when the 'h' is removed. Be careful not to use a small glottal. You may again wish to use hand gestures to help build awareness of the internal sensations. Repeat this stage until you can affect a simultaneous onset on all vowels.

3. You are now ready to apply this work to your song. A good vowel for singing with a simultaneous onset is 'oo', so try singing through the entire song on that vowel, focusing on avoiding any glottal onsets. As with the sirening exercise, sing along to a backing track to ensure you are practising in the correct key. Repeat until you are able to deliver the entire song in a simultaneous onset.

4. Now sing through the song once more. This time use the vowels of the song, but with the consonants removed. So for example, 'happy birthday to you' would become 'aa-ee eerr-ey oo oo'. Work slowly through the lyric until you can achieve a simultaneous onset on all the vowels.

5. Finally sing through the song normally with the consonants back in. Use a simultaneous onset unless the word begins with a devoiced consonant, when an aspirate onset will be required. When that is the case, glide from the consonant

onto the vowel as you did in Stage 1 of the exercise. Avoid using glottals at any stage.

Torso Anchoring

As part of her research, Estill identified the importance of the use of the muscles in the back for the healthy production of the singing voice. Try the following awareness exercise:

1. Imagine you have an orange underneath each of your armpits. Squeeze gently downwards on these imaginary oranges. You will feel an engagement in the muscles in your back below your arm. (These muscles are commonly known as the 'lats'.)

2. Sustain an 'ah' vowel on a comfortable pitch. As you do so, play with engaging and releasing your lats as described above. You may notice the sound becoming clearer and stronger when your lats are engaged. Estill described this use of the lats as 'torso anchoring'.

Here is an exercise that will encourage an appropriate use of the back muscles when singing:

1. Stand in an upright position facing a wall. Your toes should be about fifteen centimetres from the wall, with your feet parallel and resting comfortably underneath your hips.

2. Rest your palms flat against wall, with your hands slightly wider than shoulder-width apart. As you do this, don't lean forwards into the wall; stand completely upright; the gentle pressure you are applying will engage your lats. Look directly in front of you so that your eyeline is horizontal and the back of the neck is long.

3. A key to the use of torso anchoring is isolation. As you engage your lats, you need to ensure your abdominals don't begin to work unnecessarily. To practise this, whilst maintaining your physical relationship to the wall, release your abdominals using the Accent Breathing method discussed previously (i.e. 'ZZ, zz, zz' – release).

4. Maintaining the same anchored posture, sing the first line of your song. At the end of the phrase release your abdominal

wall. Be sure that you have relaxed your obliques and allowed the breath to drop in, whilst maintaining the engagement in the back. Repeat if necessary.

5. Now sing through the entire song in this manner, releasing at the points where you had previously decided to breathe. You may notice that your vocal production feels more supported and stable.

6. Sing the song again, but this time replicate the marriage of release and anchoring without using the wall to help you. Stand upright in the space, keeping the same relationship with your feet and your neck alignment. To achieve the same degree of anchoring, you may want to return to the image of squeezing oranges underneath your armpits. This will engage your lats. Remember to release after each phrase.

Adding Twang/False-Fold Retraction

As noted previously, Twang is one of Estill's six voice qualities. In its purest form it can be perceived as strident and unpleasant. However, twang isn't only a voice quality, it is also an individual resonance that can be added to other vocal set-ups. For example, twang is an important component of Opera quality. It is one of the reasons you can hear an opera singer over a full orchestra.

The amount of twang in your voice is determined by how much you narrow and tighten your AES (see p. 30), the sphincter inside of your pharynx. Try the following awareness exercise:

1. Make the following sounds: cackle like a witch, taunt like a child in a playground ('na, na-na, na, na'), quack like a duck. When you make these noises you are tightening your AES and are therefore adding twang to the voice. It is a brash noise.

2. Repeat these three sounds and become aware of the sensations in your larynx. With each of them you should notice a feeling of narrowing in the vocal tract – this is the AES. If you experience any discomfort in the larynx making these sounds, or the sound is raspy/distorted, this may be because you are constricting. Constriction occurs when your false vocal folds, which sit above your true vocal folds, close over. To free

yourself of constriction, laugh silently for a moment. You will feel a sensation of width, or space, in the larynx. Here you have altered your musculature by widening your false vocal folds. This is called retraction. If you now repeat the twang sounds, maintaining the feeling of retraction – this should get rid of the distortion and allow you to produce a clear tone.

Now that you have a physical understanding of how twang is produced, you can learn to control the amount that is added to your sound – like pushing a fader on a mixing desk.

1. Make a 'NYeh' sound on a comfortable speaking pitch with a very tight, narrowed AES – adding a lot of twang.

2. Repeat, but now clench your right fist as you make the sound. You are using your fist to help you physicalise what is happening with your AES.

3. Now slowly make four 'NYeh' sounds. With each sound gradually relax and open your fist. As you do so, also gradually relax and widen your AES. You will progress from having lots of twang in the first sound to none by the fourth. The sensation you will feel during this exercise – moving from a narrowed to a widened position in the pharynx – helps to develop the muscle memory you need to add or remove twang on demand.

Having explored this element of vocal control, you can now choose to introduce twang into your song if that seems appropriate (most pop-based contemporary musical-theatre songs will benefit from the addition of some twang). Try using the exercise outlined below:

1. Siren the first phrase of the melody on an 'ng' sound. (Twang is made with thin vocal folds, so sirening helps you add the necessary thyroid tilt to create this position.)

2. Sing through the same phrase using a staccato 'ging' sound on each syllable. Use a very tight AES. This will produce nasal twang, as your soft palate will be in a mid-position (causing some of the sound to escape through your nose).

3. Now sing through the phrase once more, but this time use a 'NYee' sound for every syllable. Your AES should remain tight

as you do this. Sing the phrase legato, rather than staccato. (The soft palate will come down each time you make the 'n' consonant, but when you lift it to produce the 'ee' vowel the sound should come out entirely through your mouth and not be nasalised. If you do this successfully you will be producing oral twang. To check the sound is oral, rather than nasal, you can pinch your nose when making the vowel – there should be no change in the sound at all. Don't pinch on the 'n' consonant or the sound will cut out.)

4. Repeat Stage 3, but this time instead of using a 'NYee' sound, put the letters 'ny' in front of the vowels of the phrase. So 'happy birthday to you' would become 'NYaa-NYee NYeerr-NYay NYoo NYoo'.

5. Now sing the phrase normally. Think about still narrowing your AES to make the twang, whilst retaining the feeling of a silent laugh to retract the false vocal folds. You should notice a brighter resonance in your sound. If you wish to add more or less twang, tighten or widen your AES as you did in the previous exercise.

6. Repeat Stages 1 to 5 for every phrase in the song.

Practising Belt

Within many musical-theatre songs there are notes that should be delivered in a Belt quality. In well-written material, belting is used for moments of musical and dramatic climax. As such, it is rare for more than one or two notes in a song to be belted. In the self-rehearsal guides appropriate moments for the use of this voice quality are identified.

Belt in its pure form is very loud. As musical theatre is usually an amplified medium, it is therefore usually preferable to add some thyroid tilt to your belt set-up. This will quieten and sweeten the voice – and help you add some vibrato – making it a more appropriate sound for singing with a microphone. The described set-up is sometimes called a 'mixed belt'. When I am vocal coaching, this is the position I am most often asked to teach, as it is a highly desirable sound in commercial singing.

Below is a system for practising a mixed belt. Before you attempt the exercise, you should engage in a thorough vocal warm-up. (If you wish, you can use the previously outlined exercises to warm the voice.) You should also remind yourself of the sensations of thyroid tilt (p. 37), torso anchoring (p. 49), false-fold retraction (p. 50). Once you have done this preparation, you are ready to try the following:

1. Stand with your feet slightly wider than shoulder-width apart so you feel grounded and have a solid foundation. Ensure your knees are free and the abdominals are relaxed.

2. Make some glottal onsets on a comfortable pitch with the thyroid cartilage in a horizontal position (i.e. 'oh oh', 'ee ee', 'eh eh'). This will put you in a Speech quality.

3. Laugh silently to remind yourself of the posture of false-fold retraction – you will notice a sensation of width in the neck.

4. Repeat the glottal onsets whilst maintaining the silent laugh posture, but this time sustain the second sound (i.e. 'oh ooohhh', 'ee eeeeee', 'eh eeehhh').

5. Now imagine you are holding the ends of a sixty-centimetre metal bar in front of your upper chest. Bend the ends of this imaginary bar downwards so your elbows finish by the sides of your body. In this position you will engage your lats and be provided with some torso anchoring, which is important when belting. Maintain this anchoring as you continue through the next stages.

6. Keeping the back of the neck long, lift your chin slightly so that you are 'looking up to the gods'. If you were in a theatre, you would be fixing your eyes on the back of the dress circle.

7. Maintaining this head/neck position, throw your voice across the room on a 'yeh' sound. This sound, like a happy yell or shout, requires you to maintain lots of retraction.

8. Still retaining the described physical posture, whimper on an 'ng' sound like a puppy. This is to remind yourself of the sensation of thyroid tilt (remember to focus on the cartilage tilting downwards and forwards).

9. Without changing your physicality throw your voice on a moaned 'yeh' sound. You are now adding thyroid tilt to the set-up and are very close to a mixed belt. (Done correctly, this sound can be quite amusing. In my studio I often describe it as 'how the Queen would belt'. It sounds like an empowered moaning.)

10. Now try Estill's famous belting phrase. In the same 'moaned' position, with an unchanged physical set-up, try exclaiming like an Italian market trader: 'Eh! Francesco!!!' (This sound should be as though you are exasperated, but not angry, with your beloved Francesco.)

11. Relax your body for a moment. Play a B♭4 on piano. Hold this pitch in your head. This is the pitch you will belt on in a moment. It is chosen because it sits in a comfortable part of the female belt register. (If you don't have access to a piano, you can find the same pitch using an online virtual piano.)

12. Repeat stages 1 to 10 whilst holding the pitch in your head. If each stage feels comfortable then try a belt on a moaned 'yeh' sound on the given male/female pitch. Remember to keep your chin lifted and back anchored. Maintain a feeling of retraction (silent laugh) in the false vocal folds. Hold the sound for as long as is comfortable. If the set-up is correct you will now be belting. It may surprise you how comfortable it feels and how easy it is to sustain the pitch for a long time. Repeat this stage a few times until it feels secure and that you are in full control.

13. If the last stage was successful, you are now ready to target the pitch that you will belt in your song. Repeat stages 1 to 12, but this time use the piano to ensure you are belting on the same pitch as the note in your song (this note will be identified in the self-rehearsal guide if you don't read music). If the belt in the song is currently too high for you, then gradually build up to this pitch in your practice, semitone by semitone. Remember, the higher you go the more thyroid tilt you will need to add (think of adding more 'moan' to the sound).

14. Once you are able to belt the requisite pitch on a 'yeh' sound, you can now target the vowel used in the song. Repeat stages

1 to 13, but this time instead of singing on a 'yeh' sound, belt on the vowel you will be singing in the song – but with the letter 'y' in front. So if you are trying to belt the word 'life' you would practise on a 'yi' sound. (If you struggle to access any particular vowel in belt, stop for a moment and try some spoken practice, moving from a moaned 'yeh' to the vowel under consideration, i.e. 'yeh, yi', 'yeh, yi', then try the singing again.)

15. Sing the phrase that contains the belt in its entirety, belting your desired note. Ensure that you add the required physicality (anchoring the torso, lifting the chin, retracting the false folds, tilting the thyroid) gradually *before* the belt – so you are already in position when the moment arrives. To achieve this, in some songs you may want to begin to alter your physicality during the preceding phrase.

16. Finally consider how you will deliver the belt in audition without 'showing' the panel your technique. Consider how you can use a gesture that is appropriate from an acting perspective to achieve the right degree of physical engagement – but so that the panel are not aware of the use of torso anchoring.

Note: When used correctly, belting is completely safe and healthy. It is also exhilarating to listen to. However, when executed poorly it can quickly tire the voice. If you feel any strain or 'scratching' of the vocal folds doing the above steps, then stop the exercise immediately and spend five minutes gently sirening on an 'ng' sound, using lots of false-fold retraction. Once you can siren through your full register, then you are usually safe to continue your practice. However, if you feel any signs of vocal fatigue, then once you have finished sirening, rest the voice and return to your belt practice another day. It is advisable to only practise belting in short sessions (no longer than twenty minutes), particularly if the set-up is new to you.

Despite this, I would encourage you not to be put off belting – even if you have not done it before. Whilst you should be careful and monitor your practice, don't be scared to experiment with your voice or to make a mistake. It is a rare student indeed who doesn't crack at times when they first learn to belt. As long as you don't practise incorrectly for long periods of time your work will be perfectly safe. However, belting can be one of the most difficult vocal set-ups – so if you find it difficult, tiring or intimidating then seek the advice of an experienced, qualified vocal coach to teach you the set-up rather than practise alone.

ACTING EXERCISES

It is a truism that a majority of candidates in a major singing audition will have good voices. Therefore if you want to excel, and stand out from the competition, you cannot simply sing well – you must also have great skills in acting through song. The following exercises will help you explore your song from an actor's perspective – and enable you to deliver the material successfully as a piece of dramatic text. All of the acting exercises are suitable for everyone.

Rehearsing as a Spoken Monologue: Images and Objectives

An excellent way to begin work on acting through song is to rehearse your performance as a spoken monologue. This temporarily frees you from the rhythmic structure of the music, allowing you the time needed in rehearsal to discover truthful impulses for the first time. However, as discussed earlier, in order to respond truthfully and spontaneously in an audition – where there are usually no other actors – you must see 'targets' in your imagination. Remember, these targets fall into four categories:

1. Something the character would see if they looked at their surroundings.

2. An image from the character's memory.

3. An image prompted by the character envisioning the future.

4. The physical behaviour of another person that your character is looking at.

Before you undertake this exercise, list on your working copy of the music the targets you'll need to see when acting the song. You may be surprised by how many there are. You will need to picture an image at all times – otherwise you will have nothing to respond to. The image will usually change every couple of lines, but in some songs may do so more frequently. The first image you see should occur before the opening line, so it engenders an impulse to start singing. For example, before the actress playing Maria can sing the first line of the title song from *The Sound of Music*, she needs to imagine a beautiful Austrian mountain range.

Once you have written down a list of images for the entire song, you are ready to undertake the exercise. You will need a friend or colleague to assist you.

1. Stand in the centre of the room. Give the working copy of your music to your partner. They should sit on the floor away from your eyeline.

2. Your partner should then read to you the first image you have written down, for example: 'an Austrian mountain range'. Picture that image in your mind, and describe out loud to your partner what you see. This should be done with your eyes open. Avoid giving intellectual answers where you are not really picturing anything. 'The large rocky mountains rise up into the summer sky' is problematic; whereas 'on the side of the nearest mountain there is a small dirt track that winds its way upwards, halfway up there is a single small tree with twisted branches and no leaves' is better.

3. To encourage you to imagine more clearly, your partner can ask you questions if they suspect that what you are describing is not truly imagined. It is helpful if they encourage you to focus on a detail, such as 'Describe the branches on the tree' or 'What do the clouds above the mountain look like?'

4. Once your partner is satisfied you have a clear mental picture of the first image on your list, they should then read out the next. Repeat Stage 3 for every image you have written down.

5. Having completed this work, act through your entire song as a spoken monologue. Allow the images you have just pictured to 'drop in' to your mind at the points you identified in the

lyric. Give yourself full permission to respond physically to those images. For example, if you had pictured someone crying, you might take a step towards them to offer comfort. If you had envisaged a clear blue sky, your impulse might be to look upwards at it and smile.

6. Rehearse your song as a monologue once more. This time, begin to play the objectives of the song, as well as seeing the images. (These objectives are outlined for you in the 'Textual Analysis' section of the self-rehearsal guides.) For example, in the opening line of 'The Sound of Music' the actress playing Maria might explore the following objective: to rejoice in the beauty of the natural world. As you rehearse, if your work is unclear, your partner should encourage you to go back and play an objective differently, or more strongly. Allow about two hours of rehearsal to explore each moment of the song till you can both play the objectives and respond impulsively to the images.

7. Finally, do a full run-through of the song, this time singing instead of speaking. See the images once more and trust yourself to respond to the impulses that are generated as a result of what you see. You shouldn't think about the objectives at this stage, instead clear your mind and trust that through rehearsal, and by seeing the images, the objectives will come to you in the moment of playing the song. Once you have finished, get your partner to feed back on what they observed.

Real Person/Imaginary Person

As mentioned in the previous exercise, if your song is directed towards another character in the musical, rather than being a soliloquy, then you will need to imagine that character's behaviour when acting it in audition. That can be difficult to sustain for the full duration of a song, but this next exercise will help you. The premise is that you work with another actor to discover what the other character's behaviour might be. You then repeat the work, but this time imagining the behaviour of the other character instead.

1. Before you start the exercise, you need to have worked on your objectives and memorised the lyrics so that you can look at the other actor.

2. Explain the given circumstances to your partner and agree an objective for them to play. It is helpful if their chosen objective works in opposition to your own, as this will create conflict in the scene and give you more to work off. For example, suppose the given circumstances are that the two characters are ex-partners and have recently broken up. If your objective is: to convince the other character to give the relationship another try, then a good choice for them to play would be: to try to avoid an intimate conversation.

3. Act through your song as a spoken scene between the two of you. Play your objectives. Your partner should also play their own objective fully and respond instinctively within the parameters of the given circumstances. So, for example, if the given circumstances were those outlined above, as you sing, your partner might choose to turn their back on you at certain points, or walk away. Pay careful attention to their behaviour and respond. At times you may feel that you are failing in your objective, which should provoke you to try something new. On other occasions you may notice that you are beginning to gain traction over your partner – which may prompt you to continue with your objective or encourage you to play a more conciliatory choice of action.

4. Now perform the song as a speech again, but this time without the other actor. Imagine the character's behaviour instead. This may include you remembering activities your partner just did, or might involve you making up something new in your head. (As you move towards a complete performance, beware of only replaying in your mind what the other actor did as this can limit your imaginative range.)

5. Finally, add the music and perform the full song, imagining the behaviour of the other character as you do so. You should find you have a much more detailed understanding of what your imaginary scene partner is doing, and will discover more impulses to respond as a result.

Incorporating Actions

As discussed earlier, playing an action (a transitive verb) on each line of your song can make your work more specific, credible and engaging. Whilst this is the strength of actioning as a system, its weakness is that it can lead to you 'getting stuck in your head'. You can end up thinking about the actions you have written down on your working copy, rather than acting spontaneously in the moment. The following exercise will help you avoid this pitfall and enable you to integrate your choices of action organically into your performance – helping you deliver a performance that is both specific and spontaneous.

Preparation

1. To undertake this exercise you are advised to purchase *Actions: The Actors' Thesaurus* by Marina Caldarone and Maggie Lloyd-Williams, available as both a book and an iOS app.

2. Firstly, you need to decide upon, and note down, your choice of actions on the working copy of your music. You will need to find a different choice for each sentence. Begin by acting out the first sentence of the lyric, whilst playing your objective. Speak the words, rather than sing them, then try and name the action you just played instinctively. For example, you may feel you were encouraging, mocking, undermining, soothing or seducing. (Remember, an action must fit into the format: 'I [action] you', or if the character is talking to themselves, 'I [action] myself'.)

3. Now look up the action you just identified in the book or the app, or using a thesaurus. This will provide you with a list of similar and related choices. For example, if you identified 'mock' as the choice you played, it would give further options such as: deride, patronise, ridicule, taunt, etc. Choose the word that you like the most from the list, the one you feel best suits your objective, and note it down clearly and legibly on your working copy. If none of them feel quite right, try another initial choice, and use the app/thesaurus again to provide further options.

4. Repeat this process, sentence by sentence, until you have noted down actions that you like for the entire song. Strive for

as much variety as possible, whilst still ensuring the actions you decide upon are logical for the character and situation. The self-rehearsal guides contain suggested actions that are appropriate for each song, but it will give you a greater sense of ownership of your performance if you are also able to identify your own choices.

Application

For this part of the work you will need the help of a colleague or friend.

1. Run your song as a spoken monologue, as you've done previously, ensuring you are still seeing images and are playing your objectives.

2. As you do this, your partner should stand about half a metre behind you with your working copy in their hand. A second or so before each sentence they should speak aloud your next action. They should do this in the form of a direct instruction. So if your action choice is 'I tempt you', and the character you are talking to is female, then you partner would simply say 'Tempt her'. If your action is 'I cross-examine myself' your partner would say 'Cross-examine yourself'. It is important that your partner says the actions loudly and clearly and doesn't worry about disturbing your work. The actions need to be delivered loud enough so that you can hear them whilst you are acting, and early enough so you have a second to process the word before it is time to play the choice. It is often necessary for your partner to say the next action whilst you are still acting the preceding sentence.

3. As your partner feeds you the actions, you shouldn't look at them – instead focus on the images you are seeing. Respond impulsively to what they say, like they are your inner thoughts.

4. Once you have completed the exercise, take a moment to clarify any hiccups. Identify any moments in which the action was incorrect, or in the wrong place. Ask if you needed a word to be spoken earlier. Change an action if you felt the chosen verb wasn't helping your performance.

5. Repeat Stages 2 and 3 again. It is usual for the first version to feel a little contrived, but by repeating the work, you will begin to take more ownership of the choices.

6. Once you have been through the process for the second time, immediately, and without discussion, act through the entire song as a monologue – this time without your partner feeding you the actions. Don't try to remember the actions you just heard, simply see your images and play your objectives. You will find that many of the actions 'stick', but you may also find you play different choices on some lines. Either eventuality is fine – don't feel obliged to stick to the actions from the exercise.

7. Finally – add the singing, ensuring you still continue to play actions now that you are no longer speaking. Get your partner to observe and feed back on what they saw. You should find your work is now much more specific.

Whispered Thoughts/Ownership of Words

This final exercise is to help you develop a deeper connection to the lyric, by allowing you to experience and find the full meaning of each individual word. You will require the assistance of two friends or colleagues.

1. Kneel on the floor with your eyes closed. Hold the working copy of your sheet music up in front of you.

2. Your two assistants should kneel either side of you, so they are in a position to whisper directly into one of your ears. One assistant should whisper into your right ear, the other into your left.

3. As you keep your eyes closed, your assistants should whisper alternative words in your ears by reading the lyrics off the sheet music. For example, if they were reading the first line of 'Happy Birthday', it would divide up as follows:

> Assistant 1: Happy
>
> Assistant 2: birthday
>
> Assistant 1: to
>
> Assistant 2: you

4. As your assistants whisper the words, they should do so with great intensity. They should aim to communicate the meaning of each individual word into your ear. Whilst they do this, you should try to clear your mind and receive the words as if you are hearing them for the first time. You may experience the exercise as though the words are your inner thoughts.

5. Once the task has been completed for the full lyric, stand up and act the full song as a monologue. You may find that you have made some new discoveries about the lyric and developed greater ownership of the words. Where previously you might have been neglecting particular words, receiving the lyric from your helpers in this way helps you to find new and fresh ways of delivering words that you might have been glossing over. Ask your assistants to feed back on this element of your performance.

The Audition

Delivering a song in an audition is different from acting on a stage. During an audition there are usually no other actors to work with; you sing to a panel rather than an audience, and you perform your song out of context. You must therefore modify the approach you would use in performance. This chapter will explore how you can do so.

When it comes to audition technique, I have often heard teachers and industry experts who claim to know the secret of how to audition successfully. However, in my role as course leader for several performing-arts programmes, I have been fortunate to lead masterclasses with many of the UK's leading casting directors. I have also sat on numerous audition panels for entry into leading drama schools. My overwhelming lesson from these experiences is this: when it comes to evaluating auditions, everyone has different preferences. It is subjective. Therefore this chapter is not simply a summary of my own opinions on auditions, rather it reflects a synthesis of the best advice I have heard from experts who regularly sit behind the audition table. So whilst I would, of course, recommend you consider these points carefully, I would encourage you to be discerning when receiving advice about auditions: it is only one person's opinion.

DO WHAT YOU DO

One of the best pieces of advice on auditioning I have heard comes from the actor Bryan Cranston, famous for the hit TV series *Breaking Bad*. You can find this short video yourself on YouTube. To summarise, Cranston's advice is: rather than going into an audition aiming to get a job (or a place at a drama school), you should simply 'present what you do'. He advocates that, rather than trying to always second-guess what the panel are after – which is completely out of your control – you should empower yourself to do what you do well, and then walk away. This is incredibly useful when preparing a song for audition. There can be a temptation to try to mould your performance into what you think the panel will want. Do they want me to sing to them, or over their heads? Would they prefer I was physically still, or used the space? Rather than hamstring yourself like this, I would suggest you follow Cranston's advice. Take ownership of the decisions you make; do what it is that you do well and make choices that you feel show you at your best. Remember: it is your audition.

PREPARATION

When I ask casting directors and performing-arts lecturers what they think is the most important factor in a good audition, they invariably give the same reply: preparation. Castings are usually friendly and supportive environments. The people behind the audition table need to cast their show, or find the right applicants for their course. *They want you to be good* – so they generally do all they can to put you at your ease so that you can demonstrate your talent and be the solution to their problem. However, though you will find that audition panels tend to be very considerate if you make a mistake through nerves – as this can happen to everyone – they can be less tolerant if you haven't prepared properly. But what should your preparation involve? Here is a checklist:

1. Ensure you know the song(s) you have prepared inside out – both musically and lyrically. When you are nervous in audition it can affect your ability to perform and you can make silly mistakes. Allied to this, your songs may be redirected in the room – which can also throw you a little. To avoid making unnecessary errors, you therefore need to know the material especially well.

2. Find out about the people on the panel. A simple internet search will allow you to research the background of a casting director you are auditioning for, find out about a

director's previous shows and achievements, or read up on the career of the course leader of the drama school you want to attend. If possible, go and watch the work of the people on the panel, or a graduation performance of the course you want to take. This kind of research will give you an insight into the type of actors, material and performance styles the panel might favour. It also gives you the opportunity to strike up a conversation about something that interested you or that you admired. This helps suggest that you take the audition seriously and have a genuine interest in the panel members and their work. If you are auditioning for a musical at school, or with your local amateur group, if possible, take the opportunity to speak to the person leading the auditions in advance to get an idea what they may be looking for.

3. Go through your song in advance with a pianist. Many auditionees fail to do this, and it really affects their performance in the room. Working with a piano in advance will allow you to be completely certain about key musical issues, such as how you pitch your first note, when you come in during the introduction, and how the vocal line fits with the accompaniment.

4. Prepare what is asked. If you are auditioning for a performing-arts course, you will often be given a clear brief about the type and length of audition song to bring with you. For professional auditions, the casting director will usually provide a breakdown (through your agent) about the style of song that is required. Presenting the right type of material gives you the best chance of showing the panel what they need to see. It can be hard to cast an actor in *Hamilton* if they audition with a song by Rodgers and Hammerstein.

5. Memorise key information about the show your audition song is from and the character you are playing. This will help you address any questions that the panel may have. They might ask about the given circumstances, or the overall context of the piece. Sometimes they may enquire

about the vocal range of the song, particularly what the top note is. Most of this information is contained within these pages, but there is further research you can do. If the show is currently running, go and see it. If that is not possible, you can watch footage of previous productions online. If you are auditioning for a full-length production, you may have been sent a script; if so, always read it in its entirety. In early-round auditions for musicals, you will normally sing material of your own choosing, rather than songs from the show you are up for. But whether you are auditioning for a professional show or for the faculty of a drama school, it is likely that the panel will know the canon very well. So if you are aware of the key information, it gives you an opportunity to demonstrate that you have done your research, are well prepared – and are therefore someone they may want to work with.

6. Dress appropriately for the audition. Deciding what to wear for a professional audition is relatively simple. A good benchmark is 'smart-casual'. You shouldn't overdress, as you need to feel comfortable to physically inhabit your song, but on the other hand, you don't want it to appear that you have made no effort. I sometimes say to my students: 'If you are not comfortable walking down the street in your audition outfit then you have probably got it wrong.' When you are auditioning for a drama school you are often asked on your invitation letter to wear loose, comfortable clothing, or dance attire, as there will usually be a movement component to the audition. However, it can be advisable to bring a change of clothing (similar to that suggested for a professional audition – i.e. smart-casual) for the singing component of a drama-school audition. In my experience, if you enter the singing audition with your hair still done for the ballet class, or wearing jogging bottoms, then it can make you appear and feel like a dancer. This can make it harder for the panel to take you seriously as an actor-singer.

THE PROCESS

When you first start auditioning, if you are not sure what to expect, then the structure of the process can be quite unsettling. There are lots of small things that can throw you on the day, which can mean that when you get to the most important part – the singing – you are not as focused as you might be. In truth, every casting is different – so some of the best advice you can have is to expect the unexpected. However, there are certain things that are fairly typical in most singing auditions, and if you enter those situations with a good understanding of the way they are likely to be structured, you give yourself the best opportunity to do well. The following sequence describes what you might expect in an early round of auditions for a big commercial musical, and how that might differ if you are taking part in a singing audition in a drama school.

1. In a professional scenario, you are brought into the room by the casting director – who introduces you to the team. In a drama-school audition this task may be done by a tutor, or by a student who is already on the course. (Alternatively you may already be in the room with a group of fellow applicants, as the whole group sing in front of each other.)

2. There is a short greeting. In a drama-school audition someone may ask your name. The panel – who could range anywhere from two to twenty people (in auditions for big-budget musicals) – will normally remain behind the table.

3. Someone, perhaps the musical director (or a tutor in a drama-school audition), will ask you what you want to sing. A choice is agreed between you and them.

4. You go over to the pianist and discuss how you would like your music played.

5. You come into the centre of the room and sing the song.

6. The panel may, or may not, ask you to sing something else, they might redirect the song, or hear you do some vocal exercises.

7. They then thank you for your time and you leave, often without any feedback.

8. The whole process normally lasts between five and ten minutes.

As you can see, this is a fairly brief opportunity for you to showcase your abilities. It is therefore important to make the most of every moment in the room. Let's consider how you should approach each stage of the process.

ENTERING THE ROOM

When I've sat on audition panels for shows, I've found that the actors that often seemed to get cast were those that came across as open, positive and professional – someone that the panel felt they wanted to work with. Although tutors at drama schools may put less emphasis on this and look more for raw potential (at this stage of their careers, few applicants are great at auditioning), the impression you make as an individual is still highly important.

As previously mentioned, in a musical-theatre audition you get very little time to put across a positive impression. It is unlike a casting for a play, where your audition slot is usually longer and you get the opportunity to talk with the director and strike up a rapport. The panel have very little time to form opinions about you, so what you do when you enter the room is crucial.

Here are a few things to try:

1. Enter with purpose. Make eye contact from the moment you come through the door and walk energetically to the centre of the room. Take control of the space. You want to appear upbeat and pleased to be there.

2. Sometimes the panel may still be talking amongst themselves about the last audition when you're coming in. If so, hold your ground in the centre of the space, breathe, and wait for them to look up. Don't wander aimlessly over

to the pianist until you have had the chance to greet them and agree your song choice.

3. Unless instigated by the panel, don't shake their hands. This process can become tiresome for them if they have to repeat it all day, so it is often not welcomed. They will offer their hand if they want to greet you in that manner.

4. Don't convey anything negative. You get to say very little in a musical-theatre audition, so opinions can be shaped by the smallest ill-thought-out comments. No one wants to hear about your sore throat or that you've had a terrible journey.

5. You will frequently be asked to prepare two songs for an audition. But when you are asked what you are going to sing, don't offer the panel a choice. Tell them which song you intend to sing. This approach is wise for two reasons. Firstly, most panels are happy for you to make this decision, as it saves time and stops them having to make the choice. Secondly, and more importantly, you will usually get to sing the song that showcases you best. (Don't worry, the panel will tell you if they want to hear an alternative!)

THE PIANIST

Once you have agreed your song choice you should make your way straight to the piano. Again, take control of this moment. Don't wait to be told. There is nearly always a time pressure in singing auditions, and your efficiency will be appreciated. As you head towards the piano it is worth reminding yourself that the performance you are about to give will rely a great deal on how well the pianist plays for you. So take a moment to greet them and ask them how they are. Be polite and professional. Taking a second to say hello costs you nothing and can help get the pianist on your side. It is important to understand that the panel may also be taking an interest in these interactions at the piano. When I am behind the table I often listen to how the singer interacts with the pianist. It gives me a sense of whether they will be somebody who I want to be in the room with.

After you have greeted the pianist, you should then explain how you would like your song to be played. If you are not very experienced at auditioning, or are not a musician yourself, it can be intimidating giving musical instructions to a professional pianist. Don't worry though – a pianist is looking for and expecting instructions about the tempo, etc. Take the time you need and don't feel rushed. Of course, the more clearly and efficiently you can communicate your requirements to the pianist, the better. To help you with this it is hugely beneficial to have laid out and marked up your music correctly in advance. As someone who has spent a lot of time sight-reading, as both a musical director and a vocal coach, I can't tell you how much easier it is when the actor has prepared their music properly and can explain clearly what they want.

Before the audition you should have done the following:

1. Marked up your sheet music. Use your clean copy to do this, rather than your working/rehearsal copy. Start by ensuring any cuts are crossed out. To mark these clearly, draw brackets around where a cut begins and where it ends. Score out the cut section with several lines unmistakably in pen. When whole pages are cut out they should be taken out entirely. If you are cutting an entire verse, and the lyrics for one verse are printed on top of the other, rule out any unsung lyrics with a ruler and pen.

2. Once you have marked the cuts, highlight any repeat marks, codas, or important dynamics with a highlighter pen. Do this in a single colour. Colour-coding is not necessary – the pianist knows what the musical instructions mean. You are simply highlighting these to draw their attention to them. If you are not sure what to highlight, seek the advice of a singing coach or music teacher, or a friend who is a musician. They can help you to mark up the music appropriately.

3. Put the marked and highlighted sheet music into a display file (a folder with in-built plastic pockets) as this makes it easy for the pianist to turn the pages. Avoid using a ring-binder, as these are very hard for quick page-turns. An alternative to using a display file is to tape the music together. If you do this, ensure you tape down the full length of the page on both sides (if you only tape one side the music can stick together), then fold the pages so the music concertinas into a book.

4. Ensure there isn't any old music lurking at the back of your display file. It is not uncommon for one of the panellists to flick through your portfolio if they didn't fancy hearing your original song choice. If there are other songs in your folder you may find they ask you to sing them instead – even if you haven't performed them for years and have forgotten half of the words!

Knowing that your music is well prepared will help you be assured in your dealings with the pianist. Here is how you should use your time at the piano:

1. Once you have greeted the pianist, put your music on the piano stand. A good trick is to enter the room with a finger tucked inside your folder at the first page of your song. This will help you find it immediately.

2. Begin by pointing out any repeats in the music. These will be easy to find as you will have highlighted them. If there are no repeats, tell the pianist: 'It goes straight through.'

3. You should then indicate your desired tempo. The best way to do this is to sing a section at the speed you require, tapping a clear pulse on your leg as you do so. It is advisable to ask the pianist to play the first note of the section before you demonstrate. This will help ensure you are singing in the correct key when you set the tempo.

4. If the sections are marked '*colla voce*', '*rubato*' or '*freely*' then the pianist will follow you at these points and it is unnecessary to provide them with a tempo. Instead give the speed for the moment when the music drops into a steady

pulse. If there is more than one tempo in your song, you should go through each one, as indicated in Step 5.

5. Once you have finished going through the music and thanked the pianist, ask them if they wouldn't mind waiting until you indicate that you are ready to sing. This will allow you a moment once you get to the centre of the room to focus your thoughts before they begin to play, and allow you to act from the first note of the introduction.

MAKING CHOICES

Once you leave the pianist you have a couple of key decisions to make. Firstly: where will you start in the space? This will often be your first time in this particular audition room, so you need to make a quick assessment of your options. A majority of auditionees will begin their song standing roughly in the centre of room, facing the panel about two to five metres from the table – depending on the size of the space. This is a standard convention, and if you make this choice it will certainly do you no harm. However, in my experience facilitating workshops with leading industry professionals, they have often revealed to my students how performers at the top of their profession make much bolder use of the space. I have witnessed casting director Neil Rutherford, who has vast experience of auditions at the highest levels from both sides of the table, encourage my students to start their performance from a corner of the audition room. On many occasions I have observed award-winning actress Rosalie Craig begin a song in an audition masterclass leaning casually against the wall or lying on the floor. Such choices give the impression that the actor is comfortable in the space. It also allows the panel to get a sense of how you might use your physicality on stage. So don't be afraid to start kneeling, or to make use of a chair; just ensure that your decisions make sense in the context of song. For example, if you are singing 'How Many Tears' from *Martin Guerre*, the character Bertrande is praying. So it would be a sensible choice to start kneeling on the floor, perhaps at a slight angle to the table, looking up towards an imaginary heaven. If you are singing 'I Don't Know How to Love Him' from *Jesus Christ Superstar*, Mary Magdalene is reflecting about her confused romantic feelings for Jesus. To portray her sense of reflection, it might make leaning against the wall, hugging your arms to comfort yourself, an appropriate starting point.

The second important decision you need to make is whether to sing directly to the panel, or not. This is a choice you should have made – and practised – in advance of your audition. Your options are:

1. To sing to the panel, making direct eye contact with them.

2. To sing to a fixed point above their heads.

3. To direct your focus to a variety of circles of attentions.

It is worth noting that leading casting professionals have different preferences when it comes to this issue. Some feel involved when they are engaged with eye contact; others prefer for you to look above them so they can sit back and assess your work without feeling they need to be directly involved in your performance. As opinions differ, the best advice is for you to make an informed choice about which style works best for your song and for you as an actor. In audition workshops with Olivier Award-winning director Timothy Sheader, I have often heard him remonstrate with students about the need for them to make clear and definite choices about where they place their focus. But what factors should determine your decision?

Singing to the Panel

This manner of presentation works particularly well if you are performing a comedy number, or a narrative song. It can also suit songs that are written as conversations with a group of other characters, or with the audience. You may discover this style suits you if you are an actor that usually thrives on interaction with other performers. Singing to the panel often has the benefit of making them feel included and engaged.

However, there are certain styles of song that don't suit this
mode of presentation. Pieces in which the content is
aggressive or confrontational can be awkward, as they can
make the panel feel as though they are the ones under attack.
Similarly, songs that are flirtatious or seductive can be a little
uncomfortable to watch. It is also worth understanding that
the panel might be making notes or whispering to each other
during your performance (they are not being rude – they are
doing their job). If you think this might throw you, then you
may want to consider one of the other styles of song
presentation. Below are a few tips for singing directly to the
panel:

1. Don't sing for too long at one individual person, as it can
   become uncomfortable for them, particularly if they want
   to make a note, or discuss you with their colleague. If you
   make eye contact with a panel member and they look away,
   or seem uneasy – shift your focus to another person. It is
   important to share your performance with the entire panel
   in any case.

2. Avoid getting too close to the table, as again this can be a
   little disconcerting for the audition panel.

3. Don't neglect thoughts that are found in your imagination,
   e.g. mental pictures that are located in the first or third
   circles of attention (see pp. 26–27). In life we rarely deliver
   an entire conversation directly into someone's eyes.

Singing to a Fixed Point

This style of presentation is perhaps the most commonly used
by musical-theatre professionals. It is a method of acting
through song where you sing to a single focal point over the
heads of the panel. For songs that are addressed to one
character, it can work particularly well, as you can put all your
focus on seeing that imaginary person. It also means you are
less likely to feel self-conscious because you are not making
eye contact with those assessing you. It also allows them to

discuss you, and write notes about you. On a different point, some actors struggle to know what physical choices to make when they are singing in audition – they worry about using too many gestures. Although I would encourage you to trust your impulses – and always move if it feels correct – this style of auditioning can help, as it lends itself to a stiller form of presentation. It also allows the panel to concentrate on your voice, which is normally the crucial component being assessed in early-round musical-theatre auditions. Below is some advice about singing to a fixed point:

1. As discussed in the previous chapter, you must see mental pictures in your imagination at all times. So if you are singing to another character, for example, you must visualise the behaviour of the person to whom you are singing. Imagine them walking into a room, winking at you, shrugging their shoulders, etc., as this will give you something to respond to.

2. Ensure your imaginary person is positioned behind the table so you are not singing on too much of an angle; otherwise the people who need to be able to see you end up looking at the side of your head.

3. When you are singing to an imaginary person, don't have them sat down, or stood on top of something. As the casting team are not privy to what you are picturing, it can appear as if you are talking to a dwarf or a giant! This can look very odd.

4. In this mode it is easy to feel physically inhibited. Always give yourself permission to move and follow your impulses.

Varied Circles of Attention

This approach is useful for songs where the character is singing in soliloquy, i.e. when they are alone. When delivering soliloquies in audition, try mixing the focus of your delivery so that you find some thoughts in the first and third circles of attention – and address the panel in other moments. This approach has the benefit of allowing you to display an element of stagecraft in your song presentation, and to demonstrate physical choices that bear a similarity to those you might do on stage. However, you need to be physically articulate to pull off this approach so that your choices make logical sense to those watching – otherwise your performance can easily be criticised as lacking in focus.

Here are some tips for this style of presentation to make your focal points specific:

1. Try putting your focus in the first or third circles when the character is remembering something, or envisaging a future event. See an image each time you do this. For example, in 'I Dreamed a Dream' from *Les Misérables* – which is a soliloquy – if you were playing Fantine, you would see images of your memories of the romantic summer you spent with Cosette's father.

2. The best thoughts to address directly to the panel are lyrics in which the character asks themselves a question, confesses a secret, or has a moment of self-discovery. In these instances, use the panel as though they are your inner-consciousness – try to seek their advice as though you are searching your own soul.

THE MOMENT OF ORIENTATION

Whichever method of delivery you decide upon, perhaps the most difficult moment of your audition is the transition between the conversational element of the meeting and the start of your performance. It is a challenge to shift quickly and successfully from talking to the pianist, to getting yourself in the necessary frame of mind to begin the song. A majority of young actors don't handle this as well as they might, and consequently the first thirty seconds of their audition song can often be acted poorly – until they get into their stride. By that point the panel may already have made an unfavourable decision.

Outlined below is a process to help you act successfully from the moment the music begins. We will use the song 'Send in the Clowns' from *A Little Night Music* as an example.

1. As you walk away from your conversation with the pianist, take a brief second to remind yourself of the immediate previous circumstances, i.e. what has happened just prior to the song. You want to focus on elements of the story that will engage you imaginatively, change your inner tempo and get you thinking as the character. In *A Little Night Music*, Desirée is in her bedroom, having just been told by her lover Fredrik that he doesn't intend to leave his young wife. If you were performing this song you might reflect on the pain and disappointment you felt just seconds ago when, for a brief moment, you thought Fredrik was going to choose to live his life with you, before realising you were cruelly mistaken.

2. Once you feel your imagination is activated, bring the first objective of your song to the forefront of your mind. Pretend that you desperately want that objective. So, with Desirée, you would focus on how much you want to make Fredrik laugh at the irony of the situation.

3. See your first image in your head. This should be the image that you respond to at the beginning of the song. This might be the behaviour of the imaginary person your character is talking to, a memory, an imagined possible future event, or an aspect of the character's surroundings. With Desirée you might imagine Fredrik smiling pityingly at you.

Once you have these three key points clear in your mind, you can indicate to the pianist you are ready. This entire process should take no more than a few seconds in total, as it can be awkward for the panel if your preparation takes too long. By readying yourself in this manner, and beginning the song in the correct mind-set, you will find it easier to act well and avoid feeling self-conscious about being watched by the panel.

ACTING THE INTRODUCTION

Once the music starts, you have your next big opportunity to make a favourable impression: by making the best use of the musical introduction. It is standard practice in audition to cut down an introduction to about two bars – and this is something you should do whenever possible. Yet even with such a short opening instrumental, it is important to recognise that the starting note of the music is the beginning of your performance and therefore the first chance the panel have to assess your acting. You should use this opportunity to stimulate the panel's interest. A good way to do this is through an imaginative use of the space. For example, in the song 'Maybe This Time' from *Cabaret*, Sally Bowles is singing to the audience of the Kit Kat Klub. So you might choose to start the song a few metres off the centre of the room, then walk into the middle of the space during the introduction, as if walking onstage towards a microphone. Making such a choice can get the panel sitting forward in their seats ready for the first lyric.

THE OPENING LINES

What you do next – in the first few lines – is crucial. You should make clear decisions in advance about what your first two actions (see pp. 25–26) will be. Although this approach is necessarily premeditated, knowing what you will play on the first line, and how the action changes on the second thought, can help set you running from the start of the song – which can be very hard to do in an audition when you are nervous. You may find that using a structured beginning can actually make you more spontaneous as the song progresses. Because you have started changing action on each new thought from the very start of your performance, you will find it easier to achieve the ideal use of actions with a different choice on every line.

FOLLOWING YOUR IMPULSES

Once you are into the flow of your song – if you have done the required preparation and rehearsal – then your job is actually uncomplicated: you merely need to see something, allow an impulse to develop inside you, and then trust your instincts enough to respond to it. Acting, though difficult to do well, is actually very simple. If instead of blocking yourself – by self-editing your choices through fear of failure – you give yourself permission to do whatever feels right in the moment, then you allow yourself a greater opportunity to be successful.

When you are acting in audition you should aim to follow this cyclical process:

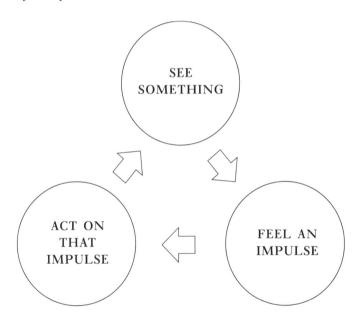

In an audition context, the instruction to 'see something' most usually refers to the mental images you will have practised, e.g. the character's memories, their visions of the future, their surroundings, or the imagined behaviour of the person to whom they are singing. When working in direct address, it refers to something you observe in the behaviour of the panel. For example, if you are working on 'Don't Cry for Me, Argentina' from *Evita*, you could imagine that the panel are your loyal supporters gathered round to hear you speak. So if one of the panellists smiles at you whilst you are singing, you could pretend they were a loyalist who was inspired by you. This might give you an impulse to galvanise them.

When you act on an impulse this can take several forms. It may cause you to move in the space, to use a gesture, or to a play an internal action – such as to comfort, to amuse, or to antagonise. A genuine impulse is a precious gift, and when one comes along you only have a split-second to take advantage of it. To do so you must act before you think. Because when you are in the moment, if you stop to analyse a choice, instead of just doing it, then spontaneity dies. Remember: *your impulse is always right*. When you are in that audition room you need to trust yourself, avoid second-guessing your choices, and give yourself total permission to follow your instincts in the moment.

EVENTS

In her fine book, *The Director's Craft: A Handbook for the Theatre*, Katie Mitchell talks about the idea of 'events'. An event is a fundamental shift. It is the instant the character makes an important discovery, takes a great decision, or has a moment of emotional catharsis. For instance, in 'Everything's Coming Up Roses' from *Gypsy*, the event occurs on the first note of the music, before the vocal line begins. Rose's eldest daughter June, the main attraction in their stage act, has just secretly eloped because she is sick of her pushy mother. In this moment Rose decides that she will therefore make her shy younger daughter Louise into a star instead. The event is marked by a drum-roll on the timpani in the accompaniment. Where there is an event in a song, this is identified in the self-rehearsal guides. As they are the most important moments in the story, they should be highlighted as the crucial moments of the narrative. You can emphasise an event successfully in the following ways:

1. Through a moment of stillness. This works particularly well when the character has a sudden realisation, or makes a fundamental internal decision.

2. By playing the strongest action of the entire song. This can highlight instances when the character finally communicates something they strongly feel – which has been suppressed for a long time.

3. By finding a genuine emotional connection at that point. This can be appropriate for moments of catharsis for the character.

CONCLUDING THE SONG

A simple way to refine and improve your audition technique is to take particular care of the moment at the end of the song, when you break out of the imaginary world of the character. You achieve this by staying in the thought-process of the song for a second or two after the music concludes, before clearly breaking character and bringing your focus back into the real world of the audition room. By marking this transition, it draws a clear delineation between yourself and the role. When you are on a panel and you see this transformation occur, it is very exciting to watch; you feel you have witnessed the end of a clear and defined piece of storytelling.

REDIRECTION

After you have performed your song you might be asked to sing it again following a piece of redirection from the panel. This might be a vocal instruction – you could be asked to belt a high note, rather than sing it in a Twang quality, for example – but more usually it will be related to acting.

When a director asks you to act your song differently, this isn't necessarily because they didn't like your original choices – it is usually an indication that they are interested in you and want to know more. A good piece of redirection will be an invitation for you to demonstrate a quality that wasn't present in your initial performance. The director, or drama-school tutor, might want you to play a different choice of action, so they may encourage you to charm, to cross-examine, to amuse, or to belittle. They might ask you to work for more stillness, or to make greater use of the space. On other occasions they may ask you to alter the given circumstances. For example: play the song as if you have just learned that your lover has abandoned you, or sing it as if you have just returned home after a romantic first date.

The redirection you are offered can sometimes be radically different from the given circumstances in the musical. This may be because the director is unfamiliar with your song, or more usually because they want to see if you can change your performance and be responsive to feedback. So even if the instructions seem strange or nonsensical, *don't ever be resistant to what is asked*. The first rule of being redirected is to respond positively to what is suggested. It is valid to engage with this redirection – to ask the panel to clarify or go further with their note – but this should always be done in a constructive and non-confrontational manner. You want to convey that you are someone who understands notes and will be good to work with.

When you act your song for the second time, you should be bold in your choices and fully engage with the redirection. However, playing a note successfully doesn't simply mean delivering only what was asked of you in a narrow, confined manner. See the note as a springboard to a wide range of new choices. This might mean starting in a different part of the room, being freer physically, and even allowing your vocal performance to alter radically. It is important to remember a basic fact: the panel witnessed your first version! They will have noted the original choices you made. So when you are redirected you should try to show something new on every line.

EXERCISES

As well as redirecting you, the panel may also ask you to sing some vocal exercises as a way of learning more about your voice. When you are auditioning for a production, this is usually because your song choice didn't demonstrate the vocal range required for the role you are being considered for. In drama-school auditions, you are often asked to sing exercises so the tutors can get a better picture of your full vocal potential. Exercises typically might include scales, arpeggios, or sirening on octave slides. The given exercise will usually be repeated, ascending a semitone at a time. When you deliver the requested exercise, give yourself the best opportunity to sing well by standing with good alignment of the head, neck and spine, with your feet directly below your hips and your weight evenly distributed. Release your abdominal wall between each repetition, as there can be a tendency for your breath to become tight as the exercise gets progressively higher. It is useful to understand that you will most usually be asked to continue progressing upwards in pitch *until your voice cracks*. Whilst this can be disconcerting, try not to let it worry you – it is just a method a panel uses to ascertain the top note of your range. You may well have sung the note the panel needed to hear several semitones before.

FEEDBACK

One of the hardest aspects of auditioning is that you rarely receive any detailed or meaningful feedback. Despite the recent #YesOrNo Twitter campaign, which has seen many leading theatres commit to informing all actors about the outcome of their audition, when trying out for many professional productions you still may not even be informed that you didn't get the job – only learning you have not got a part through the gradual passage of time. Undergoing a nerve-racking audition, and then not being told why you've been unsuccessful, can be wearing and demoralising. You can spend the weeks that follow an audition reliving it, second-guessing yourself and wondering whether you could have done something differently. Although to some extent this is unavoidable, it is also counterproductive and can make it hard to sustain yourself emotionally – whether through a season of drama-school auditions, or over a long career as a working actor.

A sensible way to manage this is to allow yourself a brief period of reflection – perhaps on your journey home from the audition – where you make a few notes on how you could improve next time around. You should then encourage yourself to forget about the audition – accept that the odds are that you will have been unsuccessful, that there is nothing you can do to change the outcome – and then ready yourself for the next opportunity. Responding in this manner can be an effective self-protection strategy that enables you to better cope with periods of uncertainty and rejection. In between auditions, if you are able to clear your mind and focus on the future, then on the occasions when the phone does ring, the positive outcomes are wonderful and uplifting surprises.

For further exercises and advice to aid you in the preparation and performance of your songs, you might look at the following books:

Acting Through Song: Techniques and Exercises for Musical-Theatre Actors by Paul Harvard

Successful Singing Auditions by Gillyanne Kayes

The Actor and the Target by Declan Donnellan

Finally, may I wish you the all very best for your audition, whatever it may be for. Remember that ultimately it is *your* audition. The exercises outlined in this book, followed carefully, will help you to prepare in the best possible way – but on the day the most important thing is to trust your own instincts and express yourself. Good luck!

PART TWO: THE SONGS

Soprano/Mezzosoprano

CLASSICAL MUSICAL THEATRE (1925–65)   90

CONTEMPORARY MUSICAL-THEATRE BALLADS (Post-1965)   124

CONTEMPORARY MUSICAL-THEATRE UP-TEMPO (Post-1965)   169

COMEDY/CHARACTER SONGS   196

'Can't Help Lovin' Dat Man'
from *Show Boat*

Music by Jerome Kern, lyrics by Oscar Hammerstein II

Choose this song if: you suit playing the romantic leading lady
and enjoy singing mezzosoprano legit material that is rooted
in a jazz tonality.

Given Circumstances

WHO ARE YOU: Julie La Verne, a mixed-race woman who most
people believe to be white. You are an independently minded,
intelligent and caring lady who is prepared to stand up for
what she believes to be right.

WHERE ARE YOU: In the kitchen pantry on board a showboat
named the *Cotton Blossom* in Natchez, Mississippi, USA.

WHEN IS IT: Late morning, a hot summer's day, 1890.

WHAT HAS HAPPENED BEFORE: The events of the story take
place approximately two decades after the end of the
American Civil War, when the North (or the 'Yankees')
defeated the Southern Confederacy. Although a key outcome
of the war was the banning of slavery in the South, racial
tensions continue to persist in states like Mississippi. Ten
years ago the white-dominated state government passed a
series of laws imposing racial segregation, and as a
consequence African-Americans still suffer extreme prejudice
under the law. Against this backdrop you were employed as
the leading lady on the *Cotton Blossom*. (This employment was
actually illegal under the state laws of the time, as a person
with black heritage was not allowed to perform for a
segregated white audience.)

This morning, about thirty minutes ago, the boat arrived at
the river dock in Natchez, Mississippi. When your boss, the

owner of the boat Captain Andy Hawks, tried to introduce the entertainers to the gathered crowd, a fistfight broke out between your husband Steve Baker (who is the leading man of the troupe) and a rough-mannered engineer named Pete. The cause of the fight was the sexual advances that Pete had been making towards you recently – which Steve objected to. After the fight had broken up and the crowd had moved on, a passing riverboat gambler by the name of Gaylord Ravenal took a romantic interest in the eighteen-year-old daughter of the captain, whose name is Magnolia. Magnolia is an aspiring performer who also happens to be your best friend. Whilst Gaylord was in the middle of talking to her he was called away to see the local judge, but not before he had made quite an impression on the young girl.

A few minutes ago you walked into the pantry to discover Queenie, one of the black women who is employed on the ship, hard at work, and Magnolia – who was sat daydreaming. Magnolia told you that she had fallen in love with Gaylord and asked for your advice. You warned her not to fall so easily for a stranger, as he might turn out to be no good. Magnolia retorted that if this proved to be case, then she would simply stop loving him. You cautioned her that it was not so simple. Your young friend then asked you why you were in love with Steve, to which you replied you didn't rightly know; there was little sense or reason as to why people fall in love – which is why she must be careful about this stranger who has just walked into her life. Magnolia then commented that these views were similar to those expressed in a song you often sang. When you gave voice to the opening section, Queenie said she was surprised that you knew a song that she had only ever heard black people sing. She has just encouraged you to sing the whole thing.

WHO ELSE IS THERE: Queenie and Magnolia.

WHO SHOULD YOU SING TO: Magnolia.

Textual Analysis

The song begins with a pre-chorus. During this opening section, you tell Magnolia that there is no logical rationale for your feelings towards Steve. Your objective at this point is: to convince Magnolia that love cannot be controlled. During the first stanza of the opening chorus you then warm to this theme. You tell your friend that you and Steve are meant for each other. Try playing the following objective at this point: to convince Magnolia of my commitment to my husband. You might explore actions such as: I urge, grip and arrest her. Your intention shifts in the second stanza, however, and becomes more light-hearted. The objective in this unit is: to mock your own foolishness. You might try to amuse Magnolia with these particular lyrics.

When you reach the bridge, you explain how you feel when your husband leaves you – and then returns. Your objective in this section: to get Magnolia to appreciate the depth of your love. You might explore actions such as: I charm, uplift and inspire her.

After the passionate outburst of the bridge there is a feeling of ease and serenity in the final section. With these lyrics you try to convey to Magnolia your complete contentment in your choice of husband. Your objective at this point is: to get Magnolia to see how happy you are in the relationship. In these final lines you might play actions such as: I soothe, calm and comfort her.

KEY MOMENTS/TOP TIPS

1. The key to this song is that, although at first glance it seems like a simple love song, in fact the lyrics also contain a message of gentle caution about the dangers of falling for a man. Keep the text active by constantly remembering that you are trying to change Magnolia's opinion about Gaylord.

2. The script indicates that Julie sings this song as part of the world of the play, but that is hard to convey in an audition.

Instead you should perform the lyrics as if they are sung dialogue, rather than the words of a song the character knows.

3. There is a wonderful musical build that occurs during the bridge. This climax needs to be matched with a strong connection to the character's emotional inner life. Let this musical release reflect the strength of Julie's feelings towards Steve.

Vocal and Musical Analysis

WHO TO LISTEN TO: Eva Gardner (dubbed by Annette Warren) on the 1951 film soundtrack.

VOCAL RANGE: B♭3 to F5.

ORIGINAL KEY: E♭ major.

ACCENT: Southern American.

STYLE OF MUSICAL: Book musical.

VOCAL SET-UP/MUSICAL TIPS

1. In the show other characters sing during the number. For the purposes of audition you should only sing the Julie's solo section, as per the suggested recording. On p. 68 of the suggested sheet music start with the last five bars, giving you a two-bar introduction before you start singing at the pre-chorus. You should then finish after you have sung the title lyric on p. 72 (just before the *poco meno* marking).

2. The delivery of the song should reflect the jazz influence of the score. To achieve this, try adding some pitch-glides and lowering the larynx to create a warm tone, as you can hear on the suggested recording.

3. Some of the notes should be 'bent' in pitch to give the music a jazz intonation – for example, on the first syllable of the word 'sister' in the opening line.

C L A S S I C A L

4. The choruses should be delivered in long legato phrases and with a consistent use of a simultaneous onset.

5. In the bridge you can afford to move the tempo forward slightly to give the song a feeling of momentum.

6. Try delivering the first two lines of last verse in Cry. Lift the larynx a little, to make the sound more vulnerable and introspective, as you can hear Warren demonstrate on the cast recording – before returning to a rich low-larynx sound.

Sheet Music

The correct sheet music for this song is available at www.scribd.com.

'Dear Friend'
from *She Loves Me*

Music by Jerry Bock, lyrics by Sheldon Harnick

Choose this song if: you have a rich, classical soprano or
mezzosoprano voice. The song offers the opportunity for you
to portray both an emotional vulnerability and lighter, more
comedic moments.

Given Circumstances

WHO ARE YOU: Amalia Balash, a highly strung and anxious
young woman in her early twenties. You are intelligent,
attractive and a lover of literature.

WHERE ARE YOU: The Café Imperiale in Budapest, Hungary.
This is a café with a romantic atmosphere, candles and dim
lighting.

WHEN IS IT: 10.05 p.m., a Tuesday, mid-December, sometime
in the early 1930s.

WHAT HAS HAPPENED BEFORE: This summer you turned up
uninvited at Mr Maraczek's parfumerie (a shop that sells
perfume) to ask for a job. You were hoping to replace a
previous salesperson, Miss Horvath, who was on maternity
leave. With the business struggling, the assistant manager
Georg Nowack told you that they were not hiring.

When Maraczek came in from the back room, he also told you
that there was no job available. However, just before you
entered, he had been insisting to a sceptical Georg that a new
product   a leather musical cigarette case – would be a big
success and that the first one would be purchased within the
hour. This would turn out to be your opportunity. Not to be
deterred, you took the initiative and managed to sell one of
the cigarette cases to a customer – by pretending it was a

candy box. Your salesmanship impressed Maraczek so much that you were offered a job on the spot.

Over the following few months, tensions began to develop among the staff at the parfumerie. In particular, yourself and Georg were constantly arguing. What you both failed to realise was that, for many months, you had unwittingly been anonymous romantic penpals. After exchanging letters for months, and never meeting, it was agreed that tonight at eight o'clock you would meet for a date with your anonymous correspondent. Neither yourself, nor Georg, had discovered each other's true identities.

With you both feeling nervous about the coming evening, just before closing time Maraczek picked a fight with Georg – saying he was unhappy that the Christmas decorations had yet to be put up. In his displeasure, Maraczek insisted that all of the employees must stay late to complete the task, but Georg told him he couldn't stay because he had an appointment. In his role as assistant manager Georg then informed yourself and the other members of staff that you would need to stay late instead. You responded by arguing but you couldn't – because you also had a date. When Georg told Maraczek this news, the owner threatened to fire him, complaining that his assistant manager was not dedicated enough to his job. In reality this was because Maraczek erroneously suspected Georg was having an affair with his wife. Incensed, Georg resigned.

You arrived at the café some time ago with your copy of the Tolstoy novel *Anna Karenina*, and a rose, so that your penpal could identify you. When Georg arrived a little later he was so nervous that he wanted to leave without even seeing his blind date, but he was encouraged to stay by your mutual colleague Sipos – whom Georg had brought along to give him courage. When Sipos pointed out the rose you were holding, Georg was shocked to discover the true identity of his penpal. He couldn't believe that – through letters – he had fallen in love with someone whom he had argued with so much in person. At first Georg wanted to leave, but Sipos encouraged him to try to make the date work. So Georg came over to your table, told you that he had resigned, and asked if you would share a celebratory drink with him. You, though, were impatient and rude and tried to get him to leave, as you still believed you were waiting for someone else. In retaliation Georg mocked you, so you hurled a series of insults at him, and a few moments ago he stormed out. You immediately regretted what you had said. With Georg having left only seconds ago, the waiter has just come over to you to tell you that it is almost closing time. After revealing to him that your date was now more than two hours late (or so you believe) the waiter has just given you a free carafe of wine for good luck.

WHO ELSE IS THERE: You are seated apart at a table – so in the main you should behave as if you are alone, but remember that there are other people in the café, and so at times you may become aware of their presence.

WHO SHOULD YOU SING TO: Sometimes you talk to yourself, at others to your absent penpal.

Textual Analysis

At the beginning of the song you are taking in the romantic décor of the café. Your objective in this opening section is: to purge your regret at the way the evening has turned out. It saddens you to be alone in such lovely surroundings. Try playing actions such as: I sadden, deflate and puncture myself at this point. You then become much more sarcastic during the first chorus. Your objective in this section is: to make light of the situation. You try to amuse yourself with the painful irony of the juxtaposition of your wonderful location – and the depressing turn of events. After this sardonic outburst, in the last two lines of the chorus you then talk to your penpal for the first time. Your objective in this brief moment is: to get your date to tell you when they will arrive.

When the second chorus begins you start to become acutely aware of the other people in the café. They are staring at you.

Your objective in the first half of this section is: to conceal the fact that you have been stood up. Everyone else in the establishment is dining with their partner, and this is making you acutely embarrassed. You therefore want to appear calm and content. With your cheeks blushing, in the second half of the chorus you address your absent date once more. Your objective here is: to convince your penpal to do the right thing. You want him to save you from your embarrassment. You might try actions such as: I beseech, entreat and charm you in order to try and achieve this.

In the final portion of the song, that occurs after the cut dialogue section (see point 3 in vocal set-up/musical tips), there are some repeated lyrics. To vary your performance, try this time delivering these to your absent friend. In the first two lines, when you explain that are trying to hide your feelings from the rest of the café, explore playing the following objective: to get my penpal to empathise with me. When you subsequently fail in this, you are driven to your final objective, which is contained within the lyric itself: I want to stop him from breaking my heart.

KEY MOMENTS/TOP TIPS

1. Explore sitting on a chair for your performance to give an indication of being at a table in a café. Try placing the chair a metre or two from the centre spot of the room and set at a 45-degree angle to the audition table.

2. When you are singing to your 'dear friend' you should use the third circle of attention, as if they are far away in your imagination.

3. Although the dialogue is cut (see point 3 below), it is handy to use this exchange to inform your interpretation of the last section. The waiter has just told you that the café is closing and that you must accept that your date is not going to arrive. This should help you find a greater sense of desperation in your final pleas for him to appear.

4. Although *She Loves Me* is a comedy, it is important to remember the stakes of this situation are high. Amalia has been waiting all of her life for such a date – so she is devastated to believe she has now been stood up.

5. It is useful to explore that in the final two lines, when Amalia implores her friend not to break her heart, she discovers that she is no longer singing to an unknown someone – that she is actually talking to Georg. This moment of self-discovery – when she realises she is truly in love with her colleague – is the event of the song.

Vocal and Musical Analysis

WHO TO LISTEN TO: Laura Benanti on the Broadway revival cast recording (2016).

VOCAL RANGE: D♭4 to F5.

ORIGINAL KEY: D♭ major.

ACCENT: As an American show, this song is most usually performed in General American. However, if you have a native Eastern European accent – it would be highly appropriate to use your own voice.

STYLE OF MUSICAL: Book musical.

VOCAL SET-UP/MUSICAL TIPS

1. The fundamental sound for this song is a legit set-up. Use a great deal of thyroid tilt, simultaneous onsets and a consistent vibrato, as Benanti demonstrates on the cast recording.

2. In the opening verse you should look to achieve a conversational tone. Whilst the highest notes in the section require you to use thyroid tilt, try employing a Speech quality on some of the lower pitches, as Benanti so ably shows.

CLASSICAL

3. There is a dialogue section in the middle of the song that should be removed for audition purposes. Cut from the beginning of bar 80 to the end of bar 99 on the suggested sheet music.

4. Stylistically, it is important to deliver long legato phrases when engaged in legit singing. Be careful to avoid glottal onsets and aim to run the vowels together. A good example of this is when you hear Benanti singing about the violins playing during the first chorus.

5. Lower your larynx slightly and anchor the torso on the higher notes to give your performance a slightly operatic sound. You can hear Benanti demonstrate this at various points throughout the song; for example, on the word 'heart' near the end of the piece.

Sheet Music

The correct sheet music for this song is available at www.scribd.com.

'I Have Confidence'
from *The Sound of Music*

Music by Richard Rodgers, lyrics by Oscar Hammerstein II

Choose this song if: you have a classical legit mezzosoprano voice and enjoy playing characters who manage to tackle their insecurities by approaching life with an upbeat perspective.

Given Circumstances

WHO ARE YOU: Maria Rainer, a flighty, free-spirited and adventurous young postulant (someone who is the process of becoming a nun), who has been struggling with the commitments of a life inside a convent.

WHERE ARE YOU: The song begins outside the gates of Nonnberg Abbey in Salzburg, Austria. It ends at the gates of Captain von Trapp's house. In between, the song takes place at various locations on the journey between the two buildings.

WHEN IS IT: 9.35 a.m., early spring, 1938.

WHAT HAS HAPPENED BEFORE: You have been a postulant for nearly six months. Since you arrived at the abbey you have been constantly getting into trouble for breaking minor rules – such as singing in the garden, which is forbidden. Your behaviour has been causing concern amongst the nuns, particularly your habit of being late. Nonetheless they are affectionate towards you and take you for what you are: an innocent and naive young girl.

Yesterday evening you returned to the abbey later than you should – having lost track of time. You had been to visit the mountains where you were raised as a girl. As a result, this morning you were summoned by the Mother Abbess – who advised that you should spend some time outside of the abbey. When you protested that you didn't want to be sent away, the Mother Abbess suggested that perhaps this might be God's will

– so that you would have the time and space to reflect on whether you still wished to become a nun. She told you that a retired naval officer, Captain Georg von Trapp, had contacted the abbey to request a governess for his seven children. The arrangement would be until September. The Mother Abbess convinced you to accept the position and said you should set out immediately, as the Captain was expecting you this very afternoon. You have just changed into ordinary clothes, packed your belongings and readied yourself for a new adventure.

WHO ELSE IS THERE: You are alone.

WHO SHOULD YOU SING TO: Yourself.

Textual Analysis

The song begins with you exiting the gates of the abbey. This is an action that fills you with contradictory emotions: excitement about the possibilities afforded by a new life in the outside world – and apprehension about the unknown. Your objective at the beginning of the song is: to imagine what the future might hold. You ponder what lies ahead of you over the coming months and try to greet it with an optimistic outlook. Actions you might play in the opening lines include: I inspire, kindle and vitalise myself. Your positivity quickly drains out of you, as you are also frightened about what may lie in store. This nervousness and apprehension irritates you, as all of your life you have wanted an adventure such as this. Your objective in this unit is therefore: to work out what is wrong with you.

Halfway through the opening section your attention drifts towards the captain and his children. As someone who has never had to raise a child before, let alone seven, the prospect of becoming a governess daunts you. In trying to battle your burgeoning self-doubt your objective in this unit becomes: to master your fears. Whilst you are grappling with your insecurities you make an important discovery about yourself (see point 2 below). In the remainder of the opening section your objective then becomes: to pluck up the courage to begin your journey. Actions you might play at this point include: I bolster, galvanise, encourage, stiffen and steel myself. You are successful in this aim – and you do indeed set off from the convent.

A long unit then occurs during the two choruses that follow. In this section you have a single objective, which is: to fill yourself with confidence. You want to make yourself feel good about the challenges that lie ahead. Because this is a very long unit, you need to employ a broad variety of actions. Possible choices include: I cheer, invigorate, compliment, enliven, bolster, boost, sustain, motivate, fortify and acclaim myself. Ultimately you are successful in this objective – and you do find the confidence you need to face your new life with the von Trapps.

KEY MOMENTS/TOP TIPS

1. To portray that you are walking out of the abbey, try starting your song while standing in a corner at the back of the space. Take a step towards the centre of the room on the first chord, as if you are stepping outside to greet a beautiful sunny morning.

2. The first event of the song occurs when you realise that you are seeking the courage that you lack. At this moment you confront – perhaps for the first time in your life – the reason you have always held yourself back from pursuing your dreams: you are petrified of the unknown.

3. In the audition room it is difficult to stage the journey from the abbey to the von Trapps' house. (The journey begins at the start of the first chorus and ends just before you ask for help near the end of the song.) You can portray that you are travelling by walking decisively from one spot in the room to another whilst you sing a couple of lines, before stopping and standing still to sing the next line or two, as if you are taking a pause on your journey to rest, considering which way you should be headed, or taking in the view. You can do this throughout the choruses. The changes of momentum in the music help indicate where you might be travelling, and where you might be still. This

movement needs to be well-rehearsed and done with conviction. If so, it can be very effective. If you struggle with it, you may be better doing a non-naturalistic version of the song where you don't move at all.

4. It is significant that the von Trapp children have lost their mother. The prospect of somehow trying to fill that void in their life makes the future particularly intimidating for Maria.

5. An important moment occurs near the end of the song, when you ask for help. At this point you should make it clear that you have just arrived at the gates of the captain's house, which you might imagine to be in the corner of the room to one side of the audition table. When you see the gates your newfound courage momentarily drains out of you, the reality of the situation sinks in, and you think of running away. The final and most important event of the song then occurs: when you resolve to face the captain and his family. You might portray this by walking into the corner of the room after you've sung the last note of the song, as if you have just walked through the gates.

Vocal and Musical Analysis

WHO TO LISTEN TO: Julie Andrews on the film soundtrack (1965).

VOCAL RANGE: B♭3 to F5.

ORIGINAL KEY: E♭ major.

ACCENT: This song is most usually delivered in Received Pronunciation. However, if you are Austrian, or Germanic, it would be appropriate to use your own accent.

STYLE OF MUSICAL: Book musical.

VOCAL SET-UP/MUSICAL TIPS

1. The beginning of the song should be delivered in a Speech quality. Keep your larynx and tongue in a neutral position,

avoid using too much thyroid tilt, and make the sound conversational. You can make use of aspirate onsets to provide emphasis on certain words, as Andrews demonstrates on the words 'I wonder'.

2. As you sing the line about longing for adventure, make your sound more legato by using simultaneous onsets and running your vowels together.

3. When you ask why you are feeling so scared, suddenly lift your larynx, tilt your thyroid cartilage and thin your vocal folds to deliver a vulnerable Cry quality, as Andrews chooses to do in her own performance. Return to a Speech quality on the next line.

4. Use a Cry quality once more on the line when you realise you are seeking the courage that you lack. This helps clarify that moment of self-discovery.

5. Affect a crescendo in the two lines that precede the first chorus. You can do this by tightening the AES a little to add some twang.

6. For both choruses you should use a legit sound – a set-up that Andrews famously excels in. Use thyroid tilt, a high back of the tongue, legato phrasing and a slightly lowered larynx. As Andrews clearly demonstrates, this set-up can include moments of Speech quality. Don't be afraid to half-speak some words for emphasis.

7. Near the end of the song, slip back into a Cry quality on the word 'alone'. When you then repeat the word, crescendo by gradually lowering the larynx, thickening your vocal folds a little and adding some torso anchoring to end with a classical soprano sound for the last line, as Andrews ably demonstrates.

Sheet Music

The correct sheet music for this song is available at www.scribd.com.

'Many a New Day'
from *Oklahoma!*

Music by Richard Rodgers, lyrics by Oscar Hammerstein II

Choose this song if: you have a bright, legit mezzosoprano voice and suit playing the spirited and quick-witted tomboy.

Given Circumstances

WHO ARE YOU: Laurey Williams, a strong-willed teenage farm girl. Although you can appear feisty and tough on the outside, you also have a sensitive and romantic nature.

WHERE ARE YOU: On the front porch of your farmhouse in Oklahoma, USA.

WHEN IS IT: Early afternoon, a Saturday, summer, 1906.

WHAT HAS HAPPENED BEFORE: For some months now you have been secretly attracted to Curly McLain, a handsome cowboy. Although he privately reciprocates your feelings, up to this point you have both been too stubborn to admit that you like each other.

Today has been a day of much activity because everyone in the locality has been preparing for the Box Social – a dance that is to happen this evening. The high point of the event will be an auction of the lunch baskets prepared by the local girls – with the highest bidder for each basket getting to share the meal with the girl who prepared it.

Earlier this morning Curly McLain came round to visit and to ask you to the dance. With both of you too proud to confess your true feelings, you began teasing each other. Curly told you that he had hired a gig to take you to the dance. As you didn't believe him, you mocked him – saying he had done nothing of the sort. He then responded by denying he had ever hired the gig, and said he'd made the whole thing up to spite you, after which you stormed off.

A few minutes ago Curly returned with a group of other young men and women from the surrounding area – notably a girl called Gertie Cummings from across the river, whom you have been jealous of in the past. Curly flirted with Gertie to try and make you jealous, and when he went to take the horses down to the river she accompanied him. Aunt Eller has just left with the boys, leaving you alone with the girls. One of them has just tried to wind you up about Curly and Gertie's relationship, so you have decided to strenuously deny that you care about him, or indeed any man at all.

WHO ELSE IS THERE: A group of your female friends.

WHO SHOULD YOU SING TO: Your female friends. In the context of an audition, you can use the panel as if they are those girls.

Textual Analysis

When the song begins, you are feeling annoyed and self-conscious. Curly's behaviour towards Gertie has embarrassed you in front of your friends. In the first verse your objective thus becomes: to assert your independence as a woman. You want to prove to your friends that you don't care about men, although, of course, secretly you have strong feelings about Curly, and this is simply an outward show to protect your wounded pride.

During the first chorus you suggest that you will kiss lots of different boys and indulge in many light romances before you look back regretfully on a past relationship. Your objective in this section is: to convince the girls that you are free-spirited. It is useful to imagine that the girls don't believe you, so you have to try actions such as: I rebuff, chide, sidestep and deflect them in order to change their minds. In the bridge that follows you then go one step further. Your objective becomes: to get the girls to agree to mock lovesick women.

For the second chorus you have identical lyrics and the same objective as in the first: to convince the girls that you are free-spirited. To find variety in your performance, try playing more light-hearted actions this time, such as: I amuse, impress, entertain, tickle and regale the girls. In the second bridge you aim to persuade the girls that in the past, when a man has rejected you, you soon found consolation in the arms of another. This section can have a cheeky and playful tone. During the last three lines you want to convince the girls that it will be a long time before you let a man worry you. However, the change in music reveals that your carefree mask slips and for a moment your true feelings are revealed (see point 4 below).

KEY MOMENTS/TOP TIPS

1. It is worth remembering that Laurey has been raised by her aunt, as she is an orphan. She would have therefore had some difficult moments in her childhood and would been brought up in a home without a male role model. That may have contributed a great deal to her being tough and wary of men.

2. Another interesting aspect of Laurey is that, having worked on the farm all her life, she is something of a tomboy – and therefore she perhaps doesn't fit in easily with the other girls. Deep down she may feel that she is not feminine or pretty enough to be of interest to Curly.

3. Explore playing with the idea that, although Laurey brags about her indifferent attitude men, she is very inexperienced romantically. She is doing this to try and hide her own insecurities.

4. During the last three lines of the song the music slows down and becomes more romantic. This suggests that, underneath Laurey's bravado, she in fact does dream of sharing her life with Curly. Explore the idea that this subtext rises to the surface in this moment.

Vocal and Musical Analysis

WHO TO LISTEN TO: Josefina Gabrielle on the National Theatre cast recording (1998).

VOCAL RANGE: C♯4 to E5.

ORIGINAL KEY: D major.

ACCENT: Oklahoma (a southern American state).

STYLE OF MUSICAL: Book musical.

VOCAL SET-UP/MUSICAL TIPS

1. In the suggested recording there are instrumental dance sections and lyrics for the ensemble. These should not be included in an audition, and are already cut in the suggested sheet music.

2. The predominant vocal set-up for this song is a legit sound. To achieve this set-up, which Gabrielle demonstrates, ensure you maintain some thyroid tilt throughout, use simultaneous onsets wherever possible, keep your soft palate raised and the back of your tongue as still and as close to the upper molars as you can.

3. A key component for delivering the music of Rodgers and Hammerstein successfully is to sing with long legato phrases. Ensure you only breathe at the punctuation, or where a capital letter denotes the beginning of a new sentence.

4. On the last page of music – when Laurey sings about the dawn, the sun, and the moon – try raising the larynx higher than you have done previously to move into a sweeter Cry quality. This will help reveal the subtext of the song, suggested above. You can then move back into a louder, richer legit sound on the last three words to show that, whilst Laurey might occasionally have romantic daydreams, she is still stubborn and independently minded.

Sheet Music

The correct sheet music for this song is available at www.musicnotes.com.

'Mister Snow'
from *Carousel*

Music by Richard Rodgers, lyrics by Oscar Hammerstein II

Choose this song if: you have a mezzosoprano legit voice, and enjoy playing idealistic, witty, comedic roles.

Given Circumstances

WHO ARE YOU: Carrie Pipperidge, a naive but cheeky young millworker in your early twenties.

WHERE ARE YOU: Sitting on a bench on a tree-lined path on the coast of New England, USA.

WHEN IS IT: Late afternoon, nearly sundown, autumn, 1873.

WHAT HAS HAPPENED BEFORE: This afternoon you visited an amusement park along the coast with your friend and co-worker, Julie Jordan. Whilst you were there you got into an altercation with the owner of the carousel: a middle-aged widow named Mrs Mullin. She had confronted Julie when your friend allowed Billy Bigelow – the handsome barker for the carousel – to put his arm around her waist whilst riding the attraction (something that was viewed as scandalous for a single woman at this time). Witnessing this, and incensed with jealousy, Mrs Mullin tracked you both down in the lane on your way home and told Julie to never return to the carousel, at which point you leapt to Julie's defence.

Shortly afterwards Billy came across the three of you arguing in the lane. Mrs Mullin then instructed Billy to not let you near the carousel again. When he found out the reason why, Billy became annoyed by Mrs Mullin's possessiveness and didn't try to prevent her when she threatened to fire him – which she eventually did. Despite being out of a job, or perhaps because of that fact, he asked Julie to have a drink with him that evening. This invitation lacked any sense of romance and Billy's manner was brusque – particularly as he asked you both to pay for his beer. With neither of you forthcoming with any money, Billy left a moment ago to buy his own drink.

After he'd gone, you tried to encourage Julie to confess how she felt about Billy. With your friend less than forthcoming, you began to tease her about how quiet and secretive she had been recently. Sensing, however, that Julie might be falling for Billy, and therefore wouldn't be single for much longer, you took this as an opportunity to tell her about your own secret relationship with Mr Enoch Snow.

WHO ELSE IS THERE: Julie.

WHO SHOULD YOU SING TO: Julie.

Textual Analysis

Note: The song begins with a spoken/sung scene in which you tease your friend for being a 'queer one'. For audition purposes this section should be cut. Instead you should begin at the start of the main song, when you first start talking about Mr Snow (as per the recommended sheet music). The analysis below assumes you have made that cut.

At the start of the song you are engaged in excited gossip; you have been longing to tell Julie about Enoch Snow for some time. In the first verse your objective is: to impress Julie with your account of Mr Snow. You do this in order to get her to approve of, and be pleased about, your choice of gentleman friend. During the second verse you are more candid and pragmatic. At this point your objective is: to paint a realistic picture of Enoch – including his faults. You amuse Julie with your frank disclosure that he comes home from work smelling of fish. However, you then try to convince Julie that you have learned to love even this unappealing aspect of him.

In the section that follows, where you tell Julie what happened last night, you reveal yourself to be an engaging storyteller. Your objective here is: to get Julie to picture Enoch's proposal, in order to win your friend's approval. You do so in an extremely evocative manner. Having relayed the joyous news of the proposal, you then want Julie to understand that it has left you feeling in a spin.

When the main melody begins you start to daydream about getting married. Your objective in the first chorus is: to imagine what your wedding day will be like. You do this in order both to delight yourself and to receive Julie's blessing. In the bridge that follows you then playfully ask Julie to picture what it will be like when you cross the threshold with your new husband. You want to amuse her by saying how you will tell Enoch that you are ready to consummate the marriage. Having enjoyed making your best friend laugh about this, during the final chorus your objective is: to convince Julie that you truly love Enoch – with all of his faults. You are completely successful in this objective, so by the end of the song you have your best friend's blessing.

KEY MOMENTS/TOP TIPS

1. On the suggested music there is no introduction. Ask the pianist to play a single 'bell note' and then you come straight in.

2. Although the song is directed towards Julie in the musical, in audition it works well as a piece of gossip sung to the panel, as though they are all your friends and confidantes.

3. The scene is set on a bench, so it might be fun to explore the beginning of the song sitting forward excitedly on the edge of chair. If you make this choice, you would be advised to stand after the first part of the song.

4. Carrie is a person who is a great deal of fun to be around. Her mode of storytelling should therefore be engaging and entertaining. Try using actions such as: I intrigue, enliven, amuse, fascinate and scandalise Julie, to convey her cheeky personality.

5. During the choruses you should picture images of your ideal wedding day in the third circle of attention.

Vocal and Musical Analysis

WHO TO LISTEN TO: Janie Dee on the National Theatre cast recording (1993).

VOCAL RANGE: D4 to G5.

ORIGINAL KEY: G major.

ACCENT: General American.

STYLE OF MUSICAL: Book musical.

VOCAL SET-UP/MUSICAL TIPS

1. The song should be sung in a legit set-up. To achieve this sound, you should use a great deal of thyroid tilt, make use of consistent simultaneous onsets and employ a degree of laryngeal lowering (similar to a Sob quality).

2. Make the tempo much broader when you arrive at the chorus. Sing in long, sweeping legato phrases and really revel in the rich, luscious melody.

3. During the bridge, when you talk about being carried across the threshold, try making use of aspirate onsets. This can help portray that this part of the story has the flavour of a slightly naughty secret.

4. The words 'here I am' are intended to be spoken. This is a nice opportunity for you to reveal Carrie's playfulness – in this moment she is fooling around about what she might say to Enoch in order to tempt him into the bedroom.

5. When delivering the high notes at the end of the song, ensure you anchor your torso and lengthen your neck to support the raised position of the larynx.

CLASSICAL

Sheet Music

The correct sheet music for this song is available at www.musicnotes.com.

'Much More'
from *The Fantasticks*

Music by Harvey Schmidt, lyrics by Tom Jones

Choose this song if: you have a strong soprano or mezzosoprano voice and enjoy playing roles that are cheeky, playful, narcissistic and adventurous.

Given Circumstances

WHO ARE YOU: Luisa Bellomy, an imaginative, spirited and romantic sixteen-year-old girl. Recently you have developed a restlessness to explore the outside world. In a trait not uncommon amongst teenagers, you have an urgent belief that you are special.

WHERE ARE YOU: In your garden.

WHEN IS IT: 3.00 p.m., a warm September afternoon, in a more innocent, mythical time.

WHAT HAS HAPPENED BEFORE: You have been raised by your father, Amos Babcock Bellomy, as, tragically, your mother died when you were small. Up to this point your life has been sheltered, with your only real friend being a boy called Matt who lives next door. Matt, who is three years older than you, has also been brought up by a single father.

When you were growing up you were a shy young girl. You were something of a daydreamer, and loved nothing more than to read a romantic novel or lie on your back in the garden studying cloud formations. In the last year, as both yourself and Matt have grown older and ever more beautiful, you have begun to fall in love. Your fathers secretly wish this match to occur, but knowing how wilful teenagers can be, they decided to pretend that they disapproved of the union, as they knew this would make you desire each other even more.

One day after school, about a month ago, your two fathers
built a wall between the two gardens with the pretence of
keeping you apart. They told you they had done this because
they were feuding. Since then, you have felt a growing sense
of longing – not only for Matt, but also for some excitement
in your life. Today you have spent a restive day alone in the
garden – yearning for an adventure.

WHO ELSE IS THERE: You are alone.

WHO SHOULD YOU SING TO: During the song you switch from
singing to yourself, and to a higher power (i.e. Fate or God).

Textual Analysis

At the beginning of the song you feel excessively bored and
fidgety. You are tired of being stuck alone in the garden and
this is making you agitated. This sense of longing leads you
into your first objective, which is: to imagine what it would be
like to do something exciting and new. You indulge these
fantasies in an attempt to relieve yourself of your insatiable
boredom. During these opening lines you are talking to
yourself. Your point of focus alters, however, when you
repeatedly sing the words 'just once', as now you begin talking
to Fate. Your objective in this lyric is: to get Fate to allow you
to have an adventure. You promise that, if your request is
granted this one time, then you will never ask again. Try
playing actions such as: I beg, implore and charm Fate.

In the next unit, when you sing about not wishing to be evil,
your intention changes. At this point your objective is: to
decide how you want to be when you are a grown woman. In
doing so you are allowing yourself to be a little self-indulgent,
precocious and silly. Your next fantasy is to imagine going out
dancing all night. Try exploring the following objective,
which should be fun to play: to dare yourself to be naughty.
When you return to singing the words 'just once' you address
Fate again and play the same objective as before: to get Fate to
grant you an adventure. To reflect your growing impatience,

try playing more dynamic actions on this occasion, such as: I urge, force and obligate Fate.

You then sing about wasting a week or so. Your objective at this point is: to indulge your own laziness. When you talk about your hair billowing to the floor, this might be a point when you end up lying on your back on the imaginary grass (see point 1 below). For the last section of the song you talk to Fate for a final time. In no mood to be denied, your ultimate objective is: to demand that Fate delivers you a fuller and more stimulating life.

KEY MOMENTS/TOP TIPS

1. Think about how physically free we can be when we are outside in a garden. Try exploring this sense of playfulness in your performance. You might choose to lie on the floor, sing flat on your back for the moment, or move dynamically in the space.

2. When talking to Fate you can use the third circle of attention, as if you are singing to the heavens. Alternatively you can sing directly to the panel in these moments as though they are Fate, and have the power to grant your wishes.

3. As an audience, we are touched and amused by a sixteen-year-old character remonstrating that she needs her life to begin – because soon she will be too old. Although this is, of course, ironic – as Luisa has her whole adult life ahead of her – try to remember how it feels to be a teenager. We can often be very impatient to grow up when we are on the threshold of being an adult. Luisa feels genuine emotional pain when she believes that her chance at life might already be gone.

Vocal and Musical Analysis

WHO TO LISTEN TO: Betsy Morgan on the Off-Broadway revival cast recording (2006).

VOCAL RANGE: B3 to F5.

ORIGINAL KEY: G major.

ACCENT: General American.

STYLE OF MUSICAL: Book musical.

VOCAL SET–UP/MUSICAL TIPS

1. On the suggested recording there is some dialogue at the beginning of the song and an extended introduction. This should be cut for audition purposes. You should instead start with the first line of singing and a two-bar introduction, as indicated on the suggested sheet music.

2. The fundamental sound quality for the song, as demonstrated by Morgan at the beginning of the cast recording, is a contemporary legit sound. Use a great deal of thyroid tilt, simultaneous onsets and legato phrasing – as you would do for a song by Rodgers and Hammerstein – but in order to stop the sound being too old-fashioned, keep the larynx raised and tighten the AES slightly to add a little twang.

3. In the two verse sections (when you talk about dancing till dawn, and doing the things you dream about) you should use a Speech quality. You can mix up your onsets and half-speak some words.

4. When you sing about your hair billowing to the floor, it is appropriate to indulge in some pitch slides, as you hear Morgan do on the suggested recording.

5. When you sing the word 'too', before you sing about the things you dream about, you should bend the pitch of the note like a jazz singer. Again, Morgan demonstrates this clearly in her performance.

CLASSICAL

6. When you repeat the title lyric at the end of the song, you should add some torso anchoring to help support these higher notes.

Sheet Music

The correct sheet music for this song is available at www.musicnotes.com.

'My Lord and Master'
from *The King and I*

Music by Richard Rodgers, lyrics by Oscar Hammerstein II

Choose this song if: you have an outstanding high soprano
legit voice and enjoy secretive characters that have a great
sense of inner conviction. The role is usually played by an
actress of Southeast Asian descent.

Given Circumstances

WHO ARE YOU: Tuptim, a rebellious, strong-willed young slave
girl from Burma.

WHERE ARE YOU: The main reception room of the Royal Palace
in Bangkok, in the Kingdom of Siam (a part of modern-day
Thailand).

WHEN IS IT: 10.00 a.m., early January 1862.

WHAT HAS HAPPENED BEFORE: A man named Mongkut has been
the King of Siam for over a decade. As is the custom in Siam,
the King has taken himself many wives during his reign – and
his power has led to him to becoming pompous, arrogant and
misogynistic. However, despite his faults, Mongkut is also a
learned man and decided several months ago that he wished
for a number of his sixty-seven children to be schooled by a
Western teacher – so he sent for a widowed schoolmistress
from England named Anna Leonowens. She arrived in
Bangkok several weeks ago. Anna proves to be unlike any
woman the King had encountered before, as she was wilful
and prepared to defy his authority. In her contract Anna had
been promised a separate house for her and her son, but on
her arrival the King's emissary, Kralahome, informed her that
this agreement was not to be honoured. Mongkut expected
her to live in the Royal Palace instead.

This morning Kralahome came to speak to the King about Anna. He informed His Majesty that the schoolmistress had been at the palace for three weeks – something the King did not know – and was now waiting to see him. Kralahome had declined to give Miss Leonowens an audience with the King prior to this due to her stubborn refusal to accept the change to her contractual arrangements.

This meeting was interrupted by the arrival of Lun Tha, an emissary from the court of Burma. Lun Tha had been granted permission by the King to study the design of the famous temple in Bangkok. To thank Mongkut for his generosity, the Prince of Burma in turn had offered yourself as a gift; you are to become another of the King's wives.

A few moments ago you were presented to the King – when you were carried in by four servants on a palanquin (a seat carried on poles). At first the King was wary that you might be a spy for Burma. You challenged his suspicions by stating you were no spy, and then asked if the King was pleased that you had been educated to speak English. With little interest in a woman's education or opinions, the King simply ignored your question before circling you to inspect your body – after which he nodded his approval to Kralahome before leaving. (What Mongkut doesn't know is that you are secretly in love with Lun Tha and have sworn yourself to him.) Kralahome has just informed you that, by nodding his head, the King is communicating he is 'pleased with you'. After which he also exited the library, followed by Lun Tha.

WHO ELSE IS THERE: You are alone.

WHO SHOULD YOU SING TO: Yourself, though in an audition you can share many of your thoughts with the panel as though they are your inner-consciousness.

Textual Analysis

When the introduction begins you are still reeling from your humiliation at the hands of the King. You are angry that he could declare he is pleased with you simply based on your appearance – without knowing anything else about you. During the first verse your objective is thus: to understand how Mongkut can form such a rash opinion. Try exploring actions such as: I query, cross-examine, interrogate, shake and agitate yourself during this section. You are disgusted at the King's behaviour.

During the bridge you then begin to articulate how the King views you: as little more than a beautiful object for him to possess. Your objective in this section is: to mock the King's misogynistic behaviour. At this point you might make choices such as: I ridicule, mimic, undermine and scorn the King. The anger this generates in you leads you to begin a new and important objective in the line before the final verse, which is: to defy the authority of the King. You are now feeling full of fight. You proudly tell yourself that, even though the King may study your body, he will never know the contents of your heart – which will always remain full of love for Lun Tha.

CLASSICAL

KEY MOMENTS/TOP TIPS

1. The song is fuelled by what must have been a humiliating experience – to be inspected like an animal or a piece of property by the King. Your anger at being treated this way would likely have been amplified because it took place in front of the man you love.

2. Tuptim is leading an incredibly dangerous double-life. If she and Lun Tha were to be discovered, they would face the death penalty. This means that the stakes in the song are incredibly high. Tuptim's sense of defiance and bravery in the pursuit of love is extraordinary.

3. Even though she is a slave, Tuptim is well educated, and notably has read a book called *Uncle Tom's Cabin* – an anti-slavery book by the American female author Harriet Beecher Stowe. This education has led her to develop strong, feminist, anti-slavery views. The righteous anger that these opinions engender should be manifest in your performance.

4. The whole song turns on the words 'so he thinks' – which is the event of the song. At this moment we should understand that Tuptim has decided that she will defy the King and continue to love Lun Tha in secret.

Vocal and Musical Analysis

WHO TO LISTEN TO: Ashley Park on the Broadway revival cast recording (2015).

VOCAL RANGE: D♯4 to A♯5.

ORIGINAL KEY: B major.

ACCENT: The correct accent would of course be a Burmese dialect – which is the best choice. However, if you have any native Southeast Asian accent, then that would usually suffice for the ears of a British audition panel. If all of these options are difficult for you, then for a UK audition you could alternatively use a Standard English accent as a fairly neutral choice in that context.

STYLE OF MUSICAL: Book musical.

VOCAL SET-UP/MUSICAL TIPS

1. You should cut the first two bars of the music to leave a two-bar introduction.

2. Try singing the first verse in a reflective Cry quality. You might make occasional use of aspirate onsets to emphasise Tuptim's sense of thoughtfulness and soul-searching at this point.

3. You should gradually crescendo during the second verse. To achieve this, add some torso anchoring, thicken your vocal folds a little, and lower the larynx to achieve a darker colour to the sound.

4. The entire song benefits from the use of long, broad, legato phrases.

5. The bridge, which is marked '*poco più mosso*', should have a feeling of momentum. Try pushing the tempo forward at this point before slowing down at the end of the section on the words 'so he thinks' to emphasis the event of the song (see point 4 above).

6. On the high A♯ in the final phrase you need to both anchor your torso and lengthen you neck – in order to support the lifting of the larynx for this high pitch.

Sheet Music

The correct sheet music for this song is available at www.musicnotes.com.

'Home'
from *Beauty and the Beast*

Music by Alan Menken, lyrics by Howard Ashman and Tim Rice

Choose this song if: you are a mezzosoprano who enjoys singing in a crossover style between legit singing and an archetypal Disney sound. The song suits actresses who enjoy playing a heroine who is strong-willed and independent.

Given Circumstances

WHO ARE YOU: Belle - a local townswoman who is blessed with exceptional beauty. A spirited, single-minded daughter of an eccentric inventor, you have a love of reading and have always longed for an adventurous life, like the characters in the books you enjoy.

WHERE ARE YOU: In the guest bedroom of the Beast's castle in a faraway magical kingdom.

WHEN IS IT: 9.30 p.m., after dinner on a winter's evening, once upon a time. (From an aesthetic perspective, fairytales that begin with the line 'Once upon a time' often contain elements that are a fantasised and romanticised version of the European medieval period.)

WHAT HAS HAPPENED BEFORE: Ten years ago, an old beggar woman visited the castle of a handsome prince. She offered him a single red rose in return for shelter from the bitter winter cold. The Prince was spoilt and selfish, and repulsed by her haggard appearance, so he dismissed her gift and tried to send her away. The beggar woman warned him not to be fooled by outward appearances, telling the Prince that true beauty was found within. When he dismissed her for a second time, she revealed herself in her true form: as a beautiful and powerful enchantress. The Prince begged the enchantress for her forgiveness, but it was too late. As she sensed he had no love in his heart, she placed a spell on the castle – transforming him into a monstrous beast and all of his servants into furniture.

As the Prince was ashamed of his new physical from, he concealed himself within the castle – a magic mirror being his only window into the world. However, the sorceress left behind the rose. It too was enchanted and she told him it would continue to bloom for many years. She said that if he learned to love another before the last petal fell – and earned that person's love in return – then he would be transformed back into a prince. If not, he would remain a beast forever.

It is now ten years later, and this morning you made your way into town to order a book from the local bookseller. Despite acknowledging your exceptional level of beauty, the townspeople also gossiped about what they consider to be your strange love of books. Whilst in town you attracted the unwanted attention of Gaston, a muscular, arrogant buffoon who, as a renowned huntsman, is the alpha-male of the town.

Upon returning home you shared your worries with your father, whose name is Maurice, about how you were viewed by the rest of the town. He assured you that there was nothing strange or odd about your love of learning. After you had helped him put the finishing touches to his latest invention, he then set off through the woods to sell his creation at a fair.

Whilst on his journey, Maurice was chased by wolves. Subsequently he became lost and stumbled upon the Beast's castle. Despite being welcomed by the servants, when the Beast discovered your father's presence he locked him away in the dungeon for trespassing.

Meanwhile back in the town you had been fighting off the advances of Gaston – who had proposed to you. You became concerned when Gaston's sidekick, LeFou, returned from the woods wearing your father's scarf. Worried that he might be in danger, you decided to go searching for your father. Eventually you discovered him locked away in the castle, but upon finding him you were yourself trapped and imprisoned by the Beast. Fearing for your life, you told the Beast that your father was unwell, and begged for his freedom. The Beast agreed that he would release Maurice – but only if you would remain imprisoned in the castle in return. When you agreed, your generosity towards your father moved the Beast, so he released you from the dungeon and took you to one of the bedrooms instead – an aesthetically more pleasing prison, but a prison nonetheless. He has just left, having ordered you to have dinner with him that evening,

WHO ELSE IS THERE: You are alone.

WHO SHOULD YOU SING TO: Yourself, though in audition you can share many of your thoughts with the panel as though they are your inner-consciousness. In the opening few lyrics, and during the closing lines, you also address the Beast.

Textual Analysis

When the song begins, the bedroom door has just shut and the harsh reality has started to set in: you have no choice but to remain in the castle for the foreseeable future. In the short pre-chorus you are in effect shouting through the door at the Beast. Your objective in this section is: to challenge the moral behaviour of the Beast. You want him to feel guilty for holding you to ransom.

The main melody then commences, and with the Beast gone you begin to talk to yourself. Your objective at the beginning of the first chorus is: to decide if you should accept your fate. You are trying to work out whether you need to learn to endure this new life, or if an alternative course of action is open to you. Halfway through the verse, when you remember a lesson from childhood, your objective changes. At that point your objective becomes: to hold true to your belief that home is where the heart is. The reality of being so far from home makes it hard for you to hold on to this point of view, and in the second chorus your objective once more becomes: to decide if you must accept your fate. This is the stage of the song at which you find it hardest to imagine how you will ever again be free. In the bridge your objective thus becomes: to wish that your fate were different.

A key change leads you into the third and final chorus. This musical build marks a shift to the following objective: to work out how long you will be kept in the castle against your will. But seemingly when you are without hope, the event of the song then occurs. At this moment you realise that, as your life has been fundamentally changed by coming to the castle, it is possible for it to alter once more. Your objective at this point is: to give yourself hope. Because you are a resolute character, you are successful in this aim – and in the final section you begin to confront your captor once more. Your objective here is: to taunt the Beast to do his worst. You defiantly state that no matter how long he imprisons you, your heart will always be free.

KEY MOMENTS/TOP TIPS

1. Belle is not your stereotypical fairytale heroine – she has a great deal of strength and conviction. You can portray these personality traits in your choice of actions when you challenge the Beast. Explore such possibilities as: I defy, oppose, confront and resist him.

2. You should address the opening section to the door where the Beast has just exited. Try imagining the door somewhere beyond the audition table.

3. As this is a bedroom, there would be places for Belle to sit down. Although you should probably start the song standing up, experiment with having a chair placed in the space, perhaps at an angle. This will allow you to explore sitting – as if on the edge of a bed – in more reflective moments, for example, at the start of the second chorus.

4. On the first line of each chorus you ask whether you must now accept the castle as your home. To show that you are struggling with this question, try playing actions that get

progressively stronger on each repetition. For example, you might play the following actions on the opening lyric of the three choruses: I question, I cross-examine, and I interrogate myself.

Vocal and Musical Analysis

WHO TO LISTEN TO: Julie-Alanah Brighten on the original London cast recording (1997).

VOCAL RANGE: A3 to F♯5.

ORIGINAL KEY: A major.

ACCENT: General American or Received Pronunciation. The song was written to be performed in General American, and you should certainly take that approach if you have a North American accent yourself, and could also do so if General American is an accent you do well. Equally, the song can work successfully in Received Pronunciation if that accent suits you better.

STYLE OF MUSICAL: Contemporary musical (legit-based).

VOCAL SET–UP/MUSICAL TIPS

1. The beginning of the song of should be delivered in a Speech quality. It is possible to play around with speaking some words, as Brighten demonstrates on the suggested recording on words such as 'monster' and 'you're a fool'.

2. From the beginning of the chorus you should use a legit sound as Brighten employs so well on the cast recording. To achieve this sound, use legato phrasing, simultaneous onsets and a good deal of thyroid tilt. Also explore lowering the larynx a little, to produce a sound that is similar to a Sob quality.

3. During the bridge you need to add additional volume. Achieve this by tightening your AES to add a little twang to your fundamental legit sound.

4. The beginning of the third chorus should be the loudest moment of the song. To help you access slightly thicker vocal folds, use glottal onsets on the words 'is' and 'this' that start the section.

5. Try delivering the last few lines in a vulnerable Cry quality, as Brighten does so well on the suggested recording.

Sheet Music

The correct sheet music for this song is available at www.musicnotes.com.

'How Could I Ever Know'
from *The Secret Garden*

Music by Lucy Simon, lyrics by Marsha Norman

Choose this song if: you have a legit mezzosoprano voice and
enjoy playing characters with dignity and grace.

Given Circumstances

WHO ARE YOU: Lily Craven, a kind, caring mother to your son
Colin, and a loving wife to your husband Archibald – who is a
hunchback. You died several years ago and now sometimes
appear to your husband as a ghost in order to try and offer
him comfort in his ongoing grief.

WHERE ARE YOU: Archibald's hotel room in Paris.

WHEN IS IT: 7.30 p.m., a humid summer evening in 1906.

WHAT HAS HAPPENED BEFORE: Several years ago you lived
happily in a cottage in a valley of the Yorkshire countryside.
One day you were at work in your garden when a passer-by
rode past. He asked if he might be able to rest there awhile, as
he had been riding for some time. You were struck by his kindly
manner and asked if he would like to come in for some tea.

After this first meeting the passer-by, whose name was
Archibald Craven, came to visit you every day to bring you
baskets of roses – for he was falling in love with you.
Although your sister Rose thought him gloomy and urged you
not to pay him any attention, you could see that inside he was
simply shy and tender. You did not care about his disability
and some months later you were married. After the wedding
you moved into Archibald's family home: Misselthwaite
Manor. Your life there was a happy one. Archibald gifted you
a beautiful walled garden, which you loved to tend, and you
had a son together: Colin. However, disaster struck when you
died suddenly a few years later.

After your death Archibald became increasingly withdrawn, and allowed his brother, Dr Neville Craven, to manage Misselthwaite. (Secretly, Neville covets the estate for himself and has always resented his brother because he was clandestinely in love with you.) Archibald refused to let go of you in his mind, and as a consequence you continued to haunt the halls of Misselthwaite.

With his grief clouding his judgement, Archibald decided that Colin should be confined to his bed after your death, as he feared that the child would suffer from the same spinal condition as himself. (In fact, Archibald discovers later in the story that Colin's spine is completely healthy. The ailments that confine your son to his room are purely psychosomatic, induced by his father's overprotectiveness and encouraged by Dr Craven, who is happy to see the rightful heir of Misselthwaite deteriorate through being unnecessarily bedridden.)

A few months ago, Mary Lennox, your ten-year-old niece, arrived at the estate from India. Your sister Rose and her husband had died of cholera, so Mary was sent to live with Archibald, as he was now her legal guardian. Since her arrival, Archibald had been avoiding Mary as she so painfully reminded him of you. Despite her own loss, and your husband's coldness, Mary was full of spirit and brought a new life and energy to the house. Encouraged by the housemaid, Martha, she went off exploring the grounds of Misselthwaite. Whilst doing so she discovered your secret garden – which she could not find the entrance to. Ben Weatherstaff, an old gardener, revealed to her that the garden had been locked since your death because it reminded Archibald of you. Martha's brother Dickon, who is also a gardener, then taught Mary to speak to the animals, notably a robin, by using a Yorkshire dialect. The bird consequently led Mary to the hiding place of the key for the secret garden, though she still did not know the whereabouts of the door. In conjunction with her adventures in the grounds, Mary had also been exploring the house. In doing so she heard some mysterious crying sounds, which she believed to be a ghost (but she will later in the story discover to be Colin).

With Mary becoming an increasingly dominant presence in the house, Neville tried to convince Archibald to send her away to boarding school. He was trying to negate anything that made his brother feel obliged to stay, as he wanted to encourage Archibald to move to Paris so he could take the house for himself. Following his brother's lead, Archibald told Mary that he was considering sending her away to school. She protested strongly against this, so he agreed to let her stay – and to allow her to tend your old garden.

With Dickon's help, Mary gradually began to bring the walled garden back to life. You then visited Colin in ghostly form – encouraging him to go outside and play in the garden. Gradually his strength began to return. Neville, who was concerned that Mary might reignite his brother's love for both the garden and for Misselthwaite – and therefore ruin his plans – warned Archibald to stay away from Mary. He said she was causing him too much pain and encouraged your husband to travel to the continent. With his brother gone, Neville then tried to pressurise Mary once more into leaving to attend a boarding school. In response she wrote to her Uncle Archibald – begging him to return to Misselthwaite to see the changes in both Colin and the garden. With Archibald struggling to decide if she should return, and still feeling haunted by your memory, you have just decided to appear to him in Paris.

WHO ELSE IS THERE: Archibald.

WHO SHOULD YOU SING TO: Archibald.

Textual Analysis

The song begins with you asking some fundamental questions of your husband. You can sense that he is upset and angry with you because when you died he felt abandoned. Your objective in the first verse is: to make Archibald realise that you didn't mean to hurt him; that you had no control over your departure from the world of the living. In this section you might explore actions such as: I awaken, coax, soothe and stir him.

You are unsuccessful in these initial attempts to get through to Archibald, though, and he remains morose. This prompts you into a different objective in the second verse, which is: to convince Archibald that you place no obligations on him. You feel that you have no right to demand that he stops grieving; he must reach that conclusion himself.

With your husband still unresponsive, during the bridge your approach becomes more direct. Your objective in this section is: to get Archibald to forgive you for leaving him. You want to help relieve him from his sense of abandonment, and yourself from feelings of guilt. Try exploring actions such as: I implore, beseech and pressurise Archibald.

The song is a moment of catharsis for both yourself and your husband: finally you are able to free yourselves from the past. During the final verse try playing the text as though it is the last words you will ever say to Archibald. Your objective at this point is: to convince Archibald that you will always be a part of him. You want him to understand that, although you are no longer physically on this earth, you will always be with him in spirit.

KEY MOMENTS/TOP TIPS

1. Although you are a ghost, you should act the song as if Archibald can see and hear you. Play your objectives and actions normally, as you would do with any piece of text.

2. A notable feature of the lyric is that it is full of questions. It is important to play each one as if Archibald might answer you back, so when he doesn't, it spurs you on to play a different action in order to get him to respond.

3. It is useful to consider how Archibald's mood changes throughout the song. At the beginning he is still racked with grief; he finds it very difficult to accept what you have to say. By the end you have finally managed to move him – he is now ready to get on with his life and look forward to the future.

134

4. Explore what happens if the event of the song occurs on the final line. The event is that, having helped Archibald to let go of his grief, you are released from the duty of having to walk the earth as a ghost – and are finally able to rest in peace. To portray this aspect of the storytelling, in the play-out of the song, try backing off a few steps then turning slowly and walking to the corner of the room, as if you are exiting the space and leaving for the last time.

Vocal and Musical Analysis

WHO TO LISTEN TO: Meredith Braun on the original London cast recording (2001).

VOCAL RANGE: B♭3 to F5.

ORIGINAL KEY: D♭ major.

ACCENT: Received Pronunciation.

STYLE OF MUSICAL: Contemporary musical (legit-based).

VOCAL SET-UP/MUSICAL TIPS

1. There is a duet section between Archie and Lily at the end of the song. This should be cut for audition purposes, as is the case in the suggested sheet music.

2. The fundamental sound for this song is a legit set-up. Ensure you use simultaneous onsets wherever possible, a good deal of thyroid tilt, and maintain a degree of torso anchoring throughout.

3. Try the first verse in a Cry quality. Explore making the sound as quiet and pure as possible with minimal vibrato.

4. The second verse needs to be slightly louder than the first. You can achieve this by adding a little twang to your legit sound, as you can detect in Braun's voice in the suggested recording.

5. Try pushing the tempo forward in the bridge to give the music a feeling of impetus.

6. Try starting the final verse very quietly – with thin vocal folds, a tilted thyroid cartilage and a raised larynx. Then start a crescendo on the word 'oh' that reaches its peak on the high F on the word 'how'. You should effect this crescendo by gradually adding some torso anchoring and lowering the larynx slightly to achieve a darker colour in the sound.

7. Sing the last line in a very quiet Cry quality.

Sheet Music

The correct sheet music for this song is available at www.musicnotes.com.

'Your Daddy's Son'
from *Ragtime*

Music by Stephen Flaherty, lyrics by Lynn Ahrens

Choose this song if: you have an outstanding mezzosoprano
voice that includes a rich lower register and the ability to belt
to a top F. The song, which was originally written for an
African-American actress, requires a deep emotional
connection to the material.

Given Circumstances

WHO ARE YOU: Sarah, a vulnerable young mother who has
suffered from an extreme post-natal illness – know as
postpartum psychosis.

WHERE ARE YOU: Your bedroom in the attic of 'Mother's'
House, Broadview Avenue, New Rochelle, New York, USA.

WHEN IS IT: 11.00 a.m., a spring morning, 1906.

WHAT HAS HAPPENED BEFORE: Four years ago, when you lived
in Harlem, you met a handsome, charismatic jazz piano player
by the name of Coalhouse Walker Jr. He played for the
renowned Jim Europe Clef Club Orchestra. You both felt a
strong mutual attraction towards each other and soon fell
deeply in love. Unfortunately, Coalhouse was something of a
womaniser and was often unfaithful to you. After you became
pregnant with Coalhouse's child, and learned of his
infidelities, you no longer wanted to see him. One day, when
he left you to see another woman, you took off without a word
or trace. You moved from New York City to New Rochelle
where you took a job as a washwoman.

Shortly after the birth of your son, whilst in the grips of a
temporary period of postpartum psychosis, you buried your
newborn child alive. This took place in the garden of a rich

white family that lived a block away from your workplace. Miraculously the matriarch of the house, referred to only as 'Mother', dug the child up whilst it was still alive. With the police threatening to charge you with murder, Mother said that instead she would take responsibility for you and your son – and take you into your home. (For a white woman to associate herself with a single black mother was an extraordinary and scandalous thing to do in this period.) The actions of Mother were particularly brave as her husband was currently away on an expedition to the North Pole. In a state of shock, you had stopped speaking.

A month or so has now passed and, unbeknownst to you, this morning Coalhouse discovered your whereabouts and set out to find you. He wanted to make amends for his past behaviour. Under the care of Mother, you have gradually been recovering from your illness, though you have still barely spoken to anyone. For the past ten minutes you have been sat rocking your baby, and have decided to tell him how you almost took his life.

WHO ELSE IS THERE: Your baby.

WHO SHOULD YOU SING TO: Your baby.

Textual Analysis

You begin the song by singing a haunting melody on an 'oo' vowel. It is useful to imagine this is a lullaby that you are singing to your son. Your objective in this moment is: to calm your child. When you start to sing the actual lyrics, you then think back to when you first met Coalhouse. You remember how you used to watch his mesmerising performances on the piano. At this point your objective is: to get your child to understand why you fell in love with his father; you paint a picture of his spellbinding musical performances. It is appropriate to explore actions such as: inspire, bewitch and captivate the child at this point. An important moment then occurs at the end of the first verse when you look at your child's hands and remember the image of Coalhouse's fingers running up and down the piano keyboard. The juxtaposition of these two images – of both your child's and Coalhouse's hands – sets off a complex chain of thoughts in your head, and you are reminded momentarily of the day you tried to bury your son. When you then return to singing on an 'oo' vowel at the end of the verse, you now not only need to comfort your child – but also yourself.

In the second verse you begin to tell your son about his father's adultery. Your objective in this section is: to get your child to comprehend why you took him from his father. You want him to empathise with you and to place the blame on Coalhouse. Moments of bitterness and sarcasm may come through at this stage. During the third verse – as the musical accompaniment becomes more driving and rhythmical – you relive the memories of running away and the period just before you tried to bury your child. Your objective at this point is: to convince your son that you were unwell. It is vital to you that he understands that you were temporarily insane when you tried to hurt him. You want him to comprehend that you were experiencing severe emotional trauma – that these weren't actions that were in any way callous.

After finally accepting what you did at the end of the verse (see point 4 below) you manage to find some sense of inner calm. For a brief moment you allow yourself to think fondly of Coalhouse. You then explain the rationale for your terrible actions (see point 5 below) before playing your final, most important objective, which is: to seek your son's forgiveness.

KEY MOMENTS/TOP TIPS

1. In advance of the audition you must make an important decision about how you will handle the given circumstance of singing to a baby. You may wish to wear an item of clothing to the audition – a small cardigan, for example – that you can remove after you have spoken to the pianist and gather up to represent a baby. If this is your choice,

you must be very convincing in handling the clothing as if it is child. An alternative is to deliver a non-naturalistic performance and direct your thoughts behind the panel's heads as if the baby is behind them.

2. In reality the child would be too young to understand anything you are saying, but don't let this throw you: you should play all of the objectives as though your son can comprehend you and is capable of exonerating you for your terrible crime.

3. As the song deals with some very dark subject matter, it is important to find moments of lightness and joy – for example, when you recall watching Coalhouse play the piano in the first verse.

4. Flaherty has scored the piano accompaniment so it drops out for a moment when you sing about burying your son in the ground. This is the first event of the song, and requires a great deal of emotional investment; it is the moment you finally accept what you have done after weeks of suppressing it in your mind.

5. The rationale that you give your child for trying to bury him alive at first seems strange: that his hands reminded you of his father's. Although the crime is, of course, very difficult to comprehend for anyone who has not had an extreme psychological disorder, such as postpartum psychosis, it is the only way Sarah can make sense of it. She tried to bury her child because he reminded her of his adulterous father, the man who broke her heart. This confession is the second and final event of the song.

Vocal and Musical Analysis

WHO TO LISTEN TO: Audra McDonald on the original Broadway cast recording (1998).

VOCAL RANGE: G3 to F5.

ORIGINAL KEY: G minor.

ACCENT: General American.

STYLE OF MUSICAL: Book musical.

VOCAL SET–UP/MUSICAL TIPS

1. The opening lullaby section should be delivered in a sweet, quiet Cry quality, with thin vocal folds and a raised larynx.

2. Once the lyric begins, the fundamental sound for the song is a legit set-up. Use a great deal of thyroid tilt, simultaneous onsets and a consistent vibrato. You should also try lowering your larynx slightly to give the music a soulful quality, as McDonald so wonderfully demonstrates on the suggested recording.

3. Explore using a Speech quality during the third verse to give your sound more weight. You will need to mix a little thyroid tilt into this set-up to allow you to advance to the higher pitches, as you can hear McDonald do on the recording.

4. When you sing about burying your heart in the ground, to the end of the verse, try using a mixed belt, as McDonald employs. At this point you need to tilt your cricoid cartilage, lift your larynx, raise your chin slightly, and add some torso anchoring.

5. During the final verse, after the a capella moment, try returning to a Cry quality. Lift your larynx as high as possible and sing very quietly here to produce an intimate and vulnerable sound.

Sheet Music

The correct sheet music for this song is available at www.musicnotes.com.

'Not a Day Goes By'
from *Merrily We Roll Along*

Music and lyrics by Stephen Sondheim

Choose this song if: you have a strong mezzosoprano voice
and enjoy singing songs about the break-up of a relationship
that require a raw emotional connection.

Given Circumstances

Note: The script for *Merrily We Roll Along* is notable because
the narrative is told with a reverse chronology. For ease of
understanding, however, the given circumstances below are
outlined in a sequential order.

WHO ARE YOU: Beth, a feminine, strong and tense woman in
her late twenties. Originally from Houston, Texas, you are
honest and kind-hearted, but can also be unworldly and naive
at times.

WHERE ARE YOU: On the steps of a Manhattan Court House,
New York City, USA.

WHEN IS IT: 1.00 p.m., autumn, 1967.

WHAT HAS HAPPENED BEFORE: In 1959 you met Franklin
Shepherd, a talented young musical-theatre composer. Frank
had been struggling, along with his best friend and lyricist
Charley Kringas, to develop his work and to get it produced.
After a creative but frustrating period in which Frank and
Charley's work was rejected by a powerful producer named
Joe Josephson (because their tunes weren't 'hummable'), the
pair decided to set up a musical revue of their own instead.
When they decided they needed a girl in the company, they
held an audition. You were successful at this casting and were
given the female role. Soon after, you became romantically
involved with Frank.

A year later Joe came along to see the revue, which was now entitled *Frankly Frank*, with his fiancée and former secretary, Gussie. On this occasion Joe was highly impressed by Frank's work, as he believed it had become more commercial. Also attending the show that same evening were your parents. They'd had strong reservations when you'd told them recently that you were going to get married. (The ceremony was scheduled for that very same evening.) They were concerned that Frank wouldn't be able to provide for you because he didn't have a 'proper job'. In truth, the wedding had not been something either of you were planning, but it had become necessary when you became pregnant. Despite this unplanned happenstance, you were both very much in love and were committed to each other. After the show the wedding went ahead as planned.

Two years later, with Frank's career starting to progress, you were both invited to a party at Joe and Gussie's house. The guests were some of the most rich and famous people in New York. Being around such guests left you feeling somewhat star-struck – an attitude that Frank found irritating. Joe and Gussie were now married, and Gussie had become a Broadway actress, though she had not yet managed to star in a big hit. At the party she deliberately spilled her drink on you before taking Frank to one side, as she wanted to be alone with him. Because of her marriage to Joe, and through her own seductive personality, Gussie had become hugely influential in the New York theatre world – which she demonstrated to a smitten Frank by securing him a top-flight agent at the party. Gussie wanted your husband to write the score for a new show entitled *Musical Husbands*, in which she would star and which Joe would produce. Initially Frank was reluctant – as he and Charley had been working for three years on a political piece that they hoped Joe would mount instead – but he soon gave in to Gussie's persuasive charm.

Musical Husbands opened in 1964 to great popular acclaim. On the opening night Evelyn, Charley's wife, went into labour. When Frank offered to go to the hospital, you urged

him to stay to enjoy the first-night party – offering to go
yourself instead. Frank's best friend Mary warned you not to
leave him alone with Gussie – but you told her that you
trusted your husband. That evening Frank and Gussie slept
together.

Today, three years later, you were at the courthouse for your
divorce proceedings with Frank – which you'd initiated when
you discovered that Frank and Gussie were having an affair.
Devastated, you demanded that you receive the lion's share of
Frank's wealth and the custody of your child: Franklin Jr.
After the trial you are intending to move back to Houston
with your son so you can be away from Frank.

Moments ago you came out of the courthouse with your
parents, and your son, to find Frank waiting there on the
steps. Upon seeing him, your parents led their grandchild
away. When the pair of you were left alone Frank asked how
Franklin Jr. was. He had not seen his son since the two of you
separated. Frank has just asked you if you still love him.

WHO ELSE IS THERE: Frank.

WHO SHOULD YOU SING TO: Frank.

Textual Analysis

It is worth considering the atmosphere between yourself and
Frank before you begin to sing. This is the first tender
conversation you have had with him since you split up. At this
point your feelings towards him are conflicted – you are not
simply angry. During the introduction, explore playing the
idea that, although he has hurt you very badly, you still love
him greatly – and as a consequence, even though you have
instigated the divorce proceedings, part of you is still
considering taking him back. In the opening lyric you might
play the following objective: to convince Frank you think about
him every day. It is possible to play warm, loving actions in this
section such as: I caress, comfort and soothe Frank.

During the second stanza, and through to the end of verse, you then confess to Frank that recently you have been spending a lot of time preoccupied with thoughts of him. Your objective in this next section is: to make Frank understand what it has been like for you since the separation. You want him to take some responsibility for the pain that he has caused.

The build in the music that leads to the climactic 'and no' suggests that this is a moment of great emotional release. From this point until the end of the song, try playing the following objective: to make Frank feel the pain that you do. You want him to suffer and to feel the consequences of his actions. In this section you can explore a visceral and animalistic range of actions, such as: I savage, maul, gouge, strike, bombard and vilify Frank. What is difficult for you is, although Frank is undoubtedly hurt by the break-up, he will never care as deeply as you do, nor feel the same level of pain – no matter what you say to him.

KEY MOMENTS/TOP TIPS

1. It is highly unusual for Sondheim to make use of repeated lyrics, as he does in this song. Unlike some other lesser writers, who might sometimes use repetition for authorial convenience, the reiteration of the exact same words is a very deliberate dramatic choice. The reason why you repeat yourself in this song is because the emotional connection to what you are saying is so strong, that saying something once is simply not enough. Try using the moments of repetition as opportunities to punish Frank – by brutally confronting him with the pain his actions have caused.

2. The song should feel emotionally raw. If accessing a strong emotional connection causes your vocal performance to become a little broken, then that is appropriate. The sound should be full of heartache, not pretty. Think of almost spitting and snarling the words at times.

3. The use of the word 'blessed' to describe the day is fascinating. There is a great deal of sarcasm and bitterness to explore with this particular lyric.

4. In the musical, immediately following the song, there is a short, tender scene where Beth asks Frank if her suspicions are correct: did he, in fact, sleep with Gussie? Frank confesses that he did, yet for a moment Beth still thinks of taking him back. It is useful to take account of this scene during the play-out of the song. Try ending the song still conflicted, rather than simply empowered, as this is a less simplistic and more interesting dramatic choice.

Vocal and Musical Analysis

WHO TO LISTEN TO: Bernadette Peters on the bonus track of the digitally remastered original Broadway cast recording (2007 [1982]).

VOCAL RANGE: D4 to F♯5.

ORIGINAL KEY: F major.

ACCENT: Texan. If you find this difficult or clumsy, then General American will suffice.

STYLE OF MUSICAL: Concept musical.

VOCAL SET-UP/MUSICAL TIPS

1. There are two versions of the lyric on the suggested sheet music. You should sing the lyrics on the lower line, which are those that Peters uses on the suggested recording.

2. The first verse should be delivered very quietly, simply and purely. Try to use a Cry quality with very thin vocal folds to portray Beth's vulnerability.

3. An important musical instruction in the opening section is '*molto rubato*' (which translates as 'very robbed' time). Sondheim is asking you to pull the rhythm around at this

point – which Peters does with great control. Try exploring how this conversational phrasing can portray how difficult Beth is finding it to say these words to Frank.

4. On the series of triplet notes that begin with the words 'thinking' and 'sweating', Sondheim asks you to sing 'with increased fury'. You want to get gradually louder during this phrase, by tightening your AES to add some twang to your sound, as you hear Peters demonstrate. You should also push the tempo forward at this point to give the music a restless quality, as if Beth's feelings are suddenly blurting out uncontrollably.

5. When you reach the climactic 'and no', the next phrase should now be very loud and full. This is best achieved by remaining in a Twang quality, rather than trying to use belt.

6. After you've sung about a blessed day, try returning to a sweet Cry quality for the next section that starts on the word 'I', before achieving another crescendo on the repetition of the words 'day after day'. Again look to achieve this by gradually tightening your AES to add twang.

7. There is an instrumental section and an extra half-verse on the recording that is not included on the suggested music. You should discount these and skip to the final repeated phrases at this point, as per the score.

8. Try making the last line the quietest of the entire song – by returning once again to a Cry quality.

Sheet Music

The correct sheet music for this song is available at www.musicnotes.com.

'Patterns'
from *Baby*

Music by David Shire, lyrics by Richard Maltby Jr.

Choose this song if: you enjoy playing emotionally conflicted characters and can belt to an E♭. The song may especially suit you if you if are an actress in your late thirties/early forties.

Given Circumstances

WHO ARE YOU: Arlene McNally, a forty-three-year-old mother of three. You struggle with panic attacks and are prone to depression.

WHERE ARE YOU: In the local park of an unspecified small university town in the USA.

WHEN IS IT: 10.20 a.m., a weekday, August 1983.

WHAT HAS HAPPENED BEFORE: Five months ago you returned from a trip to the Plaza Hotel in New York to celebrate your silver wedding anniversary, as you were married to your husband Alan twenty years ago. Returning home marked the beginning of a period of adjustment for you both, as the youngest of your three children had recently moved out – leaving the two of you alone in the house. You were excited at the prospect of having your freedom again now that all your children had become young adults. You had also been feeling a little unwell, so made an appointment to see your doctor. To your great surprise, when you went to see him he told that you that you were a month pregnant.

Alan's response to this news was unexpectedly one of delight. He felt invigorated by the prospect of having another child, but you felt differently: you were reluctant to go through with the pregnancy as you felt you were both too old to start another family. You began to discuss having an abortion, selling the family home, and moving into an apartment just for the two of you. After having three children, you felt it was now time to pursue your own dreams and aspirations – such as finishing the novel you had been writing. Because he wanted to make you happy, Alan began to make arrangements to sell the family home. However, when the estate agent came to value the house, you made an impulsive decision and told him that you no longer wanted to go through with the sale – because you were having a baby.

Five months on from that important decision, you have come to the local park. Recently the reality of your situation has begun to sink in – and so you felt you needed to get some fresh air so you could think.

WHO ELSE IS THERE: You are alone.

WHO SHOULD YOU SING TO: Yourself, though in an audition you can share many of your thoughts with the panel as though they are your inner-consciousness.

Textual Analysis

You have come to the park this morning because recently you have been feeling claustrophobic. As you are now six months into the pregnancy you understand that there is no longer any turning back, and consequently you feel trapped. Last night you couldn't sleep and spent several hours staring at the patterned wallpaper in your bedroom. The recurring shapes reminded you of the repetitive routines of motherhood (see point 1 below). You therefore play the following objective in the first verse: to work out why these patterns are haunting you. Actions you might play in this section include: I question, query and search myself. This level of introspection makes you feel annoyed with yourself. In the second half of the verse your objective thus becomes: to make fun of your own depressive mood.

The musical release that happens at the start of the first chorus reflects the emotional outburst that occurs in that moment. The pressures of impending motherhood that have been building up inside you for weeks finally reach a crescendo; you feel on the edge of a nervous breakdown. Your objective in this section thus becomes: to try and control your emotions. You want to pull yourself together.

At the start of second verse – when you complain once more about the patterns that are disturbing your sense of equilibrium – your mental state is spiralling out of control. Try playing the following objective at this point: to stop yourself from having a panic attack. In order to achieve this, you might try actions such as: I suppress, curb, throttle and muzzle myself. With the panic growing, however, you find that your ability to control your own life has been neutered; you feel like you want to run away, but lack the courage to do so. In the second half of the verse the objective therefore becomes: to criticise yourself for being a coward.

During the second chorus you are genuinely in a state of crisis. You feel that if you don't manage to control your growing claustrophobia and anxiety, you will either have a mental breakdown or leave your husband. Your objective in this section could be: to get control of your psychological state. Explore the following actions at this point: I shake, sober up, rattle and slap yourself.

In the short concluding section, your relationship to the patterns in your life changes – you now see them as a distraction from your emotional difficulties. You can play the following objective here: to try and shut out your problems. This, though, is an objective in which you are ultimately unsuccessful.

CONTEMPORARY BALLADS

KEY MOMENTS/TOP TIPS

1. To act this song well you first need to be clear what is meant by the word 'patterns'. In this context Arlene uses the word to describe two things: firstly, the physical patterns she sees around the house (e.g. in the wallpaper, or the carpet), and secondly the word is a synonym for the mundane routines of her life as a mother and housewife, such as: completing the household chores, taking the children to school, etc.

2. Try playing the song as if Arlene is seriously considering leaving her husband, abandoning her responsibilities to her family, and running away. This will make the stakes of the song very high indeed.

3. An important moment occurs when Arlene sings about tucking her feelings away again at the end of the first chorus. She feels that in the past she has had to sacrifice her own wants and desires in order to look after her children, and she is unsure about whether she wants to do that again in the future. At this moment she tries to suppress her desires once more. This is the event of the song.

4. The lyric follows an interesting dramatic arc, in that, despite spending the whole song debating whether she should run away from her marriage, by the end of the scene Arlene still has not found an answer to this fundamental question. She finds herself back where she started. Try finishing the song with a metaphorical question mark hanging in the air, as though Arlene will still be pondering her future for some time to come.

Vocal and Musical Analysis

WHO TO LISTEN TO: Beth Fowler on the original Broadway cast recording (1983).

VOCAL RANGE: B3 to E5.

ORIGINAL KEY: E minor.

ACCENT: General American.

STYLE OF MUSICAL: Contemporary musical (pop-based).

VOCAL SET-UP/MUSICAL TIPS

1. The beginning of the song should be conversational, and the use of Speech quality is therefore appropriate. In the first verse keep the note-lengths short and avoid tilting the thyroid cartilage on the top notes, as you can hear Fowler demonstrate.

2. Add some thyroid tilt the first time you sing about running away, towards the end of the opening verse. Introduce some torso anchoring at this point and use legato phrasing to transition into a legit sound on the first chorus.

3. During the first chorus tighten the AES on the top notes to add a little twang, as Fowler ably demonstrates on the word 'rise'.

4. Around the word 'shake' return your thyroid from a tilted to a horizontal position so you can transition back into a Speech quality in time for the second verse.

5. The four bars of instrumental music that precede the second verse should be cut.

6. The second chorus needs to be much louder than the first – and is best delivered in a mixed-belt set-up. From the word 'safe' onwards, gradually start to anchor your torso and lift your chin so you can tilt your cricoid on the word 'know' and open out into a belt. You can then stay in that set-up for the next couple of phrases. Try tightening the AES a little, as Fowler demonstrates, on the word 'mind', to add some extra volume to the belt by mixing in a little twang.

7. When you sing about breaking apart, return to a very plain, unadorned Speech quality. Avoid any unnecessary vibrato.

8. In the final section, which begins with the word 'patterns', sing in a plaintive Cry quality to conclude the song.

Sheet Music

The correct sheet music for this song is available at www.musicnotes.com.

'When I Look at You'
from *The Scarlet Pimpernel*

Music by Frank Wildhorn, lyrics by Nan Knighton

Choose this song if: you are able to blend a legit musical-theatre sound with the ability to belt. This song may suit you if you are used to playing the romantic lead.

Given Circumstances

Note: The musical is based on the novel of the same name, which was the first in a series of historical fiction books written by Baroness Orczy at the turn of the twentieth century.

WHO ARE YOU: Lady Marguerite Blakeney (formerly Marguerite St Just). You are the wife of Sir Percy Blakeney, who, unbeknownst to you, is secretly the counter-revolutionary known as the Scarlet Pimpernel. Formerly an actress, you are now trapped in a cold marriage – so often feel insecure and vulnerable.

WHERE ARE YOU: The drawing room of your house on the Blakeney Estate, England.

WHEN IS IT: 11 a.m., a Saturday, summer, 1792, during the period of the French Revolution.

WHAT HAS HAPPENED BEFORE: Six weeks ago you gave your final performance at the famous Parisian theatre: La Comédie-Française. On stage at the end of the performance, you announced your engagement to the Englishman Sir Percival Blakeney, whom you had met only six weeks before and who was watching from the auditorium. Immediately following your announcement, the theatre was closed by Citizen Chauvelin (who has his own romantic designs on you). Chauvelin was acting on the orders of the French revolutionary leader Maximilien Robespierre. When your friend Marie, a costume and set designer, stepped in to

protest, Percy had to save her from being arrested by
Chauvelin and his soldiers. He then helped you escape to his
native England.

With Paris falling under the shadow of the revolution, back in
England you and Percy were quickly married, as you were
both deeply in love. However, on your wedding day Percy
discovered that his friend, the Marquis de St Cyr, had been a
victim of the revolution. He had been beheaded at the
guillotine by Chauvelin. Uncertain how the Marquis had been
betrayed, Percy was given a note by Dewhurst, one of his
fellow counter-revolutionaries, which indicated that you were
a spy for the revolutionaries. (In fact, Chauvelin is
blackmailing you, though Percy does not find out the truth
about this matter till much later in the show.) Believing that
you betrayed his friend, Percy then shunned you on your
wedding night.

Following the discovery about the fate of his friend, Percy
resolved to rectify the situation in Paris. Over the coming
weeks he secretly began to disguise himself as the Pimpernel.
With the help of a group of his friends, he pulled off a series
of remarkable feats to save others from the guillotine. In
response, a furious Robespierre ordered Chauvelin to travel to
England to discover the true identity of this mysterious
masked man.

With five weeks having passed since the wedding, Percy has
remained distant from you. This morning the servants have
all been gossiping with your husband about who this
glamorous counter-revolutionary might be, without the
slightest idea of his true identity. A few moments ago your
brother Armand returned from Paris – where he has been
covertly aiding the Pimpernel. When you began to complain
to him of Percy's recent behaviour, he defended him as brave
and honourable, though he did not reveal their shared secret.
Marie, who has also recently arrived from Paris, has been busy
painting your husband's portrait. He has just shown you the
picture and asked if you recognise his likeness. He then
embarrassed you by making you repeat, in front of Marie,

a criticism you made of him the other day: that he had changed so much that you now barely recognise him. An astute Marie has just retorted that if you were to look into your husband's eyes, you would perceive who he truly is.

WHO ELSE IS THERE: Percy.

WHO SHOULD YOU SING TO: In the script it indicates that at the start of the music Marie continues to paint Percy and the room darkens around Marguerite just before she sings. This suggests that the song takes place in her inner thoughts, but for audition purposes, it is more active to perform the song as a dialogue with Percy. The textual analysis below assumes you are delivering the number as if Marie has just left you alone with Percy – and he hears and responds to what you say.

Textual Analysis

During the introduction you should prepare yourself for a difficult conversation. You have been feeling unhappy in your marriage for a while and have decided that now is the time to tell Percy how you feel – which is not an easy thing to do. Imagine there is an awkward atmosphere between yourself and your husband. In the first verse try playing the following objective: to make Percy accept that he has changed. You want him to appreciate that the connection that once existed between you both has vanished. Try approaching this with caring, loving actions such as: I comfort, soothe, stroke and sweeten Percy.

Despite your constructive intentions, you are unsuccessful in this opening objective, so in the second verse you challenge Percy more directly. The pain and rejection you feel rises closer to the surface. Try playing the following objective in this section: to make Percy remember the good times. You want him to appreciate that every time you look at him, you recall an occasion when you were happy together, and those memories are torturing you. In the bridge you then appeal to Percy's sense of compassion. Your objective in this unit is: to get the old Percy back. You promise your husband that if he were to change his current behaviour, and treat you as he used to, then you would never leave him. However, you are once again unsuccessful in your objective. During the third verse you reveal to Percy that your memories of the past are still extremely vivid. You say how, when you look at the man in front of you, it feels as if the Percy you once knew is still touching you. Your objective at this point is: to warn Percy that memories don't last forever. You want him to change his behaviour in order to save the relationship, as you doubt how long the love you once felt can keep you both together.

In the final section, when you tell Percy that you once followed him like a star, you might play the following objective: to get Percy to take responsibility for betraying the relationship. To mirror the big musical release at this point of the song (see point 3 below), you should explore strong, forthright actions such as: I challenge, accuse and expose Percy. This outburst leads to the first event of the song: when you ask yourself whether you ever really knew Percy. In that moment – for the very first time – you question if your husband ever truly loved you. Actions such as I search, cross-examine and interrogate myself are appropriate choices at this point. After this moment of introspection, your objective in the final couple of lines is: to mock yourself for your blind loyalty. You come to accept that you are trapped – because you still miss the old Percy – and this makes you incapable of leaving him now.

KEY MOMENTS/TOP TIPS

1. During the song your frequently refer to 'someone else'. You need to be clear you are talking about the old Percy you knew in the past. You are constantly comparing your husband as how he is now, to how he was before you were married.

2. Several lyrics in the song are a little unclear, as at times the lyricist strays away from dramatic dialogue into poetry –

156

for example, on the last line of the second verse. A good way to ensure these lyrics still sound like the words of a character, is to choose a defined action for that particular line and play it with conviction. This can help compensate for the somewhat purple language. For example, on the last line of the second verse you might play: I awaken you.

3. There is a significant change in the music in the final section. Your vocal performance should be fuller and more passionate at this point. From an acting perspective, imagine this is the moment when Marguerite fully releases the emotions that she has been bottling up.

4. Throughout the song Marguerite asks herself a number of questions. During your performance you should feel that you are desperately seeking answers. On each question play a powerful, searching action, such as: I cross-examine, interrogate, grill and shake myself.

Vocal and Musical Analysis

WHO TO LISTEN TO: Christine Andreas on the original Broadway cast recording (1998).

VOCAL RANGE: B3 to E5.

ORIGINAL KEY: G major.

ACCENT: Marguerite is French, so, of course, you could deliver this song in your own accent if you are native to that country, though for audition purposes the song could also be delivered in either General American (by American actresses) or in Received Pronunciation (if you are from the UK).

STYLE OF MUSICAL: Contemporary musical (legit-based).

VOCAL SET–UP/MUSICAL TIPS

1. The first verse should be performed with a reflective tone. Try singing this section in a Cry quality, with very thin vocal folds, a tilted thyroid and a raised larynx.

2. The second verse should be slightly louder than the first. Achieve this by tightening your AES to move into a Twang quality.

3. Return to a Cry quality at the beginning of the bridge (when you ask Percy if he could look at you). To achieve this, relax your AES to remove any twang from your voice. This section also requires a sense of musical impetus, so push the tempo forward a little.

4. From the word 'disappear' until the end of the bridge you want to grow gradually louder. To achieve this crescendo you should slowly remove your thyroid tilt to thicken your vocal folds. You can hear Andreas demonstrate this clearly on the suggested recording.

5. The third verse, which follows the bridge, should be delivered in a Speech quality. Use thicker vocal folds and make occasional use of glottal onsets to help you 'land' in the correct set-up.

6. The word 'me' in the line when you call yourself a fool should be belted. Remember to tilt your cricoid cartilage, lift your larynx, raise your chin slightly and add some torso anchoring at this point.

7. Following the belt, the last two lines should be sung as quietly as possible – in a sweet Cry quality.

Sheet Music

The correct sheet music for this song is available at www.musicnotes.com.

CONTEMPORARY BALLADS

158

'If I Could'
from *The Hired Man*

Music and lyrics by Howard Goodall

Choose this song if: you have a legit mezzosoprano voice and
enjoy performing songs about heartbreak and loss. You may
also want to select this song if you are a working-class actor-
singer with a native Northern accent. The song allows you to
belt to a high E♭.

Given Circumstances

WHO ARE YOU: Emily, a restless, conflicted young woman.
Although you are married, you are also secretly having an
affair with another man.

WHERE ARE YOU: Outside of a pub in the village of
Crossbridge, Cumbria, England.

WHEN IS IT: 6.00 p.m., winter, 1898.

WHAT HAS HAPPENED BEFORE: You married your husband John
in 1898 in the rural village of Crossbridge. At this time he
worked as a hired farmhand. Although John loved his work, it
was hard for him to find regular employment and earn a
decent living. Shortly after your wedding John managed to
find a job working on the farm of a landowner named Mr
Pennington. With John feeling more settled, you soon became
pregnant with your first child, a daughter, May. But despite
the birth, you quickly became dissatisfied in your marriage.
You were always working long hours and felt trapped by the
narrowness of village life.

One day John was encouraged to take a fox-hunting trip by
his brother Isaac and decided to stay away overnight. In this
moment, you yielded to a temptation you had been feeling for
some time and slept with Jackson, the handsome son of
Pennington. Afterwards, the relationship between yourself

and John began to rapidly deteriorate. He sensed a growing
distance between you – though he didn't know about your
affair. Despite your strong feelings for Jackson, you refused
his pleas to abandon your marriage and run away with him.
Eventually losing patience, Jackson recently decided to join
the army and leave for India. When you found out, you were
distraught and begged him not to leave. Soon after, John
discovered the truth about the affair – when he overheard that
Jackson, rather than his friend Joe Sharp, had visited you at
the house whilst he'd been away fox-hunting. John has just
beaten Jackson up in a fight outside the local pub where
Jackson had been celebrating his departure.

WHO ELSE IS THERE: Jackson and John are present but frozen –
but for the purposes of audition you should behave as if you are
alone. At the beginning of the song, suppose Jackson and John
are walking away in opposite directions across the hillside.

WHO SHOULD YOU SING TO: This song is a soliloquy and for
much of the time you are talking to yourself. In these
moments you might choose to address the panel as though
they are your inner-consciousness. At various points you also
address Jackson and the villagers – whom you can see, but
who are far enough away that they can't hear you. In one
moment you sing to a higher power: Fate.

Textual Analysis

At the beginning of the song you are shocked and upset. You
have just seen Jackson felled by your husband's punch and
your adultery has been exposed. In the first verse you talk to
yourself. Your objective at this point is: to wish that this had
never happened. You feel terrible about the pain you have
caused the two men you love – and would do anything to take
it away. In the second stanza, when you say that both deserved
more than this, you then take the blame on yourself. Your
objective in this short section is: to punish yourself for being
an adulterer. At this point you are full of self-loathing. Try
such actions as: I chastise, flagellate and criticise myself in

order to put this across. In the third stanza of the opening verse, which begins on the word 'suddenly', you begin to grasp the full consequences of your actions: the revelation of your adultery could cost you both your marriage and any hope of being with Jackson. Your objective at this point is: to make yourself face up this reality.

In the first chorus you continue to talk to yourself. Your objective in this unit is: to understand how this situation has come to pass. This is the fundamental question of the entire song: you want to comprehend why your actions have caused so much pain, as this was never what you intended.

Your point of focus shifts during the second verse and you begin to address Jackson. You are angry that he is leaving to join the army, so try playing the following objective: to make him feel guilty for abandoning you. In the second chorus you then question your previous decision to stay with John when Jackson asked you to run away with him. In this moment of soul-searching your objective becomes: to work out if you made the correct choice. After this moment of introspection you address Jackson once more in the first bridge (when you remind him that he saw you crying). Your objective at this point is: to get Jackson to take responsibility for his actions.

As the third verse begins, you become aware of the villagers who had gathered around to watch the fight. They are now gossiping about you and judging your actions. When you realise this, you lose your temper; for a moment you are not fully in control of your behaviour. Your objective at this point is: to make them own up to their double standards. In this unit, try such confrontational actions as: I provoke, aggravate, defy, hector and needle the villagers.

In the second bridge the song becomes epic in scale as you address Fate. Your objective when you speak to this higher power is: to get Fate to abandon you. You are now so full of self-loathing that you feel you deserve to be punished and forgotten.

The first event of the song then occurs at the beginning of the final section (see point 3 below). In the last phrases your objective becomes: to understand why your life turned out this way. The final conclusion you reach is that it is simply because you fell in love with Jackson. And that is not your fault.

KEY MOMENTS/TOP TIPS

1. During the song you never mention Jackson or John's names. This can make the song difficult for a panel to follow – particularly if they are not familiar with the given circumstances. To help make the narrative clear, imagine that Jackson is walking off in the distance to the left of the panel. Look in his direction whenever you address him. You might also wish to explain before you start singing – in no more than a sentence or two – that your husband and your lover have just had a fight, and that at some points you will be singing to Jackson, and at others to the gossiping villagers.

2. The questions that Emily asks during the song are fundamental to her future happiness. Try playing very strong actions when you ask these questions, such as: I interrogate, cross-examine, challenge and probe myself.

3. The event of the song occurs just after the words 'ask me', before the final section starts. At this moment you realise that the reason the fight occurred between Jackson and John, and that your world was shattered, was because you loved them both. You decide that this is something you could not choose or control. As a consequence, the song has a huge emotional arc. From possessing feelings of self-loathing at the beginning, by the end of the piece you have managed to find a sense of inner peace: you are able to forgive yourself for the pain that you caused the two men.

Vocal and Musical Analysis

WHO TO LISTEN TO: Julie Atherton on the Curve Theatre cast recording (2013).

VOCAL RANGE: B♭3 to E♭5.

ORIGINAL KEY: E♭ major.

ACCENT: Ideally you should work for a Cumbrian accent, though this song works well in most Northern accents.

STYLE OF MUSICAL: Contemporary musical (pop-based).

VOCAL SET-UP/MUSICAL TIPS

1. The opening of the song needs to sound both vulnerable and conversational. Try singing the first section in a Cry quality with thin vocal folds and a raised larynx. Mix in some aspirate and glottal onsets – and half-speak some words – so that the sound still feels like an extension of speaking, even though your larynx is raised.

2. It is useful to notice that the first two lines are meant to be sung quite freely (there is a marking of 'ad lib'), but then the song drops into a strict tempo on the third line. Observing this musical instruction gives the song an unexpected impetus, which reflects Emily's growing desperation. You may want to point this out to the pianist before you start singing, so that they can follow you.

3. When you repeat the words 'another love' you want to transition from a Cry to a Speech quality. Slowly remove your thyroid tilt to thicken your vocal folds and effect a crescendo at this point.

4. In the final line of the first verse you also want to crescendo. Look to achieve this by adding some torso anchoring. This will help you prepare for the first chorus, which should be delivered in a mixed-belt. For the top note of that chorus – on the word 'anger' – you should lift your chin a little and add some cricoid and thyroid tilt to help you achieve the belt set-up.

5. The second verse, when you sing about knowing that you should have been aware, has a confrontational tone. Try delivering the section in a Speech quality whilst using

some pronounced glottal and aspirate onsets for emphasis, as though you are spitting the words at Jackson. On the final line of the verse you should then crescendo in the same way you did previously: by adding torso anchoring. Return to a mixed-belt set-up for the second chorus.

6. For the first bridge section, which starts when you tell Jackson that he saw your tears, you should once again be in a Speech quality. Move into a Belt quality on the words 'go now'. During the third verse, when you challenge the villagers for staring at you, you should then repeat the confrontational tone you used in the previous verse.

7. The set-up for the second bridge, when you ask the universe to pass you by, is the same as first: you should start in a Speech quality and then transition into Belt on the words 'ask me'.

8. On the suggested recording John and Jackson also sing during the final section. You should disregard this and just sing Emily's line. This last portion of the song should be sung in an extremely quiet Cry quality. Lift your larynx very high, tilt your thyroid a great deal and thin your vocal folds. The lyric has an urgent, reflective tone – so try mixing in some aspirate onsets to reflect this.

9. The final note can be quite difficult to sustain, so before you sing it, ensure you have anchored your neck and breathe into your lower ribs. Aim to keep the ribs wide and open for as long as possible in order to control the outbreath.

Sheet Music

The correct sheet music for this song is available at www.scribd.com.

'Take Me to the World'
from *Evening Primrose*

Music and lyrics by Stephen Sondheim

Choose this song if: you have a warm mezzosoprano legit voice and want to explore an innocent, unworldly and optimistic character.

Given Circumstances

WHO ARE YOU: Ella Harkins, a beautiful nineteen-year-old girl. You are something of an outsider and, although you have been frequently unhappy, you retain a rebellious and hopeful streak.

WHERE ARE YOU: Inside a large, strange, magical Manhattan department store inhabited by a group of mysterious people who only come out once the doors are closed and all of the customers have left.

WHEN IS IT: 11.30 p.m., winter, 1966.

WHAT HAS HAPPENED BEFORE: For many years, a mysterious group of hideaways have been living in secret in the department store. The eldest, Mrs Monday, has dwelt there since the financial crash of 1897, though most of the inhabitants moved into the store following the Wall Street Crash of 1929. For various reasons they all wanted to escape from the outside world. The only way the group can remain in the store is if their existence is kept a total secret.

When you were six you became an unwilling member of this strange community. You had fallen asleep one day in the women's hats department, and when you woke up, long after the store had closed, you were confronted by Roscoe – a leading member of the group. At first he was minded to let you go. The group thought no one would believe a six-year-old telling tales about strange people living in a department store – so their secret would remain safe. However, Mrs Monday decided she wanted a maid – so you were made to stay against your will. As a consequence you have not seen daylight for thirteen years. Unlike the others in the group, you have always longed to escape. Only fear of the Dark Men – a group of sinister apparitions who turn those who try to escape into mannequins – has kept you here all these years. As the others see you as an outsider, you have been kept as a prisoner in the furniture repair shop in the basement.

Tonight your world changed dramatically when an idealistic young poet named Charles Snell slipped into the department store just before closing time. Despairing at the constant interruptions to his writing by unwanted acquaintances and annoying neighbours, he had decided he also wanted to live secretly in the department store – where he believed he would be inspired to write great new works. When you met, and you told Charles of your past, you quickly began to fall in love with each other. Charles felt you were the adventure he had been looking for all of his life. When you told Charles of your desire be free – and see the sky again – he resolved to educate you about the outside world.

In attempting to do so, Charles has just tried to play you a tape recording of birdsong – so that you can know what it sounds like – but you replied that was not enough. You wanted to hear a real bird. You have just resolved to ask Charles to take you away from the department store, even at the risk of being caught by the Dark Men and turned into a mannequin (which will eventually be the fate of you both when you subsequently try to escape together).

WHO ELSE IS THERE: Charles.

WHO SHOULD YOU SING TO: Charles. In the context of an audition, you can either sing to an imaginary Charles who is standing behind the table, or directly to the panel, as though they all have the power to take you to the outside world.

Textual Analysis

At first glance it can appear as though this song has a single overarching objective contained within the title lyric: to convince Charles to take you to the outside world. It is possible, however, to find greater textual detail. During the first half of the opening verse, for example, try playing the following objective: to encourage Charles to picture the wonderful life you could share together. You want him to envisage you roaming together in beautiful open spaces. If the first part of the verse is about encouraging Charles to envisage a shared potential future, the second half is a more of a direct instruction. In this unit explore the following objective: to make Charles educate you about life. You are desperate for him to satisfy your curiosity about what goes on outside the department store.

In the second verse you start the section by imploring Charles. You should play the overarching objective at this point: to get him to take you to the outside world. Explore actions such as: I beseech, enthuse, inspire and exhort you. Midway through the verse, it is useful to imagine that Charles is frightened about what may happen if he were to do so. In the latter half of the verse you can then play the following objective: to give Charles the courage to act. You try to do this by convincing him that you will face this together, and therefore it can be achieved. In this unit actions such as: I bolster, strengthen and reassure Charles can be useful possibilities. By the end of the song we should feel that your passion has inspired Charles, that you have been successful in your objective, and that he has agreed to try and flee the department store with you.

KEY MOMENTS/TOP TIPS

1. Although the song is directed towards Charles, much of the lyric involves Ella imagining the world beyond the department store. Ensure you have very clear, pre-prepared mental pictures of everything Ella describes (the clouds,

the crowds, etc.). You should vary your focus between seeing these images in the first or third circle of attention, and talking to either your imaginary Charles or the panel.

2. As the song doesn't have many changes of objective, it is important that you employ a large range of actions to persuade Charles to help you escape. Try playing choices such as: I implore, urge, charm, inspire, compel, quicken, persuade, encourage, galvanise, invigorate and rouse Charles. In line with the musical build, your actions should become more uplifting as the song reaches its inspiring conclusion.

3. When trying to achieve your objectives, imagine that Charles is reluctant to agree, as he wants to remain in the department store. By making him reticent, and hard to convince, it will give you a greater obstacle to overcome.

4. It is useful to remember that Ella has been imprisoned for thirteen years, and this is her first realistic chance of escape. So when she begins to picture the world, long-suppressed childhood memories are coming to the surface. Try playing the beginning of the song as though Ella is slowly recalling these images, as if from a just-remembered dream.

5. Don't forget the stakes are very high for Ella: if she is caught she will be turned into a mannequin (in effect this is like being killed). Explore playing the characteristics of being brave and daring to show that Ella is courageous in being prepared to risk this dangerous escape.

Vocal and Musical Analysis

WHO TO LISTEN TO: Lauren Samuels in *Sondheim: Women*, St James Theatre (2013).

VOCAL RANGE: B♭3 to E♭45.

ORIGINAL KEY: B♭ major.

ACCENT: General American.

STYLE OF MUSICAL: Concept musical.

VOCAL SET-UP/MUSICAL TIPS

1. This song was traditionally sung in a legit style, but it can also be interpreted in a more contemporary manner by using some Twang and a pop-set up, as Samuels does on the suggested recording. Either is valid – and depends what best suits your voice-type – though a pop style perhaps allows a greater range of voice quality to be employed.

2. Make the first verse quiet and gentle by lifting your larynx a little and thinning your vocal folds to end up in a Cry quality.

3. Throughout the song, whether you choose to sing in either a legit or a pop style, work for long legato phrases – and hold back your vibrato until the ends of the musical sentences.

4. To add a sense of urgency in the second and third verses, try using aspirate onsets to place emphasis on certain words, as you can hear Samuels demonstrate.

5. The last few lines of the song should be full and strong. If you are using a pop set-up you should transition into a mixed-belt on the word 'alone', as Samuels does on the suggested recording. Remember to tilt your cricoid cartilage, lift your larynx, raise your chin slightly and add some torso anchoring at this point. If you are interpreting the song in a legit style, explore lowering the larynx slightly and adding some torso anchoring at this point.

Sheet Music

The correct sheet music for this song is available at www.musicnotes.com.

'Crossword Puzzle'
from *Starting Here, Starting Now*

Music by David Shire, lyrics by Richard Maltby Jr.

Choose this song if: you enjoy singing comedic songs and like playing characters who are bitter, sarcastic and a little psychologically unhinged.

Given Circumstances

Note: *Starting Here, Starting Now* is a revue show, rather than a musical with a through-narrative. The given circumstances below, though derived from the lyric, are therefore invented – and could be altered to suit your needs.

WHO ARE YOU: Martha, a demanding, controlling and volatile New Yorker who has recently been dumped by her fiancé.

WHERE ARE YOU: In the living room of your tiny apartment in Brooklyn, New York, USA.

WHEN IS IT: 10.31 a.m., a Sunday, present day. Today was meant to be your wedding day.

WHAT HAS HAPPENED BEFORE: For twelve months you were engaged to a man named Hecky. You first met him when he got a job at the local bookshop where you worked. As a pair you were very different. Whereas you tended to be forthright and opinionated, he was incredibly shy. As the dominant force in the relationship you put a great deal of pressure on Hecky, and it was your idea that you became engaged.

What united you both was your mutual love of books and words. Your favourite pastime was to complete *The Sunday Times* crossword together – which you did each weekend. This activity, which at first gave you both great pleasure, soon became a cause of conflict. In recent months you had spent every Sunday morning arguing over the answers. You would bicker over who should be allowed to write in a particular word. During these mornings you could be something of a tyrant, and eventually the timid Hecky became weary of being browbeaten and subjugated. One Sunday he finally stood up to you, and shouted you down with an outburst of expletives. Soon after this argument, Hecky promptly left you. He started dating one of your work colleagues, Alice – and called off the wedding.

On Friday afternoon Hecky and Alice left work early to catch a flight, as they were off on a romantic holiday to Bermuda. Since then you have spent the entire weekend feeling bitter and resentful. You awoke this morning, had breakfast and have just sat down to indulge in your usual Sunday ritual of completing *The Times* crossword – whilst trying to forget that today was supposed to be your wedding day.

WHO ELSE IS THERE: You are alone.

WHO SHOULD YOU SING TO: The audience – which, in this situation, is the panel.

Textual Analysis

When the introduction starts, you are studying the crossword. It is a difficult puzzle and you are struggling – in large part because you are distracted by thoughts of Hecky. At the start of the first chorus, your objective is: to protest about the complexity of the puzzle. You want the audience to understand how tricky you are finding it, and how much easier it was to do the crossword when Hecky was around. When you discover that the answer to one of clues is 'gnu', your objective is temporarily: to congratulate yourself on being so clever. This moment of pleasure is short-lived, though, as your thoughts drift to Hecky and Alice. Your objective in the final two lines of the chorus thus becomes: to get the audience to think poorly of the couple. This is done with a great deal of bad temper on your part.

Your mood flips abruptly at the beginning of the first bridge. You fondly remember the Sunday mornings you shared with Hecky. In this section your objective is: to convince the audience that Hecky and yourself were very happy together.

Try playing actions such as: I charm, delight, amuse and engage the audience in this section.

Another shift occurs when you enter the word 'amorist' as one of the answers and then discover that it is, in fact, incorrect, as it is one letter too short. Making this mistake releases some of the anger you feel about your situation. This triggers your objective in the second chorus, which is: to protest that your life is unfair. You also want the audience to sympathise with you as you have had to forgo your future happiness, all because of a simple row about a crossword.

During the second bridge you once more reminisce about your mornings shared with Hecky. However, this time you do not look back on them fondly. Your objective at this point is: to ridicule Hecky. You might play actions such as: I mimic, deride and mock him. That prompts a moment of self-reflection when you realise you have been 'left on the shelf'. At this point your objective is: to decide if you were responsible for the failure of the relationship. You then try to cheer yourself up by discovering that one of the answers is 'The Statue of Liberty', but you fail in this objective and you are left asking yourself once more: why has Hecky left you?

This leads to another melodramatic outburst, and in the final chorus your objective is: to blame Alice and Hecky. You want them to take responsibility for your unhappiness. It seems you are unable to convince yourself that they are at fault, and in the last few lines you finally accept that it was your own behaviour that drove Hecky away. This epiphany is the event of the song.

KEY MOMENTS/TOP TIPS

1. This song is one of the rare occasions that you should use props. Don't inform the panel you intend to do this – just have a pen tucked in your pocket and a newspaper inside your audition folder, which you can take out when you are at the piano. Because of the opening lyric it makes perfect sense to start sitting on a chair, though you will probably choose to stand later when Martha loses her temper.

CONTEMPORARY UP-TEMPO

2. This song is written to be delivered to the audience. When singing in direct address it is helpful to make a decision about who the audience are in the mind of the character. With this song, try imagining that they are colleagues, neighbours and acquaintances – people who might gossip about you. As you are afraid of being publicly humiliated, their opinions on your failed relationship matter a great deal to you. You want to ensure they believe your own particular version of the break-up with Hecky and take your side.

3. An interesting moment occurs near the end of the second chorus when you reveal how you 'showed' Hecky. Try exposing in this moment that you were a bit of a bully towards your ex-fiancé; that you almost had a vendetta against him as your crossword-puzzle rival.

4. There is a great deal of fun to be hand in playing Martha as though she is mentally unhinged, as someone whose mood flips violently – for example, when she shifts from being angry about the memory of Hecky's four-letter-word tirade to sheer delight at discovering the answer to another clue being 'prefix'.

5. The song allows plenty of opportunity to display your abilities as a comic actress. But remember that the song is about a woman who is alone on the day she was supposed to be married. Try to connect to a genuine emotional vulnerability in the last few lines, as this will reveal another side to your performance and show the panel you can play pathos as well as comedy.

Vocal and Musical Analysis

WHO TO LISTEN TO: Loni Ackerman on the original Off-Broadway cast recording (1977).

VOCAL RANGE: C4 to E5.

ORIGINAL KEY: C major.

ACCENT: General American.

STYLE OF MUSICAL: Contemporary musical (pop-based).

VOCAL SET-UP/MUSICAL TIPS

1. The appropriate voice quality for the majority of this song is Twang. Explore having the soft palate in a mid-position to make this set-up nasal, rather than oral twang. This can help bring out the comedy of the song by creating a 'character voice' for the role.

2. Several sections of the song are written to be spoken. (In musical notation all notes with an 'x' as the notehead should be spoken rather than pitched.) The rhythm for these lines is indicated in the score – which you should adhere to quite strictly.

3. When you quote Hecky, try doing a vocal impression of your ex-fiancé, as if you are mocking him. One way to achieve this is to lower your larynx to produce a playful masculine quality.

4. Try delivering the rhyming couplet, in which you talk about being left on the shelf, in a Speech quality. Removing any thyroid tilt, and making the lyric very conversational, will help bring out the humour of this moment.

5. Explore using a crescendo during the repetition of the word 'why' till you are almost growling comically in anger.

6. In the final few lines, when you imagine how different this day might have been, try starting this section in a Cry quality with a raised larynx and very thin vocal folds to portray a sense of vulnerability. You should then crescendo in the last line by tightening your AES to move into a Twang quality once more.

Sheet Music

The correct sheet music for this song is available at www.onlinesheetmusic.com.

'The Glamorous Life'
from *A Little Night Music*

Music and lyrics by Stephen Sondheim

Choose this song if: you have a classical mezzosoprano voice. The song may suit you if enjoy playing teenage characters who are excitable daydreamers, but who are also sensitive and vulnerable.

Given Circumstances

Note: This song is from the film adaptation and is not to be confused with a completely different version of the song, which is in the original score for the stage production.

WHO ARE YOU: Fredrika Armfeldt, the grave, formal and vulnerable thirteen-year-old daughter of Desirée – a well-known actress. You have taught yourself to be self-contained around other people, yet when alone you can let your imagination run wild.

WHERE ARE YOU: In the piano room of your grandmother's large house on a country estate, Sweden.

WHEN IS IT: Early evening, late spring, 1900.

WHAT HAS HAPPENED BEFORE: Late this afternoon, your grandmother, Madame Armfeldt – who thinks that her own daughter Desirée is a fool – told you somewhat whimsically that you should come out into the garden to watch for the night to smile. She explained that the night 'smiles' three times: first on the young, then for the fools and finally on the old. As you were inquisitive about this mysterious request, you agreed that you would watch out for these smiles, though you did not know how they would appear.

An unwitting example of the fools your grandmother was describing is Fredrik Egerman, a successful middle-aged lawyer, and most likely your father (see point 1 below) – who recently married an eighteen-year-old girl called Anne. Despite being deliriously happy about the youth and beauty of his new wife, Fredrik remained sexually frustrated, as Anne has so far refused to yield her virginity to him. This evening Fredrik has bought Anne tickets to see your mother perform in a French comedy, as he would secretly like to pay Desirée a visit. Many years ago Fredrik had an affair with your mother and, to this day, she still harbours tender feelings for him. In the past your mother was a successful actress, but although she is still well-known, more recently her career has been in something of the doldrums – and now she has been reduced to taking parts in unglamorous, small-scale tours.

For the last couple of hours you have been practising the piano as instructed by Madam Armfeldt, whilst she had her pre-dinner nap. As you were playing, your thoughts drifted towards your mother, as recently you have been missing her a great deal. You have not seen her for some time, as she often seems to find excuses to avoid coming to visit.

WHO ELSE IS THERE: You are alone.

WHO SHOULD YOU SING TO: Yourself, though in an audition you can share many of your thoughts with the panel as though they are an audience of other teenage girls whom you want to rival and impress.

Textual Analysis

The song starts with you being snide about other people's mothers. You believe that they lead dull and boring lives when compared to Desirée's. Your objective in the first verse is: to demean the existence of ordinary mothers. You mock them for spending their day slaving away at household chores. Actions you might try include: I denigrate, insult and discredit the mothers.

In the first chorus you then talk about your mother's life as an actress, which you know of from the stories she tells you in the letters she sends. You spend a great deal of your time imagining her theatrical world, which you view as being incredibly glamorous – though that is far from the truth. Your objective in this section is: to indulge your fantasy of being an actress. You might try actions such as: I fascinate, bewitch, spellbind and enrapture yourself at this point. In the second half of the verse you then compare this fabulous existence (as you view it) to the lives of your friends' mothers. Your objective at this point is: to prove to the audience that your mother's life is the more exciting.

The second chorus follows immediately after the first. This creates a sense of musical impetus, which continues throughout the song, and is indicative of the fact that Fredrika has now become enraptured by her daydreams. However, it is clear that Desirée has often complained about aspects of the actor's life – such as often only having time to eat sandwiches. So your objective at the start of the second chorus becomes: to dismiss any negativity about your mother's life. You want to create a romantised version of her day-to-day existence that has no downsides. In the second half of the chorus, you then weigh up the pros and cons of having a mother who is an actress, rather than one who stays home and takes care of you all the time. The objective in this section could be: to debate which you'd prefer. For a brief moment at the end of this chorus you allow yourself to think the unthinkable: that perhaps you'd rather your mother stay at home with you (see point 3 below).

During the bridge section, when you talk about your mother's brooch and coach, you think of things about her that are a disappointment to you – that others might criticise or chatter about. Try playing the following objective in this short section: to defend your mother from other people's gossip.

The music becomes ever more joyful and exhilarating at the beginning of the third chorus – when you sing about Desirée arriving in the summer. Your objective in the first three lines of the chorus is: to brag to the audience about your mother's forthcoming visit. You continue to boast in the second half of the chorus, but now about the letters your mother sends you –

which include theatre reviews – which you feel sure that no one else in the audience receives. Actions you might play through both of these units include: I taunt, dazzle, impress and rival the audience.

Again you fantasise about your mother's life at the beginning of the fourth chorus. Try playing the following objective, which should be fun to explore: to imagine being on stage. You want to pretend that you are delivering brilliantly written speeches and receive rapturous applause. In the second half of the chorus you then return to the debate in your head about whether you'd prefer an ordinary mother to a glamorous, but largely absentee one. This time, when you state that perhaps having to see her child all the time would interfere with your mother's life, you come close to confessing how you truly feel: that you have been abandoned by your mother (and indeed your father – see point 1 below).

Lyrically, the song then takes a surprising and fascinating turn. With you at your most vulnerable, you play the following objective: to make-believe that you are a princess. In this moment you almost regress back to being a very young girl. This is a way of escaping from the painful feelings of rejection that just came rushing to the surface. Perhaps in a momentary glimpse of self-knowledge, you realise that your behaviour is foolish – because you then return to a previous, more realistic objective in order to cheer yourself up: to excite yourself and brag about your mother's forthcoming summer visit. This time, though, your manner of expressing your excitement is wrapped up in the language of adventures and fairytales – which reveals how much you need a vivid imaginary world in order to protect you from your deep feelings of rejection.

Having wrestled with the argument throughout the song of which type of mother you would prefer – an ordinary one, or your own – in the final section you triumphantly play this last objective: to completely dismiss the lives or ordinary women. At last you are able to fully embrace the life your mother leads, as you know that deep down she truly loves you. This conclusion is the event of the song.

1. Fredrika's personality is shaped a great deal by the fact that she doesn't know who her father is. Although it is never confirmed in the play, it is useful to suppose that Fredrik is her father – though he has never been part of her life. Imagine how this might have shaped her. Perhaps deep down she lacks self-confidence. It certainly means she places a great deal of emphasis on her relationship with her mother – to the point of idolatry.

2. The central conceit of the song is that, although Fredrika pretends that she is happy about the way her mother lives her life, on a deeper level she misses her and feels abandoned when she is away working. However, as a form of self-defence, she pretends that she loves the fact that her mother is an actress.

3. As with another younger character by Sondheim, Johanna in *Sweeney Todd* (see pp. 181–85), there is something a little strange about Fredrika. Explore the idea that she is the eccentric outsider.

Vocal and Musical Analysis

WHO TO LISTEN TO: Audra McDonald in *Sondheim!: The Birthday Concert* (2010).

VOCAL RANGE: C4 to E5.

ORIGINAL KEY: E♭ major.

ACCENT: As the play is set in Sweden, if you are from that country, it would be highly appropriate to use your own voice. Other Scandinavian accents would also work well. General American and Received Pronunciation are also accents that are regularly used if the show is performed in either the USA or the UK respectively, so are valid choices.

STYLE OF MUSICAL: Concept musical.

VOCAL SET-UP/MUSICAL TIPS

1. The set-up for the vast majority of the song is a legit sound. You should sing with a tilted thyroid cartilage, an anchored neck, a high back of the tongue, a slightly lowered larynx, and use simultaneous onsets wherever possible. You can hear McDonald demonstrate this expertly on the suggested recording.

2. Try not to overuse vibrato in your performance (as perhaps McDonald does a little) as it can make the character sound too old. Only deploy it at the ends of musical sentences, as you can hear McDonald do on the word 'vine', to help punctuate the musical phrasing.

3. Occasionally try making use of aspirate onsets to help convey Fredrika's excitement. You can hear McDonald use this choice on the word 'hours'.

4. Once the main melody begins, about thirty seconds into the song, embrace the rhythmical excitement of the phrases that contain the words 'ordinary mothers'. Giving these words an articulate dexterity and musical punch can again help convey the character's enthusiasm.

5. When you sing about the fact that your mother is away in a play, try raising the larynx and thinning your vocal folds to end up in a Cry quality. This can help reveal Fredrika's vulnerability about having an absentee mother.

6. In the bridge section, where you talk about your mother's brooch and coach, try using aspirate onsets to access an excited, breathy Speech quality.

7. You want to find more resonance and volume when you sing the section that starts with you talking about your mother arriving in the summer. As this is a legit song, you shouldn't do this by removing your thyroid tilt; instead add some torso anchoring to enrich your sound. It is appropriate to half-speak some words at this point, as McDonald does on the word 'brilliant'.

8. In the following section, where you talk about being a princess, you can drop into a Speech quality. During the rest of song you should sing with legato phrasing, but here you can break up the words a little to expose Fredrika's uncertainty. You can then return to the anchored legit sound for the last driving section.

Sheet Music

The correct sheet music for this song is available at www.musicnotes.com.

'Greenfinch and Linnett Bird'
from *Sweeney Todd*

Music and lyrics by Stephen Sondheim

Choose this song if: you are soprano with a classical, legit
voice. This song suits actresses who can play troubled,
psychologically complex characters.

Given Circumstances

WHO ARE YOU: Johanna Barker, the young, beautiful,
withdrawn and slightly strange ward of Judge Turpin. You are
sixteen years old.

WHERE ARE YOU: In Victorian London, at the window of your
bedroom in Judge Turpin's house on Kearney's Lane.

WHEN IS IT: 11.04 a.m., a bright spring morning, 1846.

WHAT HAS HAPPENED BEFORE: Fifteen years ago, when you
were only a year old, your father was transported to Australia
on false criminal charges. He was a barber called Benjamin
Barker (who later on would take the false name of Sweeney
Todd). A man named Judge Turpin had accused your father
of a trumped-up crime, as he lusted after your mother, Lucy.
As soon as Barker was convicted and despatched, Judge
Turpin invited poor Lucy to his house – on the pretence that
he felt to blame for her plight. In fact, when she arrived a
masked ball was underway. At the party the Judge plied your
mother with alcohol before raping her with his friend Beadle
Bamford in front of the other guests.

Today your father returned from Australia – after years of
punishment and many weeks at sea – determined to avenge
himself. Earlier this morning he visited a pie shop on Fleet
Street that sits below his old abandoned barber's shop. On his
visit there he met Mrs Lovett, the owner of the pie shop, who
recognised him at once, as she had always been secretly in love

with him. She told him that Lucy had fatally poisoned herself. (This is only partially true. Although your mother did poison herself, this failed to kill her – and she now wanders the streets as a half-crazed beggar woman.) When your father asked what had become of you, Mrs Lovett told him that he had taken you as his ward. On hearing this Todd resolved to free you, and have his murderous revenge on the Beadle and the Judge.

This morning you have been locked in your bedroom as usual by the Judge, who keeps you as a virtual prisoner in the house. Whilst he claims this is for your protection, in reality it is because he intends to marry you and fears you being stolen from him. Peering out of your window a few moments ago you saw a bird-seller, whom you talk to on a daily basis, walking in the street below. He was carrying a number of caged birds. You have just enquired about the welfare of the birds, to which the bird-seller replied that they were hungry.

WHO ELSE IS THERE: In the musical the bird-seller is present, and halfway through the song (unbeknownst to you) he is joined in the street by Anthony, a young sailor and friend of your father with whom you will later fall in love. However, for the purposes of an audition, it is better to behave as if you are alone with the birds.

WHO SHOULD YOU SING TO: The caged birds.

Textual Analysis

You are clearly fascinated by the inhabitants of the cage. As someone who is living your own life as a prisoner, you empathise with these creatures of flight who are themselves confined. It fascinates you that, despite their imprisonment, they seem to be happy and content – unlike yourself. Throughout the song it is necessary to imagine the caged birds. During the introduction you should study them with a delicate curiosity. This will then lead you into your objective for the opening verse, which is: to understand how the birds can sing when they are locked up. You are critical of them, as you do not understand why they don't seem to want to fly away. In this unit, try playing such actions as: I question, analyse, criticise and castigate the birds.

During the second verse your curiosity shifts to the meaning of the birds' song. At this point your objective becomes: to understand what the birds are saying. You hope that if you can comprehend what the birds are communicating, you might better understand yourself. When you then sing to the ringdove and robinet (in the third verse), your objective becomes: to get the birds to tell you why they agree to be captive. You wonder if they are motivated by money, or assent to be caged in order to feel safe.

In the short bridge that follows, Johanna confesses to the birds that she is unhappy in her own cage and asks the birds to help her become more 'adaptive'. Your objective in this section is: to get the birds to teach you how to cope with being a prisoner. Try more urgent actions at this point such as: I implore, beseech and urge the birds. In the short final verse, you then simplify your request to the caged creatures. Your objective is simply: to get them to teach you how to sing, as you believe this may be the route to happiness.

KEY MOMENTS/TOP TIPS

1. Although Johanna is in her bedroom, for audition purposes it is unhelpful to stage the song as if the birds are situated some metres below you. Instead imagine they are on the same level – and are situated behind the audition panel.

2. There is a popularly held theory about the characters in *Sweeney Todd* that they are all in some way insane. In this song, explore the idea that Johanna's fascination with the birds borders on the obsessive.

3. An event occurs when Johanna asks the birds if they are screaming. This is because, as a prisoner of the Judge, she feels as if she is screaming inside. Play with the idea that in this instance Johanna wonders for an instant if she is going mad.

4. A further event, and perhaps the most important, occurs when you deliver a trill on an open 'ah' vowel. At this crucial point, Johanna is trying to sing like a bird. She hopes that, if she emulates them, she too will find contentment in her captivity.

Vocal and Musical Analysis

WHO TO LISTEN TO: Sarah Rice on the original Broadway cast recording (1979).

VOCAL RANGE: A♭3 to E♭5.

ORIGINAL KEY: D♭ major.

ACCENT: Received Pronunciation.

STYLE OF MUSICAL: Contemporary musical (legit-based).

VOCAL SET-UP/MUSICAL TIPS

1. *Sweeney Todd* is performed in both opera houses and in musical-theatre venues – and is often seen as a piece that stylistically crosses both art forms. When performing this song, you therefore want to lean towards an operatic sound. To achieve this, ensure you use simultaneous onsets, a great deal of thyroid tilt, and that you anchor your torso. An operatic set-up also contains twang, which is made mellower by simultaneously lowering the larynx. Rice demonstrates this set-up very effectively on the cast recording.

2. The music is written to almost imitate bird song at points. To achieve this sound, use a light soprano voice, sing with a high larynx and decorate the top notes and ends of phrases with a good deal of vibrato, as Rice ably demonstrates.

3. The word 'stars' should be rich and full. To achieve this resonance, lower your larynx a little further on this high note and really anchor your torso.

4. In the bridge section, when you sing to the ringdove and robinet, the song briefly moves into a minor key for a couple of lines. Explore playing around with the idea that Johanna becomes mentally disturbed about her own captivity at this point.

5. If you find the trill difficult, it is possible to sing fewer notes than Rice does on the suggested recording (a musical ornament known as 'turn' will suffice). The most important factor is that this is a moment of great vocal release, as this is when Johanna fully imagines what it would be like to be free.

Sheet Music

The correct sheet music for this song is available at www.musicnotes.com.

'No Man Left for Me'
from *The Will Rogers Follies*

Music by Cy Coleman, lyrics by Betty Comden and Adolph Green

Choose this song if: you are a mezzosoprano who enjoys singing music that is jazz-based. This song could be described as a 'torch song', so suits performers who can deliver a performance with a sense of showmanship.

Given Circumstances

WHO ARE YOU: Betty Blake, the loving and long-suffering wife of Will Rogers – the real-life great American entertainment star of the first few decades of the twentieth century.

WHERE ARE YOU: In reality you are at home on your ranch in the Santa Monica Hills, California, USA. However, because of the unusual style of the show (see point 1 below), the number is set as though in a jazz bar or cabaret club (see point 2).

WHEN IS IT: About 6.00 p.m., a Saturday evening in the early 1930s, at the zenith of your husband's popularity and fame.

WHAT HAS HAPPENED BEFORE: In reality, you first met your husband in 1900 at a train station in Oklahoma – though because of the stylised theatrical form of *The Will Rogers Follies* (see point 1), in the musical this meeting takes place on a theatrical moon. After a long courtship Will proposed to you six years later. Initially you were reluctant to accept, as you were dubious about sharing your life with a man who worked in showbusiness. When he proposed again a year or so later – and promised that he would settle down – you agreed. You subsequently had four children together, and although Will never kept his promise to stop travelling, your early marriage was a happy one. You were often on the road with your family as Will's career grew from that of a vaudeville performer to a huge national star. These were happy times.

When Will's career as a movie star began to flourish you moved the family home to California. In recent times, with your husband becoming ever busier, he has been more and more frequently away from home. With you often left on your own at the ranch, this has begun to put strain on your marriage. In an incident that has now become all too familiar to you, Will has just a few moments ago departed on business, leaving you alone in the house.

WHO ELSE IS THERE: You are alone.

WHO SHOULD YOU SING TO: In the show the song is written to be sung to the audience. In an audition context you should sing directly to the panel, as though they are your confidantes.

Textual Analysis

Immediately prior to the song Will has just gone out of the door – leaving you feeling abandoned and rejected. Your objective in the opening section is: to get the audience to take your side. You want them to empathise with the plight of the lonely housewife – and there is a degree of sarcasm in your approach. You might use actions such as: I mock, amuse and entertain the audience in this short unit. As you progress into the first chorus you start to list the various activities that fill your husband's day-to-day life – and stop him spending him time with you. Your objective in this section is: to convince the audience that your marriage is unbearable. You try to achieve this by mocking Will's extravagant lifestyle.

When you arrive at the bridge, which starts with the line about the worm turning, you square with the audience about how you really feel when your husband is away. Your objective in this section is: to make the audience appreciate how difficult it is to countenance leaving your husband. You want them to understand the internal struggle you experience when you think of walking out on him – you are conflicted.

Having vented some of these concerns, in the second chorus you once more list the activities that keep your husband busy and away from home. To avoid repetition in your performance, try playing a different objective to the first chorus. You might explore the following: I want to convince the audience that Will is spoilt. By doing so you hope they will once more take your side. Having shared your inner concerns, during the final section you reach the conclusion that Will doesn't want or need you. This leads you into your final objective, which is: to convince yourself to leave your husband.

KEY MOMENTS/TOP TIPS

1. *The Will Rogers Follies* is an unusual piece in that the characters, instead of living their lives in the real world, exist within a Follies show produced by the great impresario Florenz Ziegfeld. At times during the musical you hear the godlike voice of Ziegfeld instructing the characters to get on with the show, or alter the truth of Will Rogers's life in order to make the plot more entertaining and appropriate for a Follies show. Because of this inventive theatrical conceit, the songs should be presented in a glamorous showbusiness style. This is particularly true of this number.

2. In the original production the actress playing Betty Blake delivered this number laid across a piano. This was because, even though the character is experiencing an emotional crisis, the form of the musical means this song lends itself to a cabaret-style of presentation. Try exploring characteristics that fit this type of performance, such as: seductive, charismatic and flirtatious. You may even want to start your performance leaning against the piano if it is situated near the back of the audition room.

3. During the song you battle a major obstacle: Will is a hugely likeable man and you love him deeply. So although you are incredibly frustrated, you find it hard to remain mad at him for very long.

4. The final section should have the feeling of being something of an outburst. Try playing this as if you can no longer stand being treated this way and you want your life to change.

5. The event of the song occurs on the last line – when you decide you are going to leave your husband (though in the musical Will actually makes amends before this occurs and your marriage is repaired).

Vocal and Musical Analysis

WHO TO LISTEN TO: Dee Hoty on the original Broadway cast recording (1991).

VOCAL RANGE: B♭3 to E♭5.

ORIGINAL KEY: C minor.

ACCENT: General American.

STYLE OF MUSICAL: Contemporary musical (jazz-based).

VOCAL SET-UP/MUSICAL TIPS

1. The opening section of the song should be very conversational indeed. Try singing in a Speech quality, and don't be afraid to shorten some note-lengths or half-speak some words.

2. When you reach the first chorus you should employ the predominant vocal quality required by the song, which is Twang.

3. In the bridge return to using a Speech quality. Some of the higher notes in the section (on the words 'flat' and 'grim') require you to add some torso anchoring and a little thyroid tilt in order to maintain that sound quality.

4. As the music is jazz-based it is appropriate to make some stylistic choices synonymous with the genre, for example by engaging in pitch-glides, or by 'bending' the pitch of

certain notes, as you can hear Hoty do on the word 'worms', or when she sings a little later about being lonesome.

5. The second chorus, like the first, should be delivered in a Twang quality.

6. In the final section, when you say that Will won't miss you, you should sing in a mixed belt, as you hear Hoty demonstrate on the cast recording. Ensure you tilt your cricoid cartilage, lift your larynx, raise your chin slightly and add some torso anchoring at these points.

Sheet Music

The correct sheet music for this song is available www.musicnotes.com.

'So Many People'
from *Saturday Night*

Music and lyrics by Stephen Sondheim

Choose this song if: you have a legit musical-theatre mezzosoprano voice and enjoy singing sophisticated love songs.

Given Circumstances

WHO ARE YOU: Helen, a playful, fun-loving girl in her early twenties. You are from Brooklyn, and have the adventurous spirit of a New York girl.

WHERE ARE YOU: On the porch of Gene Gorman's house, Flatbush, Brooklyn, New York City, USA.

WHEN IS IT: Early evening, a Saturday, spring, 1929.

WHAT HAS HAPPENED BEFORE: A week ago a group of young men were sitting on the porch of a house in Brooklyn. They were all commiserating with each other – because none of them had a date on a Saturday night. Suddenly the owner of the house, Gene Gorman, who is an order clerk with a brokerage house on Wall Street, came charging downstairs dressed in a tail suit. He announced that he was planning to gatecrash the Junior League Cotillion at the Plaza Hotel, Manhattan. He then persuaded his friends to lend him a hundred dollars each, so he could buy shares in what he believed to be a hot company: Montana Chem. Corp. They agreed and he promised that he would make them all rich within the week – although he didn't even have enough money for a cab. Fortuitously Gene's cousin Eugene – whose nickname is Pinhead – then stopped by the house and asked Gene to look after his Pierce-Arrow (a very expensive car), as he was taking a trip to Florida. Gene promptly jumped in the vehicle and drove off to Manhattan.

It was at the Plaza Hotel that you first met Gene. You were also trying to gatecrash the event by pretending to be a rich Southern aristocrat. However, as neither yourself nor Gene had a ticket the attendant wouldn't let either of you in. After dancing together in the hallway, Gene, who was likewise trying to keep up the pretence of being incredibly rich, offered you a lift home in his 'limousine'.

Shortly after arriving home you found Gene's driving licence, which he had left behind by accident. It had become stuck to the back of a photo he'd given you: a picture that he'd claimed was taken of him on a yacht in the Mediterranean (when in reality it was of him on a fishing boat in Sheepshead Bay). Using the address on the driving licence, you then turned up at Gene's house later that evening. When you started talking without a Southern accent, Gene realised that you had also been pretending to be wealthy. Out on the porch you both confessed that you didn't care about discovering the truth about your real financial situations – though Gene insisted that he was playing the stock market and would have a couple of thousand dollars by the end of the week.

Next day Gene took you to view an apartment on Sutton Place – an expensive area of Manhattan. Even though the property was way out of his price range he wanted to impress you, so made a spontaneous decision to lease the apartment anyway, as he was convinced that he would soon make a fortune from the Montana Chem. Corp. stock. You became angry with him, pointing out that the down payment for the apartment was needed to pay for the shares.

During the next week the stock crashed – leaving Gene in great financial difficulties. It is now Saturday once again and Gene has just told you that he has sold Eugene's car to pay for the apartment. You are very upset at him or him for doing something so selfish and reckless. At the same time you have begun to realise something important about yourself. You had always thought you would marry someone who is rich, but you have realised that that you are falling in love with Gene – even though he doesn't have a cent to his name.

WHO ELSE IS THERE: Gene.

WHO SHOULD YOU SING TO: Gene.

Textual Analysis

Just prior to the song you had a realisation: that wealth and money no longer matter to you. You are pondering this heart-warming discovery during the introduction. Your objective in the first verse then becomes: to convince Gene that you have changed. In this moment you confess that since meeting him you have altered the way you view the world. You might play actions such as: I warm, assure and melt Gene at this point.

During the second verse you begin to tease Gene. You joke that by falling for him you have had to lower you expectations. You say that even though this should have made you unhappy, it has in fact done the opposite. By lightly mocking Gene you are able to play this lovely objective: to make him understand how much you like him.

Your manner becomes more open-hearted and unguarded in the long chorus section that follows. Try playing the following objective at this point: to taunt the people who think you were wrong to fall for Gene. During this section you dismiss these people's concerns. You believe that if they could see you both together, and realise how in love you are, then they would learn that they are wrong. Appropriate actions during this portion of the song include: I provoke, defy, jibe, banish, dismiss and disregard the world. By the end of the song, with you feeling intoxicated on your own defiance, you are triumphant in the celebration of your love for Gene.

KEY MOMENTS/TOP TIPS

1. During the song Helen discovers something fundamental about herself: that in looking for a life partner with wealth and riches she was being shallow and superficial. At the beginning of the song try making this discovery uncomfortable and difficult to say out loud.

2. When you sing the title lyric you are referring to a wide variety of people in your life that you think will look down on you for choosing to be with Gene. Be specific each time you repeat the lyric about who you are referring to. It might be your parents, or other presumptuous relatives, it could be people you went to school with, or judgemental work colleagues. Picture someone different each time you deliver this particular lyric, which happens four times.

3. There is clear change of musical feel as the song progresses into the first chorus: when the music becomes much more direct and full of momentum. Let this be reflected in your acting choices: Helen is now speaking with passion about her relationship with Gene; she is talking straight from the heart.

4. The event of the song occurs at the end of the second verse, when you say that the man means more than his means. For the first time you say out loud what has been in your head for the last few minutes: that love is more important than money. By voicing it to another person, it crystallises your newfound belief: and your view on what is paramount in a relationship will never be the same again.

Vocal and Musical Analysis

WHO TO LISTEN TO: Anna Francolini (and Sam Newton) on the original London cast recording (1998).

VOCAL RANGE: B♭3 to E♭5.

ORIGINAL KEY: E♭ major.

ACCENT: General American.

STYLE OF MUSICAL: Book musical.

VOCAL SET-UP/MUSICAL TIPS

1. The song is written to be a duet, but is regularly sung as a solo in musical-theatre auditions. In this context you should sing both the male and female sections.

2. Try beginning the song in a pure Cry quality. Keep your larynx raised, thin your vocal folds, employ a lot of thyroid tilt and use simultaneous onsets so the vowels run together.

3. At the start of the second verse there needs to be a sense of musical development. Try lowering the larynx a bit so it is in a neutral position, and thicken your vocal folds. This will make your sound fuller and richer in tone.

4. When you sing the chorus, which starts with the title lyric, try lowering the larynx even further so you end up in a rich Sob quality.

5. Try suddenly flipping back into a Cry quality on the line about other people telling you that love is a thing you'll outgrow, as you can hear Sam Newton do on the suggested recording. Maintain this set-up till the end of the number to give the song a tender, subtle ending.

6. For audition purposes you should finish after you first sing the words 'you love me', as indicated on the sheet music, rather than repeat the final section as occurs on the suggested recording.

Sheet Music

The correct sheet music for this song is available at www.musicnotes.com.

'I Need a Fling'
from *Lend Me a Tenor*

Music by Brad Carroll, lyrics by Peter Sham

Choose this song if: you enjoy singing jazzy songs that
showcase a twang set-up but also allow you to belt. Originally
written for an actress in her mid-twenties, the song might suit
you if you enjoy playing excitable, ambitious, effervescent roles.

Given Circumstances

WHO ARE YOU: Maggie Saunders, the daughter of Henry
Saunders, the executive director of the Cleveland Grand
Opera Company. You have a tendency to be something of a
romantic and a daydreamer.

WHERE ARE YOU: The lobby of Cleveland Hotel, Cleveland,
Ohio, USA.

WHEN IS IT: 5.47 p.m., a Saturday, 1934.

WHAT HAS HAPPENED BEFORE: Tonight one of the world's
leading tenors, Tito Morelli, is due to perform in a grand gala
opening of Verdi's *Otello* to mark the fiftieth anniversary of
the Cleveland Grand Opera company. The show is of great
importance to your father in particular, as recently the
company has been in great financial difficulties.

With the performance fast approaching, and the show sold out,
Morelli is nowhere to be seen. With a huge potential disaster on
his hands, your father has begun to grow increasingly desperate.
Max, his long-suffering assistant and your sometime boyfriend,
began to wonder if he might have a potential solution: which
would involve him going on as the lead role. He resolved to
suggest this to your father when the right occasion arose.

Meanwhile, with Tito still not having appeared, you began to
make another plan for his arrival: his seduction. For the last

hour you have been decorating the lobby of the hotel, making it into a virtual shrine to the famous singer. Max has just rushed in from meeting with your father. Bemused, he questioned you about what you were up to. You told him about your current feelings of boredom. He has just, unsuccessfully, tried to convince you that the romantic life you share together should be exciting enough. However, despite him reminding you of the times when he took you sleigh-riding and fishing, you have just dismissed him out of hand.

WHO ELSE IS THERE: Max.

WHO SHOULD YOU SING TO: Max.

Textual Analysis

At the beginning of the song you are feeling incredibly restless; you long for romance and excitement. In the first verse your objective is: to get Max to appreciate, and empathise with, your need for adventure. Because you have been having a casual relationship with him, you feel the need for Max to give you his permission – but the way you go about this shows an almost total disregard for his feelings. Try playing actions such as: I intrigue, excite, electrify Max.

Despite your impatience, you are not entirely sure what you want to do to relieve your sense of restlessness. During the second verse, although you continue to address Max, in reality you are simply using him as a sounding board – and in fact you are talking to yourself. Your objective in this section is: to define what it is you want. In order to achieve this objective you might investigate actions such as: I search, scrutinise and cross-examine myself. In the last line of the verse you prove to be successful in your objective – and discover what it is you truly desire: a romantic fling.

This discovery proves to be a catalyst to action. In the bridge that starts at bar 98, your objective becomes: to encourage yourself to be naughty and impulsive. You might use actions such as I awaken, trigger, ignite and spark myself. After the key change, with your course of action now decided, you play one final objective: to push aside all obstacles. You are resolved to try and make Tito your lover and will let nothing stand in your way.

1. Although this song is delivered to Max, in audition it is highly possible to deliver a version directed towards the panel. If you want to take this approach, treat the panel as if they are your confidantes – who you can seek advice and permission from during the song.

2. Treat the first time you say the word 'fling' as an event. From this point onwards you have defined exactly what you want, and the rest of the song is about resolving to act upon that desire.

3. A second event occurs on the line that precedes the key change, when you talk about lighting up the sky. At this moment you decide that you are going to do whatever it takes to make Tito your lover. You become single-minded.

4. If you choose to deliver the song to an imaginary Max, it is useful to imagine how he would be behaving as you plan to seduce Tito: he would likely be distraught. In your performance try conveying a character that is completely focused on what she wants and is dismissive and unsympathetic of the emotional needs of her boyfriend.

Vocal and Musical Analysis

WHO TO LISTEN TO: Cassidy Janson on the original London cast recording (2011).

VOCAL RANGE: A♭3 to E♭5.

ORIGINAL KEY: A♭ major.

ACCENT: General American.

STYLE OF MUSICAL: Book musical.

VOCAL SET-UP/MUSICAL TIPS

1. The song begins with a duet section between Maggie and
   Max, which should be cut for audition purposes. Start
   singing at bar 36, using the preceding bar as a short
   introduction.

2. The opening verse should have a feeling of quiet, hushed
   excitement. To achieve this, sing with very thin vocal folds,
   and the tiniest amount of twang, as Janson ably
   demonstrates on the suggested recording.

3. On the word 'more' at the end of the first verse you should
   crescendo. Do this by tightening your AES a little further
   to add some more twang to your sound. This will allow you
   to deliver the second verse in a full Twang quality.

4. There is a second duet section in the middle of the song
   that should also be removed for audition purposes. To
   create a sensible musical structure you should also cut the
   third verse. In total this means cutting bars 66 to 95.

5. After the suggested cut try delivering the next section in a
   Speech quality.

6. The higher notes on the words 'lights' and sky' should be
   belted, as should the word 'sing' in the last few bars. Ensure
   you tilt your cricoid cartilage, lift your larynx, raise your
   chin slightly and add some torso anchoring at these points.

COMEDY/CHARACTER

Sheet Music

The correct sheet music for this song is available at
www.scribd.com.

'The Girl in 14G'

Music by Jeanine Tesori, lyrics by Dick Scanlan

Choose this song if: you have an outstanding, versatile voice and are capable of not only singing operatic soprano, but can also belt and perform in a jazz style. Suited to a quirky, comedic actress – this song is for the virtuosic performer.

Note: Although 'The Girl in 14G' is a well-known song in the musical-theatre-audition canon, it is not actually from a musical. It was written for the American musical-theatre star Kristin Chenoweth for her first album. The song is based on Chenoweth's real-life experiences of living with noisy neighbours when she first moved to New York. The given circumstances below, although based on the lyric, are therefore invented and may be changed if you wish.

Given Circumstances

WHO ARE YOU: Kristin, a shy, mouse-like, bookish young woman in her early twenties. As someone who can be frigid and reserved you find it very hard to assert yourself.

WHERE ARE YOU: On a window seat in your apartment, 14G, in Brooklyn, New York City, USA.

WHEN IS IT: 8.30 p.m., a summer's night, present day.

WHAT HAS HAPPENED BEFORE: Early this morning you moved to New York from Broken Arrow, Oklahoma, to take a job as a librarian. For someone as retiring as yourself, it was a shock to move to a city that was so busy and loud. Having spent the entire day unpacking your belongings, you have just managed to settle down for the evening. As a person who suffers from obsessive-compulsive disorder, you needed to get every last item of your belongings unpacked and put away before you could relax. Having completed this arduous task you have just slipped on your pyjamas, picked up your copy of *Pride and Prejudice*, and sat down to read before bed.

WHO ELSE IS THERE: You are alone.

WHO SHOULD YOU SING TO: The audition panel. At one point you also address your two neighbours.

Textual Analysis

You start the song feeling relaxed, content and perhaps the tiniest bit self-satisfied. (It is fun for the audience if you are a little bit smug to start, as it is more amusing when this attitude changes as thing start to go wrong later.) In the opening verse try playing the following objective: to welcome the audience to your new home. You want to convey how pleased you are with your quiet and comfortable abode. You might use actions such as: I impress, charm and patronise the audience. Later in the verse, when you talk about the fact that pets and parties are banned, you should now play the following objective: to teach the audience the house rules. You can lightly chide them and tell them not to disturb your peace. In the final few lines of the verse, as you reflect on sitting by the window, your objective becomes: to indulge yourself in the quiet sanctuary of your home.

Of course, your peace is then disturbed by the sound of the operatic singing coming from the apartment below. In a highly theatrical moment you should almost become the opera singer, and perform a silly, comedic impression of her. After this outburst of operatic music your objective in the lyrics that follow is: to wish that you didn't have a noisy neighbour. This objective is sustained through the remainder of the section. When you return to singing opera for a second time, on this occasion try playing the following objective: to mock the singing of your operatic neighbour.

At the start of the second verse, despite your peace being disturbed, you resolve to not let it spoil your evening. Your objective in this unit becomes: to put the problem behind you.

COMEDY/CHARACTER

You want to control your fraying nerves and make the best of the situation. Try playing actions such as: I contain, govern, curb, subdue and constrain yourself at this point. In the final few lines of the verse, when you resolve to go to bed, your objective changes once more. Try playing the following: I want to encourage myself to fall sleep.

When you're just starting to nod off, your evening is then interrupted once more – this time from the apartment above. Similar to previously, you should do an impression of your noisy jazz-singing neighbour at this point. In the following section, that begins when you mention the girl upstairs, you are clearly more frustrated at the constant noise, and so could play the following objective: to lodge a complaint about the disturbance. You want the audience to agree that you are being treated unfairly.

During the next section, where you reveal that you don't usually raise your voice, you begin to address your two neighbours directly. At first your objective is polite: to get them to listen your complaint. However, when you belt the word 'stop', your objective becomes much more direct: to get them to shut up. Having said this out loud, stood up for yourself, and found the ability to belt at the same time, in the final verse you decide to embrace your new neighbours and join them in their singing – forming an unlikely vocal trio. Your objective in the final section therefore becomes: to embrace your newfound voice.

KEY MOMENTS/TOP TIPS

1. You might want to start the song sitting on a chair to convey that you are at the window seat. It might be useful to bring a small book into the audition (ideally a copy of *Pride and Prejudice*) that you can use as a prop.

2. It is a great deal of fun to explore the physicality of both the opera wannabe in 13G and the jazz singer in 15G during your performance. Each time you sing as one of these two people, use a clearly defined physical transformation. For the girl in

15G you might play around with a stereotype of a jazz singer – perhaps with their spine curled over the microphone stand as they tilt it forwards. For the girl in 13G you might try a wildly exaggerated version of an opera singer – full of clichéd, mock-dramatic gestures (like a comedian sending up a performance of 'Ride of the Valkyries'.) You really can't go too far with these impressions.

3. Alongside these colourful physical transformations for your neighbours, it is important to have clear physicality that you return to each time you revert to 'being Kristin'. A good approach is to make her quite still, with timid or introverted body language.

4. An event occurs each time you hear one of your neighbours singing for the first time. Try to mark these moments with comedic still points that convey Kristin's dismayed reactions to her peace being disturbed. You might choose to look upwards (towards the girl in 15G), or downwards (at the girl in 13G) to convey that the sounds are coming from the flats above and below.

5. The moment where you belt the word 'stop' is the most important event of the song. At this point Kristin literally and metaphorically 'finds her voice'. She stops being a mouse-like person who is put upon by her neighbours and discovers the backbone to stand up for herself.

Vocal and Musical Analysis

WHO TO LISTEN TO: Kristin Chenoweth on her album *Let Yourself Go* (2001).

VOCAL RANGE: G3 to D6.

ORIGINAL KEY: F major.

ACCENT: General American.

STYLE OF MUSICAL: N/A.

COMEDY/CHARACTER

VOCAL SET-UP/MUSICAL TIPS

1. During the verses you should sing in a mouse-like Twang quality, as Chenoweth demonstrates so distinctly on the suggested recording. This is the main vocal set-up of the song that you should return to whenever you are using the voice of the main storyteller.

2. Quite obviously, when you are impersonating the girl in 13G you should use an operatic set-up. Some of the main features of this sound are: the use of simultaneous onsets, a great deal of false-fold retraction, a tilted thyroid cartilage, a high back of the tongue, a lowered larynx (except on the very high notes when it must rise), an anchored neck and an anchored torso. A more detailed analysis of this complicated vocal set-up is beyond the remit of this book, and so you would be unwise to tackle this song in an audition unless you have some classical singing training.

3. The sections sung by the girl in 15G should have a jazz style. To achieve this quality, try singing with a lowered larynx and explore using aspirate onsets to give a husky quality to the sound.

4. The two long notes on the word 'stop' should be belted. Remember to anchor your torso, lift your chin and tilt your cricoid cartilage at this point.

5. In the section that immediately follows the belted notes, you should sing in a Speech quality to reflect the musical structure that suggests you should 'bring the song home'.

6. The last line feels like it should be belted, but is easier to deliver in a Twang quality, as Chenoweth demonstrates on the recording.

Sheet Music

The correct sheet music for this song is available at www.musicnotes.com.

'Glitter and be Gay'
from *Candide*

Music by Leonard Bernstein, lyrics by Richard Wilbur

Choose this song if: you have an exceptional top soprano voice and have a classical singing training. As well as providing an opportunity to showcase a virtuosic voice, the material will also suit you if you enjoy playing frothy, comedic roles.

Given Circumstances

Note: Originally based on the novella by the eighteenth-century French writer Voltaire, *Candide* has been rewritten several times. The given circumstances below are those from the original 1956 version.

WHO ARE YOU: Cunegonde, the sprightly, optimistic love-struck daughter of a rich baron. You are originally from Westphalia in Northern Germany.

WHERE ARE YOU: In your lavish dressing room, in Paris, France.

WHEN IS IT: Early evening, shortly before dinner, in a fantastical time that historically bears a close resemblance to the time of Voltaire and the great Lisbon earthquake (which occurred in 1755).

WHAT HAS HAPPENED BEFORE: Several months ago you were betrothed to Candide, the illegitimate nephew of your father, Baron Thunder-ten-Tronk of Westphalia. Your father, your mother the Baroness and your brother Maximilian all looked down on Candide, as they viewed him as socially inferior. Nonetheless you were both happy together and very much in love. At that point your life seemed to be perfect, with the extent of your woes being to decide who was lovelier: your brother or yourself. This point of view was very much reinforced by your tutor, Dr Pangloss, who you all believed to be the greatest philosopher in the world. His teachings instructed you to see the good in every eventuality. Pangloss's philosophy was soon to be severely tested, as your happiness and tranquillity were disturbed when your father expelled Candide – because he did not think he was fit to marry you.

Left to wander the world alone, Candide was soon pressganged into joining the Bulgar army. When the Bulgars declared war on their traditional foe, the Abars, they selected Westphalia as their chosen battlefield. You were seemingly killed in the ensuing battle, and a distraught Candide was left to continue his journeys alone. (In reality you were alive, but your family were killed and you were raped by the Agars.) Whilst travelling through the world, Candide had many adventures. These included surviving a great earthquake in Lisbon and being put on trial by the Inquisition (an institution of the Catholic Church set up to conquer heresy) – the outcome of which was that he was flogged and Pangloss was hanged.

Unbeknown to Candide, you are in fact alive and well and recently moved to Paris. There you have become the concubine of two men, a rich Jew named Don Isaachar and the Cardinal Archbishop of Paris. You captured both their hearts and consequently they continually lavish you with expensive gifts, though you still have a melancholy heart. Sitting alone in your dressing room, you have just begun to lament your current existence.

WHO ELSE IS THERE: You are alone.

WHO SHOULD YOU SING TO: The audience, which in this situation is the audition panel.

Textual Analysis

Despite your lavish surroundings, at the beginning of the song you are despondent. You hate being trapped in what you call a gilded cage and greatly regret your social fall. From being a wealthy noblewoman you are now a virtual prostitute. Because of this, in the first verse your objective is: to wallow in your own pity. This section should be performed in a mock-dramatic fashion (as you are a wondrous attention-seeker).

A new unit begins when you say the word 'alas'. Try playing the following objective at this point: to get the audience to feel sorry for you. You do so because you don't want them to think poorly of you for sleeping with men for money and jewellery. In the second verse you seek to persuade the audience that you were forced to take the patronage of these rich men. You want to satisfy them that you had no other option after the death of your parents.

The song then abruptly changes direction. At the start of the first chorus the music becomes sprightly and upbeat. Your objective at this moment is: to decide if things are as bad as you've been saying. You eventually conclude that actually they are not, and the event of the song then occurs (see point 3 below). After the event your objective becomes: to make yourself feel merry. You do so by playing with the expensive jewellery your lovers have gifted you. Potential actions you might play in this section include: I thrill, delight, titillate, tickle and electrify myself.

Despite this outburst of revelry you swiftly fall back into a state of despair at the start of the third verse. You become very self-pitying and play the following objective: to decide if your newfound riches can compensate for the loss of your honour. During this section you might play actions such as: I cross-examine, interrogate, denigrate and reprehend myself. In this moment of contemplation, your answer to whether your jewellery can make amends for your loss of integrity is a resounding: yes. From the second chorus to the end of the song your final objective thus becomes: to indulge yourself in reckless abandon.

KEY MOMENTS/TOP TIPS

1. *Candide* is written to be performed in a buffoonish style. Your performance of this song should be heightened and laced with wit and silliness.

2. The central comedic element of the song is Cunegonde's rapacious relationship to her expensive jewellery. You

COMEDY/CHARACTER

therefore need to have some such items for you to play with in your audition (costume jewellery is perfectly acceptable). Great fun is to be wrought from concealing the jewellery on your person and then unveiling it in a comedic manner during the song. For example, you might pull out a string of pearls from the sleeve of your clothing, or pluck a ring from your bosom. This comic business should occur during the choruses and on the various cadenza, you sing on an 'ah' vowel.

3. The event of the song occurs when you first say the word 'enough' twice in a row. At this moment you resolve to stop feeling sorry for yourself and enjoy your extravagant lifestyle. Although your briefly slip back into despair at the beginning of the third verse, this is otherwise the attitude you maintain till the end of the song.

4. Explore the use of still points to mark some of Cunegonde's comedic reactions – such as the way she glares at an expensive ring, or indulges in a moment of mock-drama.

Vocal and Musical Analysis

WHO TO LISTEN TO: Kristin Chenoweth on the *Candide in Concert* DVD (2005).

VOCAL RANGE: E♭4 to E♭6.

ORIGINAL KEY: C minor.

ACCENT: Cunegonde is German, so of course you could deliver this song in your own accent if you are native to that country, though the song is more usually delivered in either General American (by American actresses) or in Received Pronunciation (if you are from the UK).

STYLE OF MUSICAL: Book musical.

VOCAL SET-UP/MUSICAL TIPS

1. For this song you should use an operatic set-up. Some of the main features of this sound are: the use of simultaneous onsets, a great deal of false-fold retraction, a tilted thyroid cartilage, a high back of the tongue, a lowered larynx (except on the very high notes when it must rise), an anchored neck and an anchored torso. A more detailed analysis of this complicated vocal set-up is beyond the remit of this book, and so you would be unwise to tackle this song in an audition unless you have some classical singing training.

2. You can make a joke out of the word 'France' by delivering it in a broad Twang quality, as Chenoweth demonstrates on the suggested recording.

3. Stylistically it is appropriate at times to do pitch-glides on certain notes. You can hear Chenoweth demonstrate this at several points on the suggested recording, notably on the word 'gilded' and the high 'ah' that occurs before the line about singing of sorrow.

4. The third verse should be spoken, as Chenoweth demonstrates on the suggested recording. Try to make this very conversational, as though you are a guest on a chatshow, confiding to the audience.

5. The top notes towards the end of the song require a great degree of torso anchoring and general physical engagement.

Sheet Music

The correct sheet music for this song is available at www.musicnotes.com.

'I Know Things Now'
from *Into the Woods*

Music and lyrics by Stephen Sondheim

Choose this song if: you enjoy playing teenage characters with naughty, mischievous, independent personalities. Although it goes reasonably high, the song is written almost entirely in Speech quality – so can suit an actress who sings.

Given Circumstances

WHO ARE YOU: Little Red Riding Hood, a greedy, streetwise and cheeky teenage girl.

WHERE ARE YOU: Outside your grandmother's house in the middle of the woods.

WHEN IS IT: Late afternoon, summer. (As *Into the Woods* is set in a fairytale kingdom, establishing the year that the piece is set is both problematic and unnecessary. Because of the feudal nature of the social hierarchy, it is sensible to assume that the story is set in a world with similarities to the European Middle Ages.)

WHAT HAS HAPPENED BEFORE: This morning you set out from your village to visit your grandmother who lives in the woods. Before you left, you visited the village Baker and his wife, whom you charmed into giving you a large quantity of cakes and pastries – which you said were for your granny, but you were to eat most of yourself.

The woods are a very dangerous and magical place, and your mother gave you strict instructions not to stray from the path. However, after you had been on your journey for a while you encountered a charming and charismatic Wolf. He secretly planned to eat you there and then, and so tried to tempt you down another path. When he heard that you were off to visit your grandmother, he hatched an alternative plot to eat you both and let you go on your way.

Further down the path you encountered the Baker. Unbeknown to you he had been sent into the woods by his neighbour, the Witch. Long ago she had placed a spell on his house that meant that he could never have children. The Witch promised she would lift the spell if he were to recover a series of items the Witch needed to make a potion. One of the items was a red cape. When the Baker saw your clothing he tried to persuade you to sell your cape, but you were unwilling because your granny had made it for you. The Baker then tried to take the cape from you, but when you had a temper tantrum and started crying, he felt guilty and gave it straight back. You promptly stood on his foot and ran off.

Shortly afterwards you arrived at your grandmother's house, and were perturbed to find the door had been left open. When you went inside you discovered the Wolf dressed in her clothes. He had already eaten your granny and promptly devoured you too. The Wolf then had a nap whilst you sat in his stomach with your grandmother.

A few moments ago the Baker, who had decided he must find you and get the cape, discovered the Wolf asleep. When he saw part of your cape hanging from the Wolf's mouth, he realised what had happened. He then promptly slit open the Wolf's stomach with a large knife, freeing yourself and your grandmother. You have just emerged into the light. Granny, who is tough and feisty like you, decided she wanted to see the Wolf die a hideous death, so resolved to fill his belly with stones. She has just dragged the Baker into the cottage, leaving you alone outside to collect the stones.

WHO ELSE IS THERE: You are alone.

WHO SHOULD YOU SING TO: The audience, which in this situation is the audition panel.

Textual Analysis

At the beginning of the song you are very pleased with yourself. You have just faced a near-death, life-changing experience and have emerged triumphant at the end of it. This outcome, allied to the arrogance of youth, has left you feeling very smug. In the opening section your objective is: to impress the audience with your naughtiness. You want to show off to them about how you disobeyed your mother – and in doing so you had a thrilling adventure with the Wolf.

During the first verse you then brag about your initial encounter in the woods with the Wolf which, although dangerous, was very exciting. A fun objective to play at this point is: to make the audience feel inferior. You want to prove that you have had an escapade that tops anything they might have experienced. With great delight and gore you then describe how the Wolf tempted you into your grandmother's house and ate you. You recount how you met your grandmother in his stomach and what it felt like when you were cut free by the Baker. An objective you can play at this point is: to frighten the audience with your horrifying tale. In order to do this, try actions such as: I scare, mesmerise, alarm, intrigue and captivate the audience.

In the second verse you are feeling cocky and self-assured. Having been on a journey of self-discovery, you now feel you have greater knowledge of the world. This enables you to play the following objective: to teach the audience a lesson in life. You can do this in a haughty manner, using action such as: I school, instruct, tutor and indoctrinate the audience. In the final section you can then revel in your ultimate objective: to congratulate yourself on being very smart.

KEY MOMENTS/TOP TIPS

1. When singing in direct address it is important to make a decision about who the audience represent in the character's world. Try pretending that the panel are other girls, slightly younger than yourself, whom you want to impress.

2. Little Red's experience with the Wolf is a metaphor for puberty and sexual awakening. In flirting with the dangers

of the Wolf, Little Red feels she has had her first truly adult experience. Her response to this is complex and multilayered. Undoubtedly it was exciting, but Little Red also misses the innocence she has lost, as she has now discovered that the world can be a dark and scary place.

3. The repetition of the words 'excited' and 'scared' is significant, as they encapsulate the two emotional extremes of Little Red's experiences with the Wolf. Give these words their full weight, meaning and colour each time you repeat them.

4. The song has a beautiful and surprising reversal in the last five words. At this point Little Red confesses that, although she has enjoyed this adventure, part of her wishes she could go back in time, to before she met the Wolf, and be innocent once more.

Vocal and Musical Analysis

WHO TO LISTEN TO: Tessa Burbridge on the original London cast recording (1990).

VOCAL RANGE: C4 to E♭5.

ORIGINAL KEY: C major.

ACCENT: When performed in the UK, *Into the Woods* is usually delivered with British accents. As Little Red is a peasant, and from a village in the countryside, it makes sense to use a regional, rural accent when you play her. For example, lots of Yorkshire, Lancashire, West Country, Irish, Welsh and Scottish accents work well. If your native accent is a rural one, then I would advise you to use your own voice when singing this song – but try turning up the strength of your dialect a little. This is generally good practice when singing to ensure the choice is clearly perceived by the audience. Accents that stereotypically denote upper class (i.e. Received Pronunciation) are not appropriate, but a Cockney or

COMEDY/CHARACTER

Mancunian accent – that can convey that Little Red is a streetwise young lady – is another possibility.

STYLE OF MUSICAL: Concept musical.

VOCAL SET-UP/MUSICAL TIPS

1. As with a great many of Sondheim's songs the vast majority of your vocal performance should be in a Speech quality. Try to keep your thyroid cartilage in a horizontal position and use the tongue positions associated with the dialect you have chosen, so that accent is clear.

2. You should try to sound like a child, so your vocal choices should be simple and uncluttered. Try to avoid using vibrato and raise the larynx slightly so you sound a little younger.

3. Aim to avoid flipping into a Cry quality on the top notes. Instead add some torso anchoring at these points, to move into an Advanced Speech quality, as you can hear on the suggested recording. Don't worry about your sound needing to be 'pretty' – it shouldn't be. The most important aspect of performing late-Sondheim material is clear communication of the lyric.

4. In the bridge section, when you describe the Wolf drawing you close, try using aspirate onsets to create a hushed, excited quality to your storytelling.

Sheet Music

The correct sheet music for this song is available at www.musicnotes.com.

'Miss Byrd'
from *Closer Than Ever*

Music by David Shire, lyrics by Richard Maltby Jr.

Choose this song if: you are an accomplished comedic actress who can play both nerdy and sexy. The song is vocally demanding and requires a range of different voice qualities – including belt – so offers a great opportunity to showcase a well-developed vocal technique.

Given Circumstances

Note: *Closer Than Ever* is a revue show, rather than a musical with a through-narrative. The given circumstances below, though derived from the lyric, are therefore invented – and could be altered to suit your needs.

WHO ARE YOU: Janie Byrd, an office secretary in her twenties who is seen by her colleagues as bland and forgettable, but who is in reality a clandestine sex-bomb.

WHERE ARE YOU: In the office of an estate agent, New York City, USA.

WHEN IS IT: 2.10 p.m., a Tuesday, July, present day.

WHAT HAS HAPPENED BEFORE: You have been working in this office for nearly six months. A major part of your job is to show potential clients around different properties that they may wish to rent or purchase. Your boss has been very pleased with your work so far as, not only are you exceptionally quiet and hardworking in the office, you have also been successful in acquiring a lot of business for the firm. However, unknown to your boss, every lunchtime for the past two months you have been sneaking off to have sex with a man named Jack, who is the superintendent of one of the apartment blocks owned by the firm. The block is just around the corner from the office.

Today you sneaked off just before one o'clock on the pretence of having a viewing for one of the basement apartments. In fact you went to indulge in an hour of wild passion with Jack. You have just returned, still flushed from the excitement of your surreptitious encounter.

WHO ELSE IS THERE: You are alone.

WHO SHOULD YOU SING TO: In the show the song is sung to the audience, so in an audition you are well advised to sing directly to the panel. Imagine they are a group of strangers that you have never met before and who you want to share your story with.

Textual Analysis

When the introduction starts, explore sitting forward on your chair (see point 1 below). Try leaning in towards the panel as if you are about to tell them a secret. You might even pretend to look around before you begin singing to check that you will not be 'overheard' by someone else in the office. In the first verse you then start by introducing yourself. Your objective in the opening half of the verse is: to intrigue the audience with your mysterious persona. You want them to think there is more to you than meets the eye. Try playing actions such as: I arouse, captivate, fascinate and tantalise the audience at this point. Having piqued their interest, and with them wondering what you will say next, in the second half of the verse your objective then becomes: to shock the audience with the revelation of your recent secret sexual lunchtime encounter. As you begin to remember and relive what happened just twenty minutes ago, this leads you to play a joyous objective in the first chorus, which is: to celebrate being in love. Here you can use actions such as: I warm, cheer, delight, comfort and uplift myself. The choruses are also a good place to play around with how you use the chair.

In the second verse, when you talk about being down in Apartment 'A', you share further and more intimate details of your story with the audience. Your objective in this section is: to impress the audience with your clandestine sex life. You want them to view you as bold, daring and liberated. At points you may also want to arouse them, though again this should be done in a very light-hearted, silly, comedic manner. During the second chorus you play a lovely objective, which is: to encourage the audience to have their own secret lunchtime encounter. Having experienced love, you want them to feel the same.

There is a tricky moment in the first three lines of the third verse, when you describe a 'floor-through-five' – which is a type of apartment. In this brief section you are describing a property. Your objective here is: to sell the apartment to a potential client. To make this clear to the audience you might want to deliver these three lines into a mobile phone, as if you are talking momentarily to a customer. The phone could have been concealed in your pocket from the beginning of the audition. For the remainder of the verse you talk about other women in the office, who you have discovered are also having sexual affairs. Your objective at this point is: to make the audience realise that the whole office is at it. You want them to stop underestimating the sexual potential of the women you work with. In the third chorus, and the long scat section that follows, you then return to your wonderful previous objective: to celebrate being in love.

KEY MOMENTS/TOP TIPS

1. It is fun to make use of a chair when performing this song as it offers possibilities for play. At the beginning of the song you might sit forward on the chair as previously suggested. As the number becomes more playful and sexual you might choose to circle around it, drape yourself across it, or stand on it (providing the chair is sturdy enough) in a provocative or joyous manner. If you decide to use a chair it is advisable to choreograph what you will do in advance of the audition.

2. A very common way for this song to be staged in performance is for the actress playing Miss Byrd to start

the number dressed as a nerdy secretary, and then to perform a (very silly and comic) partial striptease during the number, before putting her clothes back on at the end in order to 'maintain her secret'. Whilst this is not appropriate for audition, you can have some fun with removing and tossing a single garment across the room, such as a light cardigan, that you would be wearing as you entered the audition room. I have seen this work very successfully in audition. I wouldn't suggest, however, that you remove more than one item of clothing – and certainly not your blouse or trousers/skirt – as not only will this be awkward for the panel, it will leave you a lot to pick up off the floor at the end of your performance! Remember: Any such choice should be clearly comedic, rather than sexual.

3. An important element to this song is that Miss Byrd says several times that she is love. In all of the comic potential of the sexy secretary it can be easy to lose this fact. Use the choruses to reveal a more sincere emotional connection. This will help make your performance more truthful and well-rounded.

4. Right at the end of the song, in the last few bars of music, play around with returning to your office chair as if someone is about to come in and catch you talking to the audience. So when you say the final 'shh' you are asking the audience to keep your secret.

Vocal and Musical Analysis

WHO TO LISTEN TO: Jenn Colella on the Off-Broadway revival cast recording (2012).

VOCAL RANGE: F3 to G5.

ORIGINAL KEY: E♭ major.

ACCENT: General American.

STYLE OF MUSICAL: Contemporary musical (pop–based).

VOCAL SET–UP/MUSICAL TIPS

1. The sheet music indicates that the four-bar introduction should be repeated, to give you eight bars in total. This is too long for an audition, therefore scrub out the repeat marks so that the introduction is only played once through.

2. For the verses try using a modified version of Speech quality, but with the back of the tongue raised and some twang added. Clip the notes to make them slightly staccato. This set-up will give you a cute, innocent-sounding voice that portrays the nerdish office persona of Miss Byrd – and is great to alter and play around with as the song progresses.

3. At times in the song it can be fun to suddenly lower the larynx (think Marlene Dietrich singing 'Falling in Love Again') to create a moment of comedic sexiness – before flipping back abruptly to the sweet and innocent 'office girl' sound. You could try lowering the larynx in this manner when you sing about blowing the myth apart and about seals dancing in your chest in the first verse.

4. The first two choruses should be delivered in a pure Speech quality with a more neutral larynx to give you a fuller sound. Think of letting out your 'inner rock chick' in these moments to show Miss Byrd's wilder side.

5. In the third chorus, start in Speech as suggested previously, but then move up into a mixed belt when you sing the word 'love' on the high E♭. As you approach this note remember to anchor your torso, lift your chin and add some cricoid and thyroid tilt (think of making a moaning sound).

6. There are some scat lines, marked 'ad lib', at the end of each of the three choruses. If you find improvising difficult, it is perfectly valid to sing the notes that are scored on the music. The best vocal set-up for these sections is a Twang quality. Sing with very thin vocal folds, a raised larynx and a tightened AES. You should feel that you are keeping your set-up in a lifted position.

COMEDY/CHARACTER

7. This song benefits from a great deal of vocal play. For example, you might add some 'growl' at the section marked 'very funky' where you sing about the office temp. (Growl is made by constricting your false vocal folds for a moment.) Unless you are a very experienced vocalist, you may want to work with a vocal coach to help you add in these finer details.

Sheet Music

The correct sheet music for this song is available at www.scribd.com.

Alto

CLASSICAL MUSICAL THEATRE (1925–65)   222

CONTEMPORARY MUSICAL-THEATRE BALLADS (Post-1965)   248

CONTEMPORARY MUSICAL-THEATRE UP-TEMPO (Post-1965)   296

COMEDY/CHARACTER SONGS   334

'Aldonza'
from *Man of La Mancha*

Music by Mitch Leigh, lyrics by Joe Darion

Choose this song if: you enjoy playing feisty, argumentative
women who have had a tough life. As the song is delivered
almost entirely in Speech quality (it is written to be like a
sung shout) it can suit an actress who sings.

Given Circumstances

WHO ARE YOU: Aldonza, a defensive, belligerent,
confrontational prostitute. You have enormous sexual appeal
and great deal of inner vulnerability. You struggle to believe
that a man would want anything from you other than your
body.

WHERE ARE YOU: In a literal sense you are in the common room
of a stone prison vault in Seville, Spain. However, all of the
scenes in *Man of La Mancha* take place in a fictional world
located in the imagination of Miguel de Cervantes (see
below). In Cervantes's mind, this scene occurs in the
courtyard of an inn.

WHEN IS IT: Early evening, autumn, some time in the early
seventeenth century.

WHAT HAS HAPPENED BEFORE: At the beginning of the story a
man named Cervantes and his manservant were put in prison
at the hands of the Spanish Inquisition (the court of this
period responsible for maintaining Catholic orthodoxy). On
his arrival, his fellow prisoners decided to put him on mock
trial, where he was accused of the absurd crimes of being an
idealist, a bad poet and an honest man. In response to these
allegations Cervantes asked to deliver his defence in the form
of a charade, an entertainment. In that charade he would
impersonate an old country squire named Alonso Quijana. As

223

they might derive some pleasure from his performance, the prisoners agreed.

When Cervantes began his performance he explained to them that the character Alonso, having read book after book since his retirement, had become indignant at man's murderous ways towards his fellow man. Having brooded for a long time on this melancholy burden, he had therefore decided to transform himself into a knight-errant named Don Quixote and to go forth into the world to right all wrongs. Cervantes then began to act out the story of Don Quixote, of which you are a chief character. (The role of Aldonza is played in the charade by one of the female prisoners.)

The story of Don Quixote so far as it pertains to you as follows. You first met Don Quixote and his manservant Sancho at the inn where you work. One evening a few weeks ago, you were serving there whilst trying to stave off the advances of seven muleteers (a person who drives mules) when the two travellers arrived. At first sight Don Quixote was immediately captivated by your beauty. He started calling you his 'Dulcinea', which in the Spanish of the period implied an overly elegant sweetness. You dismissed his flattery as ridiculous.

A few days later, convinced of the imperative that a knight should have a lady, Don Quixote sent Sancho to court your favour on his behalf by delivering a missive (a love letter). When Sancho asked for your token you tossed him an old dishrag, but Don Quixote received this as if it were a silken scarf. As someone who was not used to romantic courtship, Don Quixote's advances threw you into confusion, and left you wondering what he really wanted from you.

In the next stage of his adventure Don Quixote asked the innkeeper to dub him a knight. Before this could happen he had to stand vigil all night in the courtyard of the inn. Whilst he was doing so, you encountered him, as you were on the way to meet Pedro, the leader of the muleteers, who had paid you in advance for your services as a prostitute. In the courtyard you confronted Don Quixote. You demanded to know why he was pursuing you. He told you that he considered it to be his quest, as he was struck by your virtue and nobility of spirit. This opinion was something you found hard to square with your life as a whore.

Whilst you were in the middle of this conversation, Pedro arrived. He was angry that you had kept him waiting and struck you. Don Quixote was shocked and angry to see you assaulted and, with the help of Sancho and yourself, he defeated Pedro and the rest of the muleteers in a fight. Immediately after the brawl the innkeeper kept his promise and dubbed Don Quixote a knight. Your suitor then surprised you by pledging that he must tend the wounds of his vanquished enemies. When he explained that a knight must be chivalrous, you reluctantly agreed to perform the duties on his behalf. However, after Don Quixote and Sancho had left, the muleteers repaid your kindness by raping you.

You have just seen Don Quixote for the first time since you were assaulted. Horrified by your bruises, he vowed to take revenge on the muleteers. Barely able to contain your anger you told him to get to a madhouse. In response he has once more called you his lady.

WHO ELSE IS THERE: Don Quixote.

WHO SHOULD YOU SING TO: Don Quixote.

Textual Analysis

The song starts with you wishing to dismiss Don Quixote's compliments and affections. When he addresses you as his lady you are in no mood to receive these words, as you currently do not feel like anything of the sort. During the first verse, in order to push Don Quixote away, you tell him that when you were a baby you were left in a ditch by your mother to die. In this section your objective is: to shock Don Quixote with the story of your childhood. By revealing your tragic upbringing you hope to dehumanise yourself in his eyes. In the second verse your attention then turns to memories of your father. Your objective at this point it is: to make Don Quixote think poorly of your father. This section can be played quite sarcastically. In the short chorus that follows, your hard, cold objective is: to ridicule your unfortunate existence.

The impulse for you to start singing the third verse is a response to Don Quixote's continuing insistence that you are a lady. (Whilst, of course, no one will be playing Don Quixote in your audition, it is useful to imagine he has just said those words of love and affection.) You refute those claims strongly by playing the following objective: to convince Don Quixote that you are a whore rather than a lady (see point 2). You can play quite savage actions at this point. Try options such as: I scold, berate, lambast and censure you.

You start the fourth verse by demanding that Don Quixote looks at you. Your objective in this section is: to make him see you as you really are. In a perverse and self-destructive way you want him to acknowledge you as the scum of the earth. After this emotional outburst in the second chorus you try to solicit Don Quixote in a mocking manner. Try playing the following objective here: to ridicule the notion of a romantic relationship.

A key change then occurs that leads you into the fifth verse. In this section you begin to attack your suitor more personally. You accuse him of showing you the sky, a metaphor for all of the grand possibilities of life. You deem this promise to be incredibly mean, as you consider such a happy existence to be perpetually out of your reach. You can play the following objective in this unit: to make Don Quixote accept that he is being cruel. This train of thought develops during the sixth and final verse, when you can play the following objective: to make Don Quixote recognise that his tenderness is causing you pain. Suitable actions for this section might include: I provoke, bait, interrogate and challenge you. With Don Quixote still unmoved – and you feeling completely exasperated – try playing this final objective in the last chorus: to provoke Don Quixote to do his worst, which in your distorted psyche means calling you his sweet Dulcinea.

1. It is possible for a performance of this song to become overly confrontational and aggressive – which can be off-putting in an audition. Look for the moments in which you can find irony and humour – where you can mock yourself and find a lightness of touch.

2. A key to Aldonza's character is that she has spent much of her adult life working as a prostitute. This has left her psychologically damaged, so she can no longer view herself positively. This is why she wants to be treated as whore, as this reinforces a deep-seated view of herself.

3. The key change is significant in the song. Use this musical development to help convey Aldonza's growing frustration – as, despite her earlier protestations, nothing she says seems to be deterring Don Quixote. From this point onwards you might lay bare Aldonza's inner struggle: that despite everything she says to the contrary, she actually really wants to believe Don Quixote.

Vocal and Musical Analysis

WHO TO LISTEN TO: Mary Elizabeth Mastrantonio on the Broadway revival cast recording (2002).

VOCAL RANGE: A♭4 to E5.

ORIGINAL KEY: B♭ minor.

ACCENT: Of course, Aldonza would have a Spanish accent. If you are from any part of Spain, or indeed even from Latin America, then this song would work well in your own dialect. However, if you are performing this material in the UK, and are not from one of those countries, then you might choose to perform the song in a regional British accent to help convey the character's earthy roots.

STYLE OF MUSICAL: Concept musical.

VOCAL SET–UP/MUSICAL TIPS

1. There is dialogue indicated on the sheet music that is meant to be spoken over the musical introduction and in between verses. This should be cut for audition purposes.

2. Before the verse that begins with the words 'for a lady' the previous two instrumental bars are scored to be repeated. This is not necessary for audition. Scrub out the repeat marks at this point and instruct the pianist to play straight through. This will leave four bars in total between the verses. You should make the same amendment before the verse that begins with the words 'you have shown'. If you don't read music, you may wish to get the assistance of a musician to help you mark these edits.

3. The vast majority of the song should be delivered in a Speech quality. The sound need not be refined or pretty, in fact it should be coarse and visceral. Don't be afraid to make raw, ugly sounds. To achieve the feeling of a musical shout you can employ a mix of aspirate and glottal onsets, and half-speak some of the words, as Mastrantonio demonstrates.

4. There are two options when you sing the higher phrases. You might tilt your thyroid and thin your vocal folds, as Mastrantonio chooses to do in her performance. Alternatively, you might move into an Advanced Speech quality by remaining in a thick vocal-fold set-up. To sing the higher notes with a thick vocal fold you will need to add some torso anchoring and a degree of thyroid tilt. You may also want to lift your chin a little at these points.

5. The final note on the word 'whore' should be belted. When using this voice quality remember to anchor your torso, lift your chin slightly and tilt your cricoid. *Note*: This is not

CLASSICAL

the set-up Mastrantonio uses on the suggested recording. If you find the belt difficult, you can alternatively tilt your thyroid cartilage and thin your vocal folds, as you can hear on the cast recording.

6. The musical structure of this song is repetitive. This makes it very simple to cut if you would like to deliver a shorter version of the song for a particular audition. A good solution involves cutting the second, third and sixth verses – so the structure of the song becomes: verse, chorus, verse, chorus, verse, chorus. To make this cut, you should scrub out all repeat marks on the music, delete all of the first-time bars (bars denoted with a number 1 and a bracket above them), and instruct the pianist to play the entire piece of music straight through once. Score out any lyrics you won't be singing with a ruler and pen.

Sheet Music

The correct sheet music for this song is available at www.scribd.com.

'The Boy Next Door'
from *Meet Me in St. Louis*

Music and lyrics by Hugh Martin and Ralph Blane

Choose this song if: you have a rich alto voice and enjoy
playing characters that are naive and enjoy to fantasise. The
song has a limited range, so can suit actresses who sing.

Given Circumstances

WHO ARE YOU: Esther Smith, the lively, attractive seventeen-
year-old daughter of Alonso and Anna Smith.

WHERE ARE YOU: By the window seat in the bedroom of your
house, in St. Louis, Missouri, USA. (*Note*: This is the setting
from the film, rather than the stage musical.)

WHEN IS IT: 5.20 p.m., a warm afternoon, midsummer, 1903.

WHAT HAS HAPPENED BEFORE: This afternoon has been very hot
and sunny. It has also been a chaotic day in your household. A
couple of hours ago your bright, six-year-old sister Tootie was
engaged in banter with the postman, whilst your other younger
sister Agnes, who is twelve, practised her stilt-walking. Your
brother Lon, who is two years older than you and is studying at
Princeton, became excited when he received a letter from his
university friend, and your grandfather, like Tootie, was
excitedly looking forward to St. Louis's forthcoming World Fair.

The most of important event of the afternoon occurred when
Katie, the family cook, persuaded your mother to have dinner an
hour early – which was unusual. She made the excuse that this
was because she had to visit her sister. In fact, you had put her
up to it. The reason for this was your eighteen-year-old sister
Rose was expecting a phone call from the millionaire Warren
Sheffield at 8.30 that evening. Rose didn't want the call to come
in the middle of dinner. She wanted her privacy because she was
hoping that tonight Warren would propose to her.

You have just been sitting out on the porch with Rose. Next door you saw your neighbour John Truitt, to whom are you madly attracted but have never spoken, wearing a baseball mitt and playing catch with his friend. You were both enjoying eyeing the handsome John when Agnes came out to tell you your mother wanted the pair of you to go upstairs and make your beds. Unfortunately, by the time Rose had shooed Agnes off, John had left – apparently totally unaware that you'd been watching him. When you dismissed him as not being very neighbourly, Rose suggested you invite him to Lon's going-away party. You despaired that this wouldn't be till August - which right now seems to you a lifetime away. Rose then left, after which you both headed upstairs to your separate bedrooms. You are now sitting by the window dreaming of John.

WHO ELSE IS THERE: You are alone.

WHO SHOULD YOU SING TO: Yourself, though in an audition you can share many of your thoughts with the panel as though they are your inner-consciousness.

Textual Analysis

When the song begins you are achingly lovesick. Your objective in the first verse is: to come to terms with how you feel about John. Seeing his beautiful smile in the next-door garden has had a profound effect on you: you are dumbstruck. As a teenager with no experience of love, you are now left trying to make sense of these feelings.

At this point of the song you debate in your head what seems an insurmountable problem: how can anything happen between yourself and John if he doesn't even know you exist? You conclude that this situation is impossible, and in the couple of lines that precede the chorus your objective becomes: to make yourself give up on love. Choices such as: I deflate, disappoint and dispirit myself can be good to play. Although this objective seems counter-intuitive, you are doing this to lower your expectations and thus avoid having your heart broken.

At the beginning of the chorus you then begin to ask yourself
some direct questions. Your objective at this point is: to work out
how to cope with your predicament. You wonder how you can
continue to function if you never have any contact with John.
Try exploring such actions as: I question, query, check and vet
myself at this juncture. These moments of self-reflection lead
you into the event of the song (see point 3 below), after which
your objective becomes: to spur yourself into action. As an
audience, from this point until the end of the song, we should be
clear that Esther will now do whatever it takes to get her man.

KEY MOMENTS/TOP TIPS

1. To convey that Esther is sitting at a window seat, you
   might use a chair. If you choose to do so, place it at the
   front of the space, with its back turned towards the panel
   on a slight angle. During the introduction you can then run
   in a few paces, as if you catch a glimpse of John out of the
   window, and then sit on the chair.

2. The great irony for the audience is that Esther feels as if
   she has no chance of ever meeting John – even though she
   lives next door! The more you play up her sense of
   despondency and hopelessness, the more fun you will have
   with the song.

3. The event of the song occurs near the end of the lyric
   when you resolve that you can't ignore John any longer.
   You might try standing from your window seat at this point
   to highlight the moment of decision.

Vocal and Musical Analysis

WHO TO LISTEN TO: Judy Garland on the original film
soundtrack (1944).

VOCAL RANGE: A♭3 to B♭4.

ORIGINAL KEY: D♭ major.

ACCENT: General American.

STYLE OF MUSICAL: Book musical.

VOCAL SET–UP/MUSICAL TIPS

1. Stylistically the song should have a jazz influence in its vocal delivery. To achieve this try singing the song in a Sob quality with a lowered larynx, as Garland demonstrates on the suggested recording.

2. The song has a long instrumental section that is not appropriate for audition. You should cut the sheet music so you finish singing on the word 'door', just before the instrumental begins.

3. In this song it is stylistically appropriate to employ pitch-glides between two notes, as Garland demonstrates throughout the recording. For example, between the words 'just' and 'adore'.

4. Try pausing slightly on the top notes, as Garland does on the words 'I' and 'my' near the beginning of her performance.

5. Employ a Speech quality when you sing the phrase on a single pitch about yourself and John both living in Kensington Avenue. You can make your sound comically mundane and bored at this point, as Garland demonstrates.

6. During the chorus, sing with long legato phrases; use simultaneous onsets wherever possible and try to run the vowels together.

7. You can sustain a lengthy pause on the word 'display' near the end of the song.

Sheet Music

The correct sheet music for this song is available at www.scribd.com.

'Far from the Home I Love' from *Fiddler on the Roof*

Music by Jerry Bock, lyrics by Sheldon Harnick

Choose this song if: you enjoy playing strong-willed, opinionated characters. Although the song is delivered in a legit style, the range is just above an octave – so the song is not overly demanding from a vocal perspective.

Given Circumstances

WHO ARE YOU: Hodel, the second eldest daughter of Tevye, a poor Jewish milkman. Although not formally educated, you are an intelligent, sparky girl with a quick tongue and an inquisitive mind. Brought up in a deeply traditional manner, you are beginning to challenge the orthodoxies of your religion and society. You are seventeen years old.

WHERE ARE YOU: At the local railway station, which is a long walk from the tiny village of Anatevka in Russia where you grew up – and your family all still live. The station would be virtually unrecognisable as such to us today, no more than a wooden bench beside a railway track – the land deserted as far as the eye can see.

WHEN IS IT: Early morning, winter, 1905.

WHAT HAS HAPPENED BEFORE: When you were growing up it was the tradition that all marriages within the Jewish faith must be arranged by a matchmaker and approved by the father of the bride. A few months ago your elder sister Tzeitel broke from this tradition when she begged your father to let her marry the man she loved – Motel, the poor tailor – rather then rich butcher Lazar Wolf whom the matchmaker had proposed. After a crisis of conscience your father reluctantly agreed.

Around this time Perchik – a revolutionary student from the city of Kiev – had come to your village. With no money, and

CLASSICAL

nowhere to stay, your father agreed to provide him with food and shelter, in return for which Perchik would educate you and your sisters. In your entire life you had never left the village and Perchik's lessons helped open your mind to the great changes that were going on in revolutionary Russia. He taught you how the old traditions were being blown away in Kiev and the other great cities. At the wedding of Tzeitel and Motel, Perchik broke another of these traditions by dancing with you (men and women were traditionally forbidden from dancing together).

A few weeks later Tevye was forced to bend his traditional views still further when you and Perchik decided to marry. Not only was your marriage not arranged, but you didn't even ask your father for his permission – only his blessing. However, seeing that you were in love, Teyve once more relented. Shortly after you became engaged, Perchik was arrested for revolutionary activities and was deported by the authorities to the frozen wastelands of Siberia – where he was to be imprisoned. After much soul-searching you resolved that you must leave your home in Anatevka to be near your husband. This morning your father walked with you to the railway station. On arrival you confessed that Perchik is in Siberia, something you had been keeping from your father. Tevye has just asked you how you can choose to abandon your family and journey the thousands of miles to that Arctic wilderness.

WHO ELSE IS THERE: Tevye.

WHO SHOULD YOU SING TO: Tevye, until the last couple of lines when you sing to yourself.

Textual Analysis

When the introduction begins your father is clearly distressed. He doesn't understand your decision to leave and needs an explanation as to why you're abandoning your home and family. When you begin singing you find you don't have an explanation to give. In the first stanza your objective is: to make Tevye understand how difficult it is to explain your decision. You should then imagine that your father is distressed by what you have just said – because he sees your decision as uncaring. This will give you the impulse to play the following objective in the second stanza: to reassure Tevye that you were happy in the family home. Try playing gentle actions, such as: I warm, ease, comfort, console and sustain my father at this juncture.

In the bridge, as the music soars, you become absorbed in positive, heartening memories of your times with Perchik. However, your objective in the first two lines is: to prove to Tevye that this was not what you intended. For the second two lines of the bridge your objective then becomes: to make Tevye comprehend how scared you feel.

At the start of the third verse, when you say how melancholy your choice is, you are temporarily overwhelmed with feelings of hopelessness and despair. Your objective here is: to get your father to appreciate how heart-wrenching your choice is. Try actions such as: I awaken, alert and shake my father. When you say then that you must go, which is the event of the song (see point 4 below), your objective should be: to assert your independence.

After this moment of defiance, with the decision made, you briefly sing to yourself. When you ponder what it will be like to be wandering across the country, your objective is: to reflect upon the unlikelihood of your situation. This moment should have a sense of irony; you might even try to amuse yourself. In the final line, after you have a realisation on the word 'yet' (see point 5 below), you then play this ultimate objective: to make peace with your decision.

KEY MOMENTS/TOP TIPS

1. You cannot underestimate the stakes of the decision Hodel is making: she has never left her tiny village and now is travelling thousands of miles, simply to be near a man who will be in prison. It is also likely that she will never see her family again. It is important to recognise not only the difficulties that Hodel is facing during the song, but also the courage needed to overcome them.

2. Listen to a recording of the piano accompaniment. You will hear how the harmonic structure in the verses keeps shifting between a major and minor key. The minor sounds forlorn and despondent, the major more uplifting. This is a good barometer of the changes in Hodel's thought processes: she moves between despair and trying to raise the spirits of both herself and her father. The musical changes reflect her inner turmoil.

3. At some point during the bridge it is useful to visualise Perchik in your imagination, perhaps in the midst of one of his inspiring moments as your teacher.

4. The event of the song occurs when you say twice that you must go. Here, for the first time in your life, you clearly – but gently – defy your father. At this moment he should understand that your mind will now not be changed.

5. On the word 'yet' Hodel has an important realisation: that her home is no longer with her family, but with Perchik. You might choose to mark this discovery, which is an event, with a moment of stillness, as if Hodel has been struck by something she has never felt before.

6. This song is a rite of passage for Hodel. During your performance, through her growing sense of resolve, we should almost see her change before our eyes from being a teenage girl into a young, independent woman.

Vocal and Musical Analysis

WHO TO LISTEN TO: Laura Michelle Kelly on the Broadway revival cast recording (2004).

VOCAL RANGE: C4 to E5.

ORIGINAL KEY: C minor.

ACCENT: Russian/Yiddish. In many productions Hodel is performed with a General American accent – including on the suggested recording – though, of course, there is no logical reason for this, beyond the fact that the musical was written by Americans. However, if you are struggling with the Russian/Yiddish accent you could copy this choice.

STYLE OF MUSICAL: Book musical.

VOCAL SET-UP/MUSICAL TIPS

1. The verses should be delivered in a legit set-up. Sing with a tilted thyroid cartilage, thin your vocal folds and make use of simultaneous onsets wherever possible, as Kelly suitably demonstrates.

2. During the bridge, which starts with the word 'who', you should gradually get louder. Achieve this by tightening the AES to add some twang to your sound. Once you reach the word 'helpless', gradually relax the AES once more so that you decrescendo and end up in a quiet, vulnerable Cry quality in time for the word 'dreams'.

3. When you twice assert that you must go, try using aspirate onsets to help portray Hodel's sense of conviction at this point.

4. To clarify the moment of discovery that occurs on the word 'yet', separate this word by putting a fractional breath before and after it.

5. Sing the last line in a pure Cry quality. Lift your larynx very high and thin your vocal folds as much as possible.

Sheet Music

The correct sheet music for this song is available at www.scribd.com.

CLASSICAL

'I Get a Kick Out of You'
from *Anything Goes*

Music and lyrics by Cole Porter

Choose this song if: you enjoy playing stylish, sophisticated
roles, which require a sense of wit and a warm-hearted
portrayal. The song suits a strong alto voice, rooted in Speech
quality.

Given Circumstances

Note: The libretto for *Anything Goes* has been rewritten
several times. The given circumstances below are from the
Beaumont Theatre version that was reworked in 1987 by
Timothy Crouse and John Weidman.

WHO ARE YOU: Reno Sweeney, a glamorous, sexy, evangelist
turned nightclub singer.

WHERE ARE YOU: In a smoky Manhattan bar.

WHEN IS IT: 10.30 p.m., a Tuesday, 1934.

WHAT HAS HAPPENED BEFORE: This evening you were due to
have a drink with your friend Billy Crocker – a handsome
young stockbroker on Wall Street. However, Billy, who is very
popular with the ladies, completely forgot your date. This
reflected the unwelcome truth that, whilst most other men
regularly fall for your seductive charms, Billy only sees you as
a friend.

A few minutes ago Billy arrived at the bar where you'd been
waiting. He was meeting with his boss, Elisha J. Whitney.
Whitney – who is due to travel to England tomorrow on the
SS American – had instructed Billy to run around town all day
making preparations for him. Despite his attempt to do all
that was asked, Billy had forgotten to bring his boss's
passport. As he was not best pleased by this news, Whitney

told Billy to bring the passport to the docks tomorrow – and then left.

As Whitney headed out the door you spotted Billy at the bar. He was asking the barman, Fred, if Hope Harcourt (a beautiful heiress with whom he has fallen in love) had called for him. She had not. When you headed over and greeted him, Billy was immediately apologetic that he had stood you up. He explained that his day had been incredibly stressful, before ordering you both a conciliatory cocktail. You were worried that Billy's Wall Street job was turning him into a unhappy bore, so you have just decided to try and convince you to come with you to London tomorrow aboard the *SS American* (on which you will also be a passenger).

WHO ELSE IS THERE: Billy.

WHO SHOULD YOU SING TO: Billy.

Textual Analysis

In the opening lyrics you are frank about your current view of the world. Your objective in the first two lines is: to confess that you have grown indifferent to life. You do this in a flippant, almost defensive manner, as you don't want to expose the true depth of your feelings in front of Billy. But though you often feel down on your luck, being with Billy makes you think differently. In the remainder of the pre-chorus your objective becomes: to convince Billy that only he can cheer you up. You want him to feel needed – so that he will agree to sail on the *SS American* with you.

In the first chorus you compare Billy to the buzz that can be gained from drinking alcohol. You ask him to explain why you get a thrill out of being with him, when drinking does not have the same effect on you. Your objective in this section is: to get Billy to understand why he has such a powerful effect on you. In the second chorus, you then talk about people who take cocaine for fun. Your objective in this moment is: to ridicule those who need drugs to make them happy. It is true

CLASSICAL

that you have probably tried such illegal substances yourself – but you recognise they did nothing to help with your melancholy.

A feature of your personality is that you rarely betray your true feelings, but in the bridge you go against your usual behaviour and play the following objective: to convince Billy that you are in love with him. You do so in order for him to take pity on you, as you know these feeling are not reciprocated. By doing so, you expose your vulnerability. You do this only fleetingly, though, and you quickly change the subject at the beginning of the third chorus – by talking about flying. The lifestyle you lead is glamorous and profligate, so it is probably not at all unusual for a rich gentleman to take you flying in his plane. During this section your objective is: to convince Billy that your extravagant lifestyle means nothing to you. In the final line you then say very simply, for a final time, that what really matters to you is him.

KEY MOMENTS/TOP TIPS

1. It has been said of Porter's lyrics that in them you hear the lyricist, rather than the character. You could also argue that they are autobiographical. As a gay man who was often required to hide his sexuality behind his opulent lifestyle, Porter certainly has parallels with Reno. Despite her allure and apparent self-confidence, underneath she clearly has a sense of underlying melancholy, tragedy even. On a relationship level she is lonely – which is reflected in her mistakenly making Billy the object of her affections.

2. Despite the subtext described in the previous point, on the surface Reno is being upbeat and positive throughout the majority of the song: she is trying to cheer Billy up. In order to portray this, try exploring actions such as: I amuse, delight, tickle, flatter, charm and seduce Billy.

3. The event occurs in the final line of the song. At this moment Reno relinquishes any claim she might have on Billy's heart. She indicates that, although she loves him,

she accepts that her feelings will never be reciprocated and they will always be just friends.

Vocal and Musical Analysis

WHO TO LISTEN TO: Sutton Foster on the Broadway revival cast recording (2011).

VOCAL RANGE: A3 to D5.

ORIGINAL KEY: C major.

ACCENT: General American.

STYLE OF MUSICAL: Musical comedy.

VOCAL SET-UP/MUSICAL TIPS

1. The bright, upbeat musical setting of the song contrasts with the lyrics in which Reno reveals she is tired of life. This indicates that she is covering up her underlying feelings – and is solely focused on lifting Billy's spirits.

2. Try delivering the pre-chorus in an oral Twang quality, as Foster uses on the suggested recording.

3. When you reach the first chorus, try shifting to a Speech quality, so there is more 'core' to the fundamental sound. You will need to relax your AES and release your thyroid tilt.

4. When you sing the word 'kick' explore using a very clear, defined consonant on the final 'k' – to give the word an almost onomatopoeic quality.

5. During the choruses there are several phrases that finish with a sustained note. Try beginning these pitches with a horizontal thyroid cartilage so you are singing with a very straight tone, then tilt the thyroid at the very end of the note to introduce the vibrato. You can hear Foster demonstrate this beautifully on the word 'cocaine'.

CLASSICAL

6. During the bridge, try bending the pitch of some of the notes to give them a 'moaned' quality. You can hear Sutton Foster do this clearly on the suggested recording on the words 'time' and 'clear'.

7. Try singing the last line much quieter, with a raised larynx, a tilted thyroid cartilage and thin vocal folds – so you end in a Cry quality that reveals Reno's underlying vulnerability.

Sheet Music

The correct sheet music for this song is available at www.musicnotes.com.

'Just You Wait'
from *My Fair Lady*

Music by Frederick Loewe, lyrics by Alan Jay Lerner

Choose this song if: you enjoy singing comedic songs that
require both a playfulness and a short temper. The song sits
mainly in a speech register, so can work for actresses who sing.

Given Circumstances

WHO ARE YOU: Eliza Doolittle, a loud-mouthed, wilful
Cockney flower girl from Lisson Grove in London, who
works in Covent Garden.

WHERE ARE YOU: The study of Professor Henry Higgins's
house, Wimpole Street, Marylebone, London.

WHEN IS IT: 4.30 p.m., April, some time in the Edwardian era
(between 1901 and 1910).

WHAT HAS HAPPENED BEFORE: Several weeks ago you were
selling flowers in Covent Garden. The evening performance
at the Royal Opera House had just finished, and the rich
patrons were waiting for taxis underneath the arches of the
market. Whilst they were loitering you tried to sell one of
them a flower: a fellow by the name of Colonel Pickering. He
explained that he couldn't because he only had threepence –
but he nonetheless gave you the money he did have out of
charity. When this transaction took place you quickly became
concerned, as you noticed that a rich gentleman, a stranger by
the name of Professor Henry Higgins, was noting down
everything you were saying to Pickering. You were worried
that Higgins was a policeman and that he would arrest you for
begging. When you proclaimed your innocence to him,
Higgins explained that you had nothing to fear as he was not a
policeman at all – he was a phoneticist: he studied people's
accents.

The Professor went on to lament the fact that, in his eyes, so many people – such as yourself – could not speak English properly. He then announced a theory to an absorbed Pickering: that a person's speech was what truly defined their social status. Afterwards he joked with the Colonel, who was fascinated by Higgins's ideas, that within six months he could teach you how to speak 'properly' and pass you off as a lady at the upcoming Embassy Ball. They then left together.

The next day you turned up at the door of the Professor's house. After hearing last night's conversation you had decided that you wanted to take elocution classes so you could become a lady and work in a proper flower shop. When you asked him if he would teach you, Higgins agreed, but warned you that he would prove a hard taskmaster. He then decided to formally accept Pickering's wager and train you for the Ball.

Since then you have been living in Higgins's house. He has been subjecting you to long and exhaustive speech lessons, often working you for twelve hours a day. In these sessions the Professor has been trying to get you to speak in a heightened form of Received Pronunciation. (This dialect was fashionable amongst the upper classes at the time, and was perceived to be the 'right way' to speak.) The lessons involved you doing boring and repetitive exercises in order to produce sounds that are not ordinarily present in your own accent – such as the letter 'h'.

A few minutes ago you came into the study to discover Higgins talking to your father, Alfred Doolittle. Your father had heard that you were staying with the Professor, and had come to save your virtue. However, when Higgins offered your father five pounds if he would let you stay, Doolittle promptly took the money and left. The Professor then asked you to continue practising your vowels, but you flatly refused. Higgins has just replied that if you do not learn to pronounce your vowels properly by the end of the day, you will be denied lunch, dinner and chocolates.

WHO ELSE IS THERE: You are alone.

WHO SHOULD YOU SING TO: To the absent Henry Higgins.

Textual Analysis

When the song begins you are furious with the Professor – he has humiliated you. As he has only just walked out of the door, your anger is fresh, and his sudden departure has denied you the opportunity to vent your frustrations at him directly. This leaves you stewing, and so you begin to plot how you might gain some measure of revenge. During the first two verses your objective is: to warn Higgins that a disaster will soon strike him down. You want him to panic that, when something does go wrong, you will not be around to help. In the first verse you forewarn him that you will not save him if he faces financial ruin, in the second you caution him that you will not aid him if he were to fall ill. You become particularly inventive when you begin to imagine what would happen if Higgins were drowning. You could explore actions such as: I taunt, heckle and ridicule Higgins in this section.

By the time you reach the bridge, your imagination is running riot. You imagine that you will be so famous that you will be friends with the King of England. Your objective from this point until the end of the song is: to indulge your fantasy of Higgins's fatal demise. In this section try playing actions such as: I delight, entertain, amuse, delight and cheer myself. Ultimately you are completely successful in this objective, as, having begun the song humiliated, by the end you are feeling triumphant. You are certain that one day soon you will have your revenge.

CLASSICAL

KEY MOMENTS/TOP TIPS

1. Even though Higgins is not there, you should still focus your objectives towards him during your performance. This is the imaginary conversation that you would like to have with your tormentor if he were present. Try directing much of the song to where you imagine Higgins has just exited, which should be somewhere behind the panel.

2. Because Eliza is angry at the start of the song, she is not able to think rationally. Explore playing with this obstacle:

that at times she is so frustrated it makes it hard for her to think clearly and come up with a plausible method of revenge.

3. There is a great deal of fun to be had when you twice sing on an extended 'ooh' sound. These are opportunities to really embody the delight Eliza takes in plotting against Higgins. It can be fun to use a sweeping pitch-glide at these points.

4. When you sing the words of the King, try doing a silly impression of His Majesty. To achieve this you might explore singing in a rough Received Pronunciation (Eliza still hasn't mastered the accent yet). You could also explore making him sound old and doddery, lower the larynx to achieve a deeper tone, or speak-sing his sections.

Vocal and Musical Analysis

WHO TO LISTEN TO: Julie Andrews on the original London cast recording (1959).

VOCAL RANGE: A♭3 to E♭5.

ORIGINAL KEY: C minor.

ACCENT: Cockney.

STYLE OF MUSICAL: Book musical.

VOCAL SET-UP/MUSICAL TIPS

1. It is appropriate to use Speech quality for the vast majority of the song. Make use of both glottal and aspirate onsets and don't be afraid to half-speak some words, as Andrews does on the cast recording.

2. The accent is incredibly important in this song. A Cockney dialect in Edwardian times would likely have been much stronger than its modern equivalent, so make your accent very thick indeed.

3. In the middle section you should continue using a Speech quality wherever possible. However, you will need to tilt your thyroid cartilage for some of the higher phrases. Ensure you maintain the dialect at these points and still speak some words. This is important as otherwise the section can sound too refined, and you will lose the working–class tone of Eliza's voice.

4. When you tell the imaginary firing squad to get ready, take aim and fire, those three syllables should be shouted rather than sung.

5. The last few lines should sound almost like a sung shout. To achieve this, avoid tilting your thyroid cartilage, as this will make your sound too sweet. Instead use thick vocal folds and add some torso anchoring to allow you to finish in an Advanced Speech quality, as Andrews clearly demonstrates.

Sheet Music

The correct sheet music for this song is available at www.musicnotes.com.

CLASSICAL

'Breathe'
from *In the Heights*

Music and lyrics by Lin-Manuel Miranda

Choose this song if: you have an excellent contemporary musical-theatre voice and can belt to an F. The song may suit if you enjoy exploring sensitive, conflicted characters. The role was originated by a Hispanic actress.

Given Circumstances

WHO ARE YOU: Nina Rasario, an intelligent, open-hearted, principled university freshman. From a poor Dominican-American background, you are the first in your family to make it into higher education.

WHERE ARE YOU: On the street outside the apartment of your honorary grandmother in Washington Heights, Manhattan, New York City, USA.

WHEN IS IT: Early morning, 3rd July, the hottest day of the year, present day.

WHAT HAS HAPPENED BEFORE: Last year you were awarded a scholarship to Stanford University. As a bright high-school student, you had always been very ambitious and worked incredibly hard to earn this opportunity. Your parents, and indeed your entire community, were tremendously proud of your achievement in being accepted to such a prestigious institution.

However, when you arrived in California you found university life a struggle. Your scholarship did not cover your living costs and you had to work two jobs in order to support yourself. As a result your studies began to suffer, and when you achieved poor results in your mid-term exams the dean of the university called you into his office to inform you that your scholarship had to be rescinded. As a result, four months ago, in March, you took a leave of absence. Despite these difficulties you failed to reach out to your parents, Kevin and Camila. During the last few months you have been sleeping on friends' couches, trying to work out how on earth to confess to your family.

Last night you flew across the country to return home for summer. Shortly after dawn you arrived back in Washington Heights. You have just got back to the neighbourhood where you grew up. You were greeted on the street as a returning hero by three people who you have known all of your life: Usanavi, the owner of the local bodega (a shop), his cousin Sonny, and Abuela Claudia – who is like a grandmother to you, and indeed the entire community. You failed to tell them that you had left university. With Usanavi and Sonny returning to work, Abuela Claudia has just gone inside to make you a sandwich, leaving you on the street – trying to summon the courage to tell everyone your bad news.

WHO ELSE IS THERE: You are alone.

WHO SHOULD YOU SING TO: Yourself, though in an audition you can share many of your thoughts with the panel as though they are your inner-consciousness.

Textual Analysis

Note: The song contains an introductory section where other members of the community sing in Spanish. For audition purposes this should be cut, along with the first time you sing the words 'just breathe'. You should instead start singing at the beginning of the first verse with a two-bar introduction (containing the D♭ and A♭ chords). The textual analysis below assumes you have made this cut.

At the beginning of the song you look around the neighbourbood. It is many months since you have been home, and you reflect on the people you grew up with. Your first objective is: to work out how to tell your friends and family about the loss of your scholarship. They have all built you up as a great success story, so you ruminate over how hard it will be to disappoint them. When you sing the word 'breathe' – which is extended over several bars – you try to do exactly that: take a deep breath. Your objective at this point is: to try and calm yourself down.

During the second verse you think back to what it was like to grow up in the neighbourhood. Your objective in this section is: to cheer yourself up with happier memories. You are unsuccessful in this objective, though, and during the last line of the verse you again try to work out what you might say to your loved ones.

There then follows a section where you have short vocal interjections and the ensemble would usually sing. At this point you begin to resent the expectations that were placed on you by the rest of the neighbourhood. You feel they put a level of pressure on you that was unfair. Your objective here is: to take pity on yourself. As the music builds into the dynamic bridge section a new unit begins. Your objective here is: to question whether you made the right choice going to Stanford in the first place. You punish yourself for what you see as your failure. In the bridge, try playing actions such as: I chastise, criticise, mock and condemn myself.

Having reached a very low point at the end of bridge – as you begin to wonder if your life will now amount to anything – you manage to gain some courage at the beginning of the third verse when you tell yourself to straighten your spine. Your objective in this section is: to pull yourself together. You try to convince yourself that everything will be fine. Explore playing actions such as I repair, reassemble, galvanise and freshen myself at this point. You will fail in this objective too, and in the final few lines you ask yourself some fundamental questions: How will my parents react? Can I actually face up to these people? In these moments your objective is: to work out if you can follow through on your decision to come clean. This time you are successful, and you do find the courage to confront your family. You are then left with you an ultimate objective on the final word: to keep breathing – in order to settle your nerves.

KEY MOMENTS/TOP TIPS

1. It is important to consider that, due to her long flight and a great deal of worrying, Nina has probably not slept. Explore playing with the idea that her tiredness contributes to her nervousness. She is at her wits' end.

2. You sing a line of Spanish in the second verse. In English this translates as: 'I love you, I want you.'

3. The interjections from the ensemble are written as though they are voices in Nina's head. Although they will, of course, not be heard in the audition, it is useful for you to act as if these thoughts are nagging at you at this point. In the section that starts with you singing the word 'hey', the Spanish ensemble lines translate as follows: 'I'm not worried about her.' 'Look, there is our star!' 'She really makes the grade!' Imagine you can hear those voices in your mind.

4. The event of the song occurs before you sing the final word, having just thought about letting your parents down. At this moment you discover the courage to walk into Abuela Claudia's apartment – so you can begin the process of telling your friends and family.

5. The physical storytelling centres on you trying to find the courage to walk through a door. Explore having an imaginary door to the side of the audition table. You can finish the song by walking off into the space, as if you are going through that door.

Vocal and Musical Analysis

WHO TO LISTEN TO: Mandy Gonzalez on the original Broadway cast recording (2008).

VOCAL RANGE: F3 to F5.

ORIGINAL KEY: B♭ major.

ACCENT: General American.

STYLE OF MUSICAL: Book musical.

VOCAL SET–UP/MUSICAL TIPS

1. After the introductory ensemble section, which should be cut (see above), there are other occasions during the song at which the chorus also sing backing vocals. You should ignore these lines for audition purposes – though this doesn't require you to make any further cuts in the piano accompaniment.

2. The first verse should be delivered in a Speech quality. Try not to tilt the thyroid cartilage too much on the higher notes of this section. Keeping it in a horizontal position will make you sound very conversational, as Gonzalez ably shows.

3. When you sing 'just breathe', sing with a long legato line – using simultaneous onsets.

4. The second verse and the start of the bridge should be delivered in an oral Twang quality. In this quality remember to keep the thyroid tilted, the larynx high and the soft palate high to avoid nasality.

5. The next section of the song, which begins in the bridge when you say you remember being a child and stops on the word 'horizon', should be delivered in a mixed-belt quality. As this is an extended section to be delivered in this set-up, you must ensure you remain incredibly physical. You will need to anchor the torso, lift the chin and tilt the cricoid cartilage for the entire time. For the highest notes you also need to add some thyroid tilt, as these pitches require you to progress towards the top of the female belt register.

6. For the final line of the bridge, which follows the word 'horizon', try lifting the larynx, relaxing your AES and tilting the thyroid cartilage so you arrive in a thoughtful Cry quality, as Gonzalez demonstrates on the cast recording.

7. You should start a crescendo on the word 'standard' that builds to the conclusion of the song. Achieve this crescendo by tightening your AES to arrive in an Oral Twang quality.

8. Deliver the last two words in a very pure Cry quality.

Sheet Music

The correct sheet music for this song is available at www.musicnotes.com.

'I'm Here'
from *The Color Purple*

Music and lyrics by Brenda Russell, Allee Willis and Stephen Bray

Choose this song if: you have an outstanding soulful voice with a high belt. Written originally for an African-American actress, this is a huge torch song that enables you to showcase a very powerful performance.

Given Circumstances

WHO ARE YOU: Miss Celie, a thirty-seven-year-old African-American woman. Fiercely loyal to your sister and children, you are painfully shy and have long suffered from low self-esteem – caused by decades of abuse at the hands of the men in your family.

WHERE ARE YOU: On the porch of your house, Memphis, Tennessee, USA.

WHEN IS IT: 11 a.m., a spring morning, 1932.

WHAT HAS HAPPENED BEFORE: In 1909, when you were fourteen years old, you fell pregnant for the second time. Tragically the father of both your children was your own father, Alphonso, who had raped you as a young girl. When you went into labour your newly-born daughter, whose name was Olivia, was taken from you by Alphonso – just as he did with your first child, Adam.

This hard upbringing was made worse when a local widower named Albert, who was known as 'Mister', came to see your father because he was looking for a new wife. Mister was really interested in your pretty younger sister Nettie, but when Alphonso refused to let Mister marry her, he agreed to take you instead – not because he was attracted to you, but because he desperately needed someone to clean the farmhouse and look after his children.

Your new life at Mister's farm was a misery. He treated you as a virtual slave, and you lived constantly under the threat of physical violence. Your life briefly took a turn for the better when Nettie, whom you love dearly, moved in with you and Albert. She had grown tired of trying to fight off your father's sexual advances towards her and wanted to pursue her dream of becoming a teacher. Unfortunately Mister still had his own sexual designs on Nettie – which was his real motivation for letting her stay. When he tried to seduce her she fought him off – but as a consequence he threw her out. As she was leaving, Nettie promised to write to you, but Mister swore that he would never let the two of you see each other again.

A decade later, in 1920, Mister's eldest son Harpo brought home a woman named Sophia. Sophia was strong both of will and body. When Harpo found that he could not control his future wife you advised him that he should beat her – which perhaps revealed how your worldview had been shaped by the abuse you had suffered at the hands of men. However, when Harpo tried to follow your advice, he ended up being beaten himself by Sophia, who promptly moved out to live with her sisters.

After Sophia had gone, Harpo began an affair with a waitress known as Squeak (her real name is Agnes) and they set up a juke joint together. Soon afterwards they invited a successful and attractive jazz singer called Shug Avery to come to town and sing at Harpo's. Shug and Mister had been having an intermittent affair since long before you met Albert, but when Shug arrived she was in such poor health that you had no choice but to nurse her. Through the intimacy you shared, for the first time in your life you started to have romantic feelings for another human being. Shug told you that you were beautiful and encouraged you to find the strength to stand up to Mister – and a sexual relationship began to develop between you both. After her performance at Harpo's, Shug returned with you to the farm. There she discovered a great

number of letters that Albert had hidden away. When you
recognised the handwriting as belonging to Nettie you
realised that your sister was alive – and that Mister had been
keeping you from communicating with each other for all of
these years. On reading the letters you discovered that Nettie
was in Africa, where by a miraculous turn of fate she was
living with the missionary family who had adopted your
children.

In the year of 1932 your life took a significant turn. Shug had
arrived for a visit with her new lover, Grady, for Easter. With
you finally having reached the end of your patience with
Mister, you told him that you were leaving for Memphis with
Shug (Squeak also decided to leave Harpo and join you on the
journey). When Albert tried to prevent you going, you cursed
him.

In Memphis you finally started to receive some of the good
fortune you rightly deserved. You began corresponding
regularly with Nettie and discovered you had a gift for making
trousers, which in this period were now worn by both men
and women. Using this newfound skill you set up business in
your own shop. The sense of independence this gave you was
enhanced when shortly afterwards you inherited your
childhood home – enabling you to possess your own property
for this first time.

Unbeknown to you, a reformed Mister was now in the process
of trying to help Nettie, Olivia and Adam return to the
United States so that you can be reunited with them.
Although this future happiness will soon come to pass, you
had one more blow to endure. A few moments ago Shug has
told you that she has fallen in love with a nineteen-year-old
jazz musician called Germaine and that she will be leaving
with him. As you are still in deeply love with Shug, this news
has left you feeling crushed.

WHO ELSE IS THERE: Shug Avery.

WHO SHOULD YOU SING TO: Shug Avery.

Textual Analysis

Note: In the musical Celie only sings to Shug for the first half of the song. For the purposes of audition it is clearer if the entire song is directed to her. The analysis below assumes that decision has been made.

For any performance of this song, it is vital to appreciate that Miss Celie is not someone who usually stands up to people. So these words are like the first she has ever spoken as her true self. At the beginning of the song you should therefore struggle for the courage to open your mouth. Your objective in the first two lines is: to assert your independence from Shug. You do this at first in a very quiet, understated way – but with a great deal of resolution and conviction.

What then follows is a list of the things in your life that give you strength. These include your new material possessions, such as your house, and those things you hold only in your heart, like the knowledge that you have a family in Africa who love you. Your objective in listing these things to Shug is: to show her that you are strong. You want her to understand that you are a different person now and can survive without her. Actions you could play might include: I assure, convince, undermine, confront, resist, encounter and defy Shug.

In the next unit, which starts when you say you are going to take a deep breath, you now speak with growing conviction and confidence. Your objective at this point is: to boast about your future. You want Shug to understand that you are going to live your life to the full and not be held back by anyone. Try playing actions such as: I thwart, outwit and confound Shug. This section can be delivered with humour and wit. The emotional arc of the song reaches its peak when you defiantly say that you will sing out – which is a moment where you rejoice in your newfound self-confidence. In the section that follows you can play this wonderful objective: to celebrate being alive. After the most difficult of lives, you have finally reached a point at which you are able to find a sense of joy, pride and dignity in being who you are.

1. An important moment takes place when you say that your eyes see things as they really are. This is the one time in the song where you allow yourself some bitterness and anger towards Shug. With this lyric you are saying that you now see Shug as she really is: someone who lets you down.

2. As suggested above, during the song Celie lists the things in life that give her strength: her sister, her children, her house, her chair, her hands, her eyes. For each of these prepare a clear image – an invented memory – that you can recall during the song. For example, you might see an image of Nettie playing games with you when you were young, or a piece of clothing from your shop that you proudly made with your own hands.

3. The event of the song occurs when Celie says that she is beautiful. If you are to perform this song successfully, it is crucial to appreciate that Celie has spent her entire life being told she is ugly. She was raped by her father, and has suffered years of abuse at the hands of Mister. Therefore for her finally to be able to value herself is the most profound discovery. It is the event, not only of the song, but also of the entire musical.

4. Celie undergoes a massive emotional journey during the song, from someone who has never made herself heard, to a woman who is newly empowered. Try reflecting this in changes to your physicality. Perhaps at the beginning of the song you could be very still, your body language may be closed off and introverted, you might find it hard to make eye contact with Shug. By the end of the song your physicality might include you stepping forward in the space and using defiant and confident gestures.

Vocal and Musical Analysis

WHO TO LISTEN TO: Cynthia Erivo on the Broadway revival cast recording (2016).

VOCAL RANGE: E3 to G5.

ORIGINAL KEY: G major.

ACCENT: General American.

STYLE OF MUSICAL: Book musical.

VOCAL SET–UP/MUSICAL TIPS

1. The beginning of the song should be delivered in a Speech quality, but with a slightly lowered larynx, to give your voice a soulful tone. The rhythmical delivery can also be quite fractured, to reflect the fact that Celie is just beginning to 'find her voice'. All of this is demonstrated by Erivo on the suggested recording.

2. When you start to sing about having got your house, your vocal delivery needs to develop, as the song has more musical momentum at this point. To increase your volume, tighten your AES slightly to add some twang to the Speech set-up, as Erivo demonstrates. Keeping the larynx slightly lowered will stop the sound becoming too shrill.

3. When you sing about showing your heart, you need to progress into a mixed belt. This complicated vocal set-up is used frequently throughout the rest of the song. To move from a Speech quality to a mixed belt you should do the following: add some torso anchoring, lift your chin slightly, remain in a thick vocal-fold set-up but add both thyroid and cricoid tilt – so the belt has a 'moaned' quality. You can hear Erivo clearly click into this position on the words 'close to' and 'are now' a few phrases later.

4. There is a long instrumental section that is not suitable for auditions and should be cut. After singing the bar that contains the words 'really are now' on p. 4 of the sheet music, you should cut all the following instrumental bars, so the piano comes back in at the bar when you sing 'I'm gonna' at the top of p. 5. You will therefore have a single sustained chord between those two phrases.

5. Try singing the words 'I'm gonna' at this point in a vulnerable Cry quality. Lift your larynx at this point, thin your vocal folds and use a good deal of thyroid tilt.

6. You should then alternate between the aforementioned Speech quality (with some twang added) and the mixed-belt set-up for the next big musical section – going into belt on the higher notes such as on the words 'sing out' and 'living'.

7. When Celie is finally able to say that she is beautiful, the vocal delivery should be very simple and exposed. Try delivering this in a breathy Speech quality, making use of some aspirate onsets. This can help convey the discovery Celie is making about herself.

8. The last three words of the song should be belted. *Note*: The riff that Erivo sings on the final note is optional. If you prefer you can choose to simply sustain the high D.

Sheet Music

The correct sheet music for this song is available at www.musicnotes.com.

'Lying There'
from *Edges*

Music and lyrics by Benj Pasek and Justin Paul

Choose this song if: you want an audition piece that allows
you to explore material with emotional and psychological
depth. The song is vocally demanding and allows you to
showcase a range of voice qualities.

Given Circumstances

Note: *Edges* is a revue show, rather than a musical with a
through-narrative. The given circumstances below, though
derived from the lyric, are therefore invented – and could be
altered to suit your needs.

WHO ARE YOU: Betsy, an emotionally conflicted woman in her
early twenties. You suffer from chronic insomnia.

WHERE ARE YOU: In the bedroom of the apartment you share
with your boyfriend.

WHEN IS IT: 4.07 a.m., a muggy weekend, summer, present day.

WHAT HAS HAPPENED BEFORE: Two years ago you were engaged
to be married to a high-flying journalist named Jerry. The
relationship was serious, and you had a date set for your
wedding, but as the day of the ceremony approached you
realised that you were not really in love with Jerry. So, with a
month to go, you broke off the engagement.

Six months later you began dating Frankie. You had known
each other throughout your engagement to Jerry – as you
were work colleagues – but you had only ever seen Frankie as
a friend. Frankie had always secretly been fond of you, and
when you became single he was very persistent in his attempts
to get you to go on a date with him. Over time he gradually
wore you down and soon you became his girlfriend.

Three months ago you moved in with Frankie. Unlike Jerry, who sometimes treated you poorly, Frankie was always the perfect gentleman and treated you as an equal and a partner. He would go out of his way to try and make you happy. In recent months you have become more and more irritated by Frankie's gentle manner, with his kind gestures only serving to annoy you. The tetchiness you feel towards him has been exacerbated by the fact you have been suffering from chronic insomnia.

This evening you came home from a shopping trip to find that Frankie had surprised you with a candlelit dinner. This lovely, thoughtful gesture perversely made you feel crabby and resentful. With a blameless Frankie unsure what was wrong, you both went to bed around eleven o'clock. After initially falling asleep, you have now been awake for the last few hours, worrying about why you always seem to react so negatively to Frankie's kindness and love.

WHO ELSE IS THERE: Frankie, but he is asleep.

WHO SHOULD YOU SING TO: At some points you sing to the sleeping Frankie, at other times to yourself.

Textual Analysis

When the introduction plays you are watching Frankie sleeping. As you have now been awake for several hours, you wish that you could also fall asleep. Your objective in the first stanza is: to make Frankie understand your need for rest. You want him to empathise with you, to appreciate how exhausted and stressed you have been feeling. For a moment you recognise how ironic it is that he is sleeping soundly when you are desperate for sleep. In the second stanza your objective then becomes: to imagine what Frankie might be dreaming about. In this section you can play gentle actions, such as: I warm, comfort, calm and soothe myself.

In the next section, which begins with the word 'despite', there is a clear musical change. The piano accompaniment becomes more restless, and this reflects your feelings of inner turmoil. Your objective at this point becomes: to vent your frustration. You do this by trying to take out your annoyance on your sleeping boyfriend. Actions you might play in this moment include: I blame, ruffle, agitate and chide Frankie.

At the start of the second verse you tell Frankie how – even though you want the relationship to work – your efforts to try to do so are wearing you down. A good objective to play at this point is: to get Frankie to agree to let you go. You want him to release you from your commitment to him so you can be at peace. The music then develops when you say the words 'you'd think'. At this point your tone becomes quite sarcastic. Your objective in this moment is as follows: to make Frankie understand that you don't feel the way he does. Try playing these actions at this juncture: I madden, awaken, defy and shake Frankie. Perhaps saying these things out loud causes you to feel genuine anger towards him for a moment.

After this brief outburst, in the bridge that follows you then begin to reflect on all of the good things about Frankie, such as his eyes. You consider for an instant whether you are about to make a mistake if you choose to end the relationship. Explore playing the following objective at this point: to find a reason to stay with Frankie. Despite your best efforts, you are unsuccessful in this objective, perhaps because tiredness and irritability overcome you (see point 3 below).

At the beginning of the third verse, you look at Frankie sleeping peacefully and realise that, even though you are having severe doubts about the relationship, it is not his fault: he has always treated you well. An objective you might play at this point is: to get Frankie to understand why you must put yourself first. This selfishness has the effect of making you feel guilty, and for a moment you want to wake Frankie in order to try and save the relationship – but you realise you can't, because you are not in love with him. In the final section you should therefore play this objective: to make peace with your decision to leave Frankie.

1. Even though in actuality Frankie would be lying down, this is hard to convey to an audition panel without another actor to sing to. When you address Frankie, imagine him at eye level standing behind the panel. If you look downwards this can appear very strange, as though you are singing to someone who is very short!

2. Even though, of course, Frankie would wake up if you were to be singing next to him in real life, the theatrical conceit is that this is an internal monologue that only the audience can hear – so Frankie sleeps soundly throughout the song.

3. The fact that Betsy is suffering from insomnia should be central to your performance. Her lack of sleep means she is short of patience.

4. An event occurs when you ask: Am I fulfilled? Play this moment as though you are taken by surprise by the question. It is something you have never considered before – and the answer to the question is: No.

5. The song requires an imaginative use of the audition space. You might wish to start the song sitting on a chair, placed at an angle in the space. This can help convey that you are sat beside a bed. You may want to play with sometimes being physically still, and at other moments moving tetchily around the room as though the claustrophobia of the situation has overtaken you.

6. A second event occurs at the end of the song when you say that you wish that you could love Frankie. This is the first time you realise that you are not in love with him.

Vocal and Musical Analysis

WHO TO LISTEN TO: Farah Alvin on the original Off-Broadway cast recording (2007).

VOCAL RANGE: G3 to E5.

ORIGINAL KEY: C major.

ACCENT: General American.

STYLE OF MUSICAL: Revue.

VOCAL SET–UP/MUSICAL TIPS

1. The opening section should be delivered in a gentle Twang quality. Sing with a tilted thyroid cartilage, a narrowed AES, and make use of simultaneous onsets to produce legato phrases.

2. When you reach the word 'despite', transition into a Speech quality. In order to achieve this take out your thyroid tilt, thicken your vocal folds and produce a louder sound.

3. For the higher notes that follow (when you say you can't sleep and breathe), add a little thyroid tilt and some torso anchoring to your set-up to progress into an Advanced Speech quality.

4. Try lifting your larynx suddenly for the phrase when you ask if you are fulfilled. This helps clarify this as a moment of self-reflection. (Use the same vocal choice near the end of the song when you say that you wish you could love Frankie.)

5. Return to a Twang quality at the start of the second verse, and then shift into a Speech quality in the next section, which starts when you repeat the words 'you'd think'. Once more you will need to use an Advanced Speech quality for the higher notes that follow.

6. When you sing about Frankie's eyes, you want to use a more romantic tone. Try singing in a sweet Twang quality and use legato phrasing at this point, as you can hear Alvin demonstrate.

7. In the phrase containing the word 'night', gradually release your thyroid tilt to thicken your folds, achieve a crescendo

CONTEMPORARY BALLADS

and move into a Speech quality. You should then anchor your torso, lift your chin slightly and tilt your cricoid cartilage so you can belt the words 'can't' and 'sleep'.

8. Start the third and final verse in a quiet Cry quality. Then, on the word 'bet', transition into a Speech quality (as described in point 7) before once more belting the highest pitches on the words 'can't' and 'sleep', as Alvin demonstrates.

9. Use a warm Twang quality for the very last line.

Sheet Music

The correct sheet music for this song is available at www.musicnotes.com.

'Now That I've Seen Her'
from *Miss Saigon*

Music by Claude-Michel Schönberg, lyrics by Alain Boublil and Richard Maltby Jr.

Choose this song if: you enjoy singing big emotional power ballads. The song gives you the opportunity to showcase a belt to an E. (*Note*: This song has also been titled 'Her Or Me', and was cut from the 2014 London production altogether and replaced with an alternative song called 'Maybe'.)

Given Circumstances

WHO ARE YOU: Ellen, the American wife of Chris, an ex-GI. You are in your early thirties. Whilst you can be caring and generous, in order to keep your husband you are also capable of being selfish and manipulative.

WHERE ARE YOU: Your hotel room (room 317) in Bangkok, Thailand.

WHEN IS IT: Afternoon, spring, 1978.

WHAT HAS HAPPENED BEFORE: In 1975, before he'd met you, your husband Chris was serving in the US army in the Vietnam War. The conflict was nearing its conclusion as the South Vietnamese army, who the USA supported, were facing defeat at the hands of Communist Vietcong. In Saigon there was an air of defeatism and resignation amongst the Americans, who had never previously lost a war in the history of their nation. Many of the soldiers were choosing to plunge headlong into a lifestyle of hedonism to escape the reality of the military situation.

In a tacky Saigon bar named Dreamland, Chris had gone drinking with his friend John. John offered to buy Chris a prostitute to cheer him up, but Chris had grown very cynical of this kind of lifestyle and wanted to be left alone. A seventeen-year-old girl named Kim had started working at the bar as a prostitute, and Chris was struck by her innocence and guilelessness. That night he went back to her place and they had sex.

The next morning Chris found he was in a state of confusion and turmoil. He realised he was falling for Kim, and he was angry that this was happening now – with him soon due to leave for home. His feelings of affection towards Kim were exacerbated when he discovered that she had been orphaned by the war and had never before slept with a man for money. When he offered payment, Kim refused. Overtaken by his impulsive feelings for Kim, Chris decided to take some leave from the army so that they could spend the next few days 'playing house' together. This was an incredibly dangerous idea, as Saigon was on the brink of falling to the Vietcong.

When he heard of Chris's plan, John wanted his friend to return to the US Embassy straight away, but Chris convinced him and, reluctantly, John covered for him for a day. During that time Chris and Kim had an improvised, unofficial Vietnamese wedding. Later that afternoon Chris returned to the Embassy to organise the paperwork necessary to take Kim back to America with him – stating that he would marry her officially as soon as they got to the United States.

Soon afterwards Chris was called back to the Embassy, and he left Kim behind to pack her belongings, as he figured they would get plenty of notice before the Vietcong mounted their final attack on Saigon. When Chris was at the Embassy the assault on the city began and the building was placed on lockdown. With Chris powerless to leave, and Kim unable to get into the compound, he was eventually forced to get in a helicopter and leave her behind.

Upon returning to the United States, Chris had an emotional breakdown. With Vietnam having fallen to the Communists, he tried desperately to find out what happened to Kim. He could get no word, and for a year barely spoke to anyone except John. However, after those difficult twelve months had passed, he met you – and soon you began a romantic relationship together. You were very patient, loving and sympathetic to what Chris had endured in Vietnam. You both fell in love and a year later were married – though Chris never told you about Kim.

A couple of months ago John, who now works for a charity who help the half-Vietnamese children of American soldiers, told Chris that he had received news of Kim. She had escaped to Bangkok, was alive, and she'd had a child called Tam. He also told him that Tam was his son. Chris agonised about whether he should tell you that he'd had a child with another woman. John convinced him that he should – and that he should bring you with him to Thailand.

The three of you arrived in Bangkok today. This morning John managed to track Kim down and told her that he would go to fetch Chris and bring him to her. Even though she was clearly still deeply in love with Chris, John chose not to tell Kim that you and Chris were now married. When Kim found out from her old pimp, who was known as The Engineer, that Chris was staying in the hotel, she decided that, rather than wait, she would go there to see him.

A few minutes ago Kim arrived at your room. She discovered you there alone, as Chris had already left to go and find her. At first you mistook her for the maid, but when she explained she was looking for Chris, you realised who she was. You then broke the news to her that Chris was your husband. She was devastated. When you informed her that you and Chris had agreed to offer financial assistance for Tam, Kim instead begged you to take her son to America with you – so he could have a better life. You said that was impossible. Moments ago Kim just yelled in your face. She still believes that Chris is her husband, and she said that if he will not take Tam to America, then he must come to her place tonight and tell her so to her face. She has just left, leaving you shell-shocked.

WHO ELSE IS THERE: You are alone.

WHO SHOULD YOU SING TO: Yourself, though in an audition you can share many of your thoughts with the panel as though they are your inner-consciousness.

Textual Analysis

When the song begins you are in shock. You have just heard these revelations about Kim and Chris's past (see point 1) and you don't know how you to take them. Your objective in the first stanza is: to make sense of your emotional response. Chris's secrecy has left you feeling betrayed, and you are struggling to come to terms with it. You quickly realise that you must snap out of this mood, and in the second stanza your objective becomes: to pull yourself together. Actions you might play at this point include: I galvanise, sustain and embolden myself. You are successful in this objective, so in the first chorus you show much more resolve. You now realise that Kim is a threat to your marriage, and therefore cannot simply be ignored. Try playing the following objective at this point: to make yourself face up to reality. You now know that another woman loves your husband, and she will do all she can to win him back. You might try the following actions in the first chorus: I awaken, activate and spur myself.

During the bridge you begin to reflect on what meeting Kim was like. You analyse your impressions of her behaviour and expressions. Your objective at this point is: to decide what Kim's true feelings are towards Chris. You conclude that they clearly both loved each other – so you must be prepared to fight for your husband (see point 2 below).

Meeting Kim has made you face up to a massive problem with your marriage: Chris has been keeping secrets since he first met you. Your objective in the final chorus thus becomes: to resolve to have it out with Chris. You decide you are going to make him share his experiences of Vietnam – even if doesn't want to – because you now believe that if he is not able to be honest, then your marriage may not survive.

1. It is highly significant that Ellen did not know about the improvised wedding ceremony that took place between Chris and Kim. Whilst she was prepared to take Chris's child into her life, she has now learned that her husband has been harbouring a massive secret. During the song she is forced to consider whether she can now trust him.

2. An event occurs when you swear that you will fight. At this moment you decide that you will battle to keep Chris, and that you are prepared to be ruthless in order to get what you want.

3. In the musical Chris returns at the end of the song, and he and Ellen then have a huge argument. We should feel that, by the conclusion of the number, you have readied yourself to confront him.

4. Ellen says during the song that she doesn't hate Kim. It is interesting to explore the prospect that she is not being truthful with herself when she makes this statement. What if she actually has something of a vindictive nature and resents Kim as the ex-lover of her husband? That can be very interesting to play.

Vocal and Musical Analysis

WHO TO LISTEN TO: Clare Burt on the original London cast recording (1989).

VOCAL RANGE: F♯3 to E5.

ORIGINAL KEY: E major.

ACCENT: General American.

STYLE OF MUSICAL: Contemporary (pop-based).

1. The first verse of the song should be quiet and reflective. Try singing the section in a Cry quality, with a raised larynx and thin vocal folds. This opening part of the song also wants to sound conversational – so make use of aspirate onsets and short note-endings to achieve this tone.

2. In the line containing the word 'truth', you want to begin to build in intensity as you progress towards the first chorus. To achieve this, shift into using only simultaneous onsets to make the phrasing smooth, connected and legato – and gradually remove your thyroid tilt to thicken your folds and effect a crescendo.

3. The first chorus should be delivered in a rich Speech quality – but still maintaining the legato phrasing you have just established.

4. During the second verse, repeat the vocal set-ups used in the first, i.e. start in a Cry quality, then initiate a crescendo on the last two lines. However, this time deliver the entire verse with legato phrasing to achieve a sense of musical development.

5. The remainder of the song should be delivered in a strong Speech quality.

6. The word 'lied' should be belted. Remember to anchor your torso, lift your chin slightly and tilt your cricoid cartilage at this point.

Sheet Music

The correct sheet music for this song is available at www.musicnotes.com. (*Note*: There are two versions available with differing lyrics. This version begins with the words: 'There are days'.)

'Out of Love'
from *Adventures in Love*

Music by Zina Goldrich, lyrics by Marcy Heisler

Choose this song if: you are looking for a number with subtle and detailed acting content. The song deals with the break-up of a relationship, but the storytelling involves humour and irony, as well as pathos. As the song sits comfortably in a speech register, it is suitable for an actress who sings.

Given Circumstances

Note: *Adventures in Love* is a revue show, rather than a musical with a through-narrative. The given circumstances below, though derived from the lyric, are therefore invented – and could be altered to suit your needs.

WHO ARE YOU: Fiona, a sensitive, heartbroken woman in her mid-twenties. You are a romantic at heart, but have the ability to view the world with pragmatism and perspective.

WHERE ARE YOU: In the living room of the apartment you used to share with your ex-partner in New York City, USA.

WHEN IS IT: 11.32 a.m., a Saturday, autumn, present day.

WHAT HAS HAPPENED BEFORE: Two years ago you started a new job in a junior post of a major law firm. After being in the position for a few months, you began to have a relationship with one of the young lawyers, whose name was Tom. This was not your first major relationship, having had three others in the last five years, but after six months it felt like the most important of your life – and so you moved in with Tom.

Although you were both a little concerned that working and living together might put a strain on your relationship, in fact the first three months went incredibly well. After that initial honeymoon period, Tom got promoted, and this led to him travelling away from home a lot. You never had any major arguments, there was no infidelity that you knew of, but gradually you sensed a growing distance between you.

A month ago Tom confessed that he felt he had fallen out of love with you. You didn't feel ready to end the relationship and tried everything you could to salvage it. But Tom had made up his mind. Last week he told you that he thought it best that you move out. You then spent a few days staying at your best friend Jenny's place. Today, with Tom away for the weekend with work, you have returned to the apartment to pack the last of your belongings.

WHO ELSE IS THERE: You are alone.

WHO SHOULD YOU SING TO: The audience – which in this situation is the audition panel.

Textual Analysis

You start the song by commenting ironically on some of the practicalities that occur at the end of a relationship, like the packing of belongings and cleaning of closets. Your objective in this first section is: to normalise the break-up. You want to convince the audience that you are coping well with the separation. Try playing light actions in this section such as: I amuse, humour and entertain the audience. In the last two lines of the first verse a new unit occurs – and you should play a different objective: to convince the audience that you put everything you had into the failed relationship.

You are finding life disorientating now that you are single again - as you are unsure of what to do with your time, or how to make sense of yet another break-up. Your objective in the second verse is therefore: to test out your break-up theories on the audience. You want them to tell you if the assumptions and solutions that are buzzing around your head are correct. At this point try exploring actions such as: I question, interview and query the audience.

A significant flip occurs in the first bridge, when you suddenly start addressing Tom – even though he is not present.

Bitterness rises to the surface and you feel resentment towards him. At this point you can explore playing the following objective: to provoke Tom into a confrontation. Actions that might be suitable at this point include: I aggravate, antagonise, mock, infuriate and nag Tom. Of course, this objective is futile, as Tom is not present – it is an imagined conversation that you would like to have with your ex-boyfriend.

Your message in the final verse is a positive one: that we learn from the painful things that happen to us in life. Try playing the following objective in this section: to convince the audience to be positive in the face of adversity. You could try some of the following actions here: I inspire, uplift, hearten and cheer the audience. In the second half of the verse, you reveal how challenging you have found the break-up. Your objective in this final section, until the surprising reverse on the last line (see point 3 below), is: to get the audience to pity you.

KEY MOMENTS/TOP TIPS

1. When singing in direct address it is important to make a decision about who the audience are in your imagination. In this situation try pretending that the panel are a group of girlfriends of a similar age to you. They are people you can confide in – but whom you can also advise. You can share with them the lessons that life has taught you.

2. It is tricky to make it clear that you are suddenly talking to Tom in the bridge section. As these lyrics are quite confrontational, it is not appropriate to address them to a member of the panel. Instead deliver this section to an imaginary Tom standing behind the audition table, or into the air as though you are half-talking to yourself.

3. The event of the song occurs when you say that you are currently functioning with only half of a soul. At this moment we should finally understand the depths of your feelings for Tom.

4. The last line provides an interesting and surprising conclusion to the song. In this moment, we should realise that, although Fiona has just confessed how hard she has found the break-up, she is now trying to deny what she just said. She pretends that what she has just told us is from hearsay, rather than personal experience.

Vocal and Musical Analysis

WHO TO LISTEN TO: Natalie Weiss in the cabaret show *Marcy and Zina and Friends: The Songs of Goldrich and Heisler* (2017).

VOCAL RANGE: A3 to C♯5.

ORIGINAL KEY: A major.

ACCENT: General American.

STYLE OF MUSICAL: Revue.

VOCAL SET-UP/MUSICAL TIPS

1. For the purposes of an audition, the introduction is too long. You should cut the first four bars to leave a four-bar introduction.

2. The voice quality suitable for almost the entire song is Speech. On the higher notes, however, you will need to modify your musculature to move into an Advanced Speech set-up. In order to do this, you should add a little torso anchoring and some thyroid tilt to give a slight moaned quality to your sound. You can hear Weiss demonstrate this set-up when she sings about there being so many ways of being beaten into the ground.

3. The tone of the song should be very conversational. To achieve this it is appropriate to cut the note-lengths short, half-speak some words and make use of aspirate and glottal onsets. You can hear Weiss make use of all of these technical approaches on the suggested recording.

4. In the final verse you want your sound to be quieter and more reflective than previously. To achieve this, try using lots of aspirate onsets to take you into a breathy Speech quality, as Weiss chooses to do in her performance. You can hear this clearly when she sings about functioning with half of a soul.

5. Try delivering the next line – about wanting to scream – in a Cry quality. Use simultaneous onsets to run the vowels together, a tilted thyroid cartlage, a raised larynx and thin vocal folds. This will help portray the character's vulnerability in that moment.

Sheet Music

The correct sheet music for this song is available at www.musicnotes.com.

CONTEMPORARY BALLADS

'Wait a Bit'
from *Just So*

Music by George Stiles, lyrics by Anthony Drewe

Choose this song if: you enjoy playing characters who are on a journey of self-discovery, and want to sing a number that requires a variety of different voice qualities – including belt. (*Note*: The musical is based on the *Just So Stories* by Rudyard Kipling.)

Given Circumstances

WHO ARE YOU: The Kolokolo Bird. As a flightless species, you often feel like an outsider, and dream of being able to soar like the other birds.

WHERE ARE YOU: In a jungle in South Africa.

WHEN IS IT: The original stories are set in 'the High and Far-Off Times', which suggests that the song is set in a fantastical time. As Kipling's book was published in 1902, you might suppose the song is set in the early-Edwardian era. It is afternoon, summer.

WHAT HAS HAPPENED BEFORE: You were first brought into existence by the Eldest Magician – who created all of the animals. At the moment of creation he bid all of his creatures to venture out into the world and play together – so they could learn who they truly are. You all obeyed his command except Pau Amma, the crab, who decided to be disobedient and play only by himself. Skulking in the deepest waters, he grew so large that soon the Eldest Magician could no longer control him. Twice a day Pau Amma would go hunting for food and in doing so would flood the land, as he had grown as tall as the smoke of three volcanoes.

A few weeks ago the elephants gathered around the watering hole to discuss the problem of the giant crab. Their gathering was interrupted by Elephant's Child who bombarded them with questions that they found to be a nuisance. When the elephants heard the sound of Pau Amma approaching, they decided to head for higher ground, away from the flooding. Elephant's Child concluded that he wouldn't hide, instead he would track down the giant crab and try to make him stop. The Eldest Magician encouraged you to join Elephant's Child on this quest, and you both set out for the far-off Limpopo River. When Pau Amma caused another flood you both jumped into a treetrunk, which you used as boat. This boat was to take you on a series of adventures – where you met various other creatures that had suffered because of the giant crab. Eventually these adventures led you to the High Veldt, where your group was joined by Giraffe and Zebra, who were fleeing from the predatory Leopard and Jaguar.

Your continuing search then took the four of you into a great jungle. There Elephant's Child discovered how the jungle light could camouflage the animals below – and prayed to the Eldest Magician to help him make magic. The Eldest Magician responded by causing the beams of light to fall in a manner that hid Giraffe and Zebra from their hunters. In doing so the light permanently changed their hides, giving them their distinctive stripes.

The animals of the High Veldt, upon hearing of Giraffe and Zebra's extraordinary transformation, came to the jungle and were themselves transfigured in their own special ways. The Eldest Magician was delighted, as this was exactly what he had always intended: that each animal should have its individuality. Elated with the way they now looked, the animals decided to hold a huge party. The celebrations were interrupted by the arrival of Pau Amma. When Elephant's Child politely asked the crab to stop terrorising the other animals, Pau Amma responded by saying he would do no such thing. Instead he would step up his hunting sprees to seven times a day. With Elephant's Child feeling that he had made matters worse, you stepped in with words of encouragement. You urged him to continue the journey to the Limpopo River, and promised that you would help him find a solution to defeating Pau Amma.

The journey ahead was difficult, and soon you lost your way. You have just had a heated argument with Elephant's Child, as he blamed you for losing the path. In retort you mocked him, saying that he had no idea how to stop Pau Amma – even if you did manage to find him. This served to make Elephant's Child more argumentative. He has just called you a freak for being a bird that can't fly – before running off, leaving you feeling alone and forlorn.

WHO ELSE IS THERE: You are alone.

WHO SHOULD YOU SING TO: Yourself, though in an audition you can share many of your thoughts with the panel as though they are your inner-consciousness.

Textual Analysis

During the musical introduction you are reflecting upon the criticisms you have just received from Elephant's Child. They have left you feeling rejected and deflated, which leads you to play your first objective, which is: to find out what is wrong with you. You want to comprehend why you are failure in life. Actions you might play at this juncture include: I cross-examine, study, scrutinise and interrogate myself. This thought process develops in the third and fourth lines of the opening verse, which form a new unit. Your objective in this unit is: to understand why you never take action to resolve your problems. You want to appreciate what it is about your personality that leads you to hold yourself back. Having grown a little frustrated with yourself, in the first chorus you then ridicule yourself for never trying to fly. Your objective at this point is: to mock your own failings. Try playing the following actions here: I deride, shame and satirise myself.

In the second verse you then ask some fundamental questions of yourself. You explore the idea that perhaps you don't have what it takes to fulfil your dreams: maybe you will never be able to fly. Your objective at this point is: to work out if you are good enough. In pursuing this objective, you are trying to decide if you should give up on your ambition of flight, or continue to strive for what you want. This unit continues into the second chorus (until you ask yourself if you are just not fit to fly). After this lyric, you then begin to reflect on a moment when you stood on the edge of the cliff, and had the chance to jump off and fly – but froze. Try playing the following objective in this moment: to comprehend why you held yourself back.

After this moment you watch some other birds fly past (see point 3 below), and are filled with a renewed sense of hope and purpose. Your objective for the final section of the song thus becomes: to stiffen your resolve. You affirm to yourself the newfound belief that you will fly one day – you just need to be patient.

KEY MOMENTS/TOP TIPS

1. Because the song frequently involves you asking questions of yourself, there is a danger that your performance can become too introspective for an audition. A way to circumvent this problem is to ask those questions of the panel, as though they are able to offer you help and advice. Make the text a dialogue, rather than a monologue.

2. It is important to be clear that in the chorus, when you refer to things that 'she says', you are talking about yourself. You are criticising yourself for the negative thoughts that often run through your head.

3. During the instrumental section, imagine that you see a passing flight of birds. This sight should set off a complex set of reactions within yourself. These including feelings of melancholy, but more importantly, seeing the other birds provides you with a sense of hope that one day you may fly yourself.

4. The journey of the song should involve you moving from feelings of deflation and self-doubt to a renewed sense of purpose. In the final line, when the Kolokola Bird resolves

CONTEMPORARY BALLADS

to wait a little more, try playing that moment as if you now believe that your future will be a positive one. This is the event of the song.

Vocal and Musical Analysis

WHO TO LISTEN TO: Julie Atherton on the world premiere cast recording (2006).

VOCAL RANGE: F♯3 to D5.

ORIGINAL KEY: E major.

ACCENT: The song can work well in a variety of British regional accents. A Yorkshire dialect, as demonstrated by Atherton on the suggested recording, is a good example of a successful choice.

STYLE OF MUSICAL: Book musical.

VOCAL SET-UP/MUSICAL TIPS

1. The first verse and chorus should be sung with a sense of vulnerability and reflectiveness. Trying delivering this section in a Cry quality with a raised larynx and your thyroid tilted. In particular, ensure you maintain this lifted set-up on lower pitches, such as at the beginning of the chorus. During this section you may also explore using some aspirate onsets on certain words to give the voice a thoughtful quality.

2. Deliver the start of the second verse in a Speech quality with thicker vocal folds. This will make you a little louder than first time around and give the song a sense of progression.

3. On the third line of the second verse (when you sing about your expectations not being great), try lifting your larynx and suddenly tilting your thyroid cartilage to make the line much quieter and more introspective. You can then take the tilt out and thicken your vocal folds on the last few

words of the verse to arrive back in a Speech quality in time for the start of the second chorus. To help yourself really 'land' in this quality, try employing some small glottal onsets on the words 'am' and 'I'.

4. The words 'fledge' and 'edge' that occur just before the instrumental should be belted. To achieve these top notes, add some torso anchoring and raise your chin slightly during the preceding line so you are already in the correct physical position. You then need to tilt your cricoid cartilage.

5. The instrumental section is too long for an audition. You should cut bars 71 to 73.

6. The first phrase after the instrumental section should be sung very quietly in a Cry position. Crescendo gradually during the following line by slowly tightening the AES so that by the time you reach the highest phrase (about him making you feel like you can soar) you are in a loud Twang quality. After you have sung the word 'soar', immediately relax the AES so you can sing the last two lines in a sweet and gentle Cry quality.

Sheet Music

The correct sheet music for this song is available at www.scribd.com.

'Where is the Warmth?'
from *The Baker's Wife*

Music and lyrics by Stephen Schwartz

Choose this song if: you have a rich alto voice and can belt to a
C♯. The song is originally written for an actress in her late
twenties and enables you to explore a character who is
unhappy in her love affair and consequently is about to make
a life-changing decision.

Given Circumstances

WHO ARE YOU: Genevieve Castagnet, the beautiful younger
wife of Aimable, a middle-aged baker. You are bored by your
provincial life and long for adventure.

WHERE ARE YOU: A hotel room in a rural village in Provence,
France.

WHEN IS IT: Early afternoon, October 1935.

WHAT HAS HAPPENED BEFORE: In September you moved from
Marseilles to a sleepy provincial village with your husband –
who had come to fill the vacant post of local baker. The job
had been unfilled for seven weeks after the previous
incumbent died, so your arrival had been eagerly anticipated
by the villagers, who had been without bread for that entire
period. When you both arrived you were greeted by the
Marquis, who mistook you for Aimable's daughter. Despite
the embarrassment this made you feel, it didn't dampen your
husband's mood as he was very optimistic about the new
bakery. This was the first time you had both owned your own
home, and the new appointment meant you would no longer
have to work as a waitress, as you had done previously.
Despite his optimism about work, your husband had a
tendency to fret about your relationship. Often he would fuss
over you needlessly, and tell you that he loved you so

frequently that you would have to remind him that you were already his, and he didn't need to be so clingy.

The bakery opened the day after your arrival and was a great success; the villagers were delighted with the bread that Aimable produced. After they had passed on their congratulations at the opening, the villagers' conversation returned to the relationship between you and your husband. Some of the men of the village joked about his good fortune, but you stood up for him by reminding them that your husband had not just selected you – you had also chosen him.

When left alone afterwards you reflected that with this marriage you had much to be grateful for. Your previous relationship had been an affair with a married man named Paul – which had left you deeply unhappy. Having just determined to commit your heart anew to Aimable, your resolve was then tested by the arrival of a handsome young man named Dominique. He was the chauffeur of the Marquis and had been sent to the bakery to fetch his employer's order. Like the Marquis himself, he at first mistook you for Aimable's daughter. When you corrected him, he was incredulous that you should have chosen to marry a much older man. Dominique then began to make subtle advances on you – which you somewhat unconvincingly rebuffed.

Two weeks later you encountered Dominique again in the village square. He had been pursuing you on a daily basis since you first met, and he once more tried to seduce you. Yet again you refused him. That evening, when you were in bed with Aimable, your persistent suitor came to your bedroom window to sing a serenade. Your husband mistakenly thought Dominique was singing in praise of his bread, but you realised his true intentions. When you went downstairs in order to send him away, Dominique kissed you, and finally persuaded you to run away with him that night.

Next morning, when he discovered your disappearance, at first Aimable refused to believe that you had abandoned him – so he told everyone that you had simply gone to visit your mother. Over the next few weeks, after he had accepted you had really gone, he began to turn to drink. But as he was on the verge of letting his business fall apart, Aimable instead resolved to live his life with dignity, even if that meant being without you.

Today you have spent the morning making love to Dominique in a hotel room in a nearby village. Despite the strong sexual attraction you feel towards him, you have recently begun to feel uneasy about the relationship. A few moments ago Dominique suggested that you both move to Paris. You were reluctant, because you had started to intuit that you don't want to be away from your husband. In this reflective state you have just spotted a girl outside the window. She was carrying a cat that resembled the one you used to keep with Aimable – whose name was Pompom. When you tried to explain that you missed Pompom – because you used to have make-believe conversations with her – Dominique failed to understand why this was important to you. You have just turned back to look at him and have discovered that he has fallen asleep whilst you were pouring out your heart to him.

WHO ELSE IS THERE: Dominique – though he is asleep so he can't hear you.

WHO SHOULD YOU SING TO: Yourself, though in an audition you can share many of your thoughts with the panel as though they are your inner-consciousness.

Textual Analysis

When the song begins you are focused on Dominique – your sleeping Adonis. He is most likely naked and you can see his beautiful face and muscular chest. In the opening stanza of the first verse your objective is: to revel in his good looks. You find him incredibly attractive and, even with the internal tensions you are experiencing about the relationship, he still has a powerful sexual effect on you. In the final line of the verse, when you sing the title lyric, your objective changes and you ask the key question of the song. Your objective is: to discover if Dominique really loves you.

As you progress to the second verse, you start to reflect on how Dominique and yourself are perceived as a couple. Try talking directly to the panel at this point. Your objective in the first stanza of this second verse (when you ask them to look at the pair of you) is: to get the panel to acknowledge that you are a dazzling couple. You are beginning to realise that this superficial reasoning is not a strong enough motive for you to stay with your lover. In the second stanza of the verse, your objective thus becomes: to get the audience to confess that they can tell that you're unhappy.

During the bridge there is a feeling of momentum. Your thoughts start to rush more quickly through your mind, and your objective changes once again. In this section you want to work out if you feel love for Dominique, as well as passion. In a key moment of discovery you discover that you don't – your feelings for him are purely sexual.

Having reached this conclusion you then turn on yourself in the third verse. Your objective at this point becomes: to make a mockery of yourself. You feel that you should be overjoyed to be with Dominique, but instead your mood is perversely wintery and cold. Try playing actions such as I shame, deride and ridicule myself in this section. You then repeat the title lyric twice. In this moment, try playing the following objective: I want to decide if I should be in this relationship. The event of the song then occurs: you conclude that you want to go back to Aimable. In the final three lines, try playing the following objective: to bid farewell to Dominique.

CONTEMPORARY BALLADS

KEY MOMENTS/TOP TIPS

1. Although in reality Dominique is asleep in the bed, this is difficult to convey in audition. When you sing about the way he looks, which you do frequently, imagine your lover is standing behind the table at eye level. If you look downwards at an imaginary bed it can look peculiar.

2. Metaphors about temperature are the key to the lyric. 'Fire' and the fact you are 'feverish' are both synonyms for sexual passion. This contrasts with the word 'warmth' which in this context is used to mean love. References to 'December' and 'snow' symbolise the cold detachment you feel at times towards Dominique.

3. At the end of the scene Genevieve exits, leaving Dominique sleeping. To convey this, you may want to walk away towards a corner at the back of the space during the final bar of music to punctuate the end of the narrative.

Vocal and Musical Analysis

WHO TO LISTEN TO: Patti LuPone on the original cast recording (1976).

VOCAL RANGE: G♯3 to C♯5.

ORIGINAL KEY: A major.

ACCENT: General American.

STYLE OF MUSICAL: Contemporary musical (pop-based).

VOCAL SET–UP/MUSICAL TIPS

1. The first two verses of the song should be very conversational. Use a Speech quality and sing with short note-endings and minimal vibrato, as LuPone demonstrates on the suggested recording.

2. The bridge, when you talk about being feverish, should have a feeling of momentum – so you might wish to push the tempo forward at this point (though this is not the case on the cast recording).

3. When you sing about feeling that the fire is there in the relationship, the top notes should be belted, as should the word 'man' near the end of the song. Remember to tilt your cricoid cartilage, lift your larynx, raise your chin slightly and add some torso anchoring at these points.

4. The unusual section of instrumental music near the end of the song (where you can hear bells in the accompaniment) is very important. It signifies the event of the song – where Genevieve decides to leave Dominique and return to her husband. Try to mark this with a change of inner tempo – you should feel as though your heartbeat is quicker and your mind is racing at this point.

5. The final note is scored to be sung quietly (in a Cry quality). As an alternative, you may wish to belt this line instead, as LuPone does on the recording.

Sheet Music

The correct sheet music for this song is available www.musicnotes.com.

'Woman'
from *The Pirate Queen*

*Music by Claude-Michel Schönberg, lyrics by Alain Boublil
and John Dempsey*

Choose this song if: you enjoy playing dynamic, passionate,
articulate women. The song offers the opportunity to
showcase a strong alto voice – with the use of Twang,
Advanced Speech and Belt qualities.

Given Circumstances

Note: *The Pirate Queen* references some real-life historical
figures and events, but for narrative purposes, liberties were
taken by the authors with the timeline of events. The given
circumstances that appear below therefore work within the
context of the show, but are not always historically accurate.

WHO ARE YOU: Grace O'Malley, daughter of Dubdhara – the
leader of the O'Malley Clan. You are feisty, independent and
opinionated, and long to be a sailor like your father.

WHERE ARE YOU: Clew Bay, County Mayo, Ireland.

WHEN IS IT: 10.07 a.m., spring, 1558.

WHAT HAS HAPPENED BEFORE: Recently King Henry VIII of
England decided to conquer Ireland. This aggression
prompted the various feuding clans of Ireland to take arms
against him. As part of this action the O'Malley Clan of
seafarers and pirates – led by your father – decided to plunder
English treasure ships returning from India, China and the
Caribbean.

Yesterday your father christened a new ship: *The Pirate
Queen*. As he was preparing to set sail you were playing
around in the rigging with Tiernan, a sailor and another
member of the clan, with whom you are secretly in love.

When your father caught you he was displeased, as he was afraid that you would fall and hurt yourself. (Your mother died when you were very young, leaving your father to raise you on his own. As a consequence he has always been overprotective of you, as this incident demonstrates.) Despite your father's displeasure, you pleaded with him to be allowed to join the expedition. Your entreaties were dismissed – because you are female.

Your father has just sent you to shore with the other women. On the shoreline you have been remonstrating with Tiernan about your father's decision, rightly arguing that you are as capable a sailor as he is – and that the only reason you are not being allowed to sail is because of your sex.

WHO ELSE IS THERE: Tiernan.

WHO SHOULD YOU SING TO: Tiernan.

Textual Analysis

Despite your urgent desire to join the ship on its maiden voyage, at the beginning of the song your arguments are controlled and considered. You are extremely articulate. In the first verse your objective is: to get Tiernan to appreciate the obstacles a woman faces. You want him to understand that the freedoms he takes for granted are not available to you, and that a woman faces many additional challenges if she wants to pursue her ambitions in a male-dominated world. During this section you might play actions such as: I question, cross-examine, awaken, sober and stimulate Tiernan.

At the start of the first chorus you tell your lover that you long for adventure in your life. Your objective at this point is: to get Tiernan to take your ambitions seriously. You want him to acknowledge that your desires are as valid as his. In the middle of the chorus you then demand very directly that Tiernan should look you in the face. Try playing the following objective at this point: to get Tiernan to see you as you really are. You want him to appreciate that you are not like the other women in the clan who are willing to be subservient to the men in their lives.

You start the second verse by making a point about sexual equality. In fact, this is a very modern point of view for a woman from the sixteenth century. Your objective here is: to convince Tiernan that you are as good a pirate and sailor as he is. Having forced him to acknowledge this truth, you can then play this objective in the second half of the verse: to get Tiernan to agree that sexism against women is unfair. You want him to concede that it is unjust that he has the freedom to do precisely what he wishes, whereas you are denied the same liberties. With you now in the full flow of your argument, you should try the following objective in the final chorus: to convince Tiernan to help you become a sailor. You might try actions such as: I inspire, rally, provoke, uplift and challenge Tiernan. These fervent proclamations lead to the event of the song, which occurs on the final line, when you resolve that nothing will stand in the way of your ambition. (In the next stage of the story you secretly stow yourself away on the ship – thus beginning a series of events that will eventually lead to you becoming the captain of *The Pirate Queen*.)

KEY MOMENTS/TOP TIPS

1. A useful supposition that can help you act the song well is to imagine that Tiernan is reluctant to agree with you. During your performance, imagine you are speaking to a man who does not want to listen. Picture Tiernan walking away from you, laughing at your ideas, dismissing you with a gesture of the hand. Such images will give you the impulses necessary to argue with vigour.

2. In the musical, as in real life, Grace goes on to be a famous and successful captain of a pirate ship. This would suggest she was physically capable. To reflect this fact, make your performance physically dynamic. Don't be afraid to move boldly in the space or make use of strong, committed gestures. To counterbalance this, you can also convey Grace's natural sense of authority through stillness at times.

3. There are two possible previous circumstances you could pursue with regard to the information you share with Tiernan. Firstly, you could suppose that these are arguments that you have had with him before. It is perhaps more interesting to imagine that you have never shared these feelings out loud to anyone, that they have been bottled up inside you for years. This second version may help give your arguments more urgency.

4. In the script there is some spoken dialogue that occurs after the first chorus. This should be cut, although this means that there is a short piece of instrumental music during which you are not speaking. You need to make a choice about what to do with that music. One possibility is that you are so exasperated at the end of the first chorus (when you say that you would rather be damned to hell than not fulfil your potential) that you walk away from Tiernan during the instrumental music before deciding to come back and win your argument. In the audition, try storming off towards a back corner of the room, before coming back to address your imaginary Tiernan (who should be located behind the panel) just in time to deliver the second verse.

CONTEMPORARY BALLADS

Vocal and Musical Analysis

WHO TO LISTEN TO: Stephanie J. Block on the original Broadway cast recording (2007).

VOCAL RANGE: E3 to E4.

ORIGINAL KEY: A minor.

ACCENT: An Irish accent would be appropriate for this song, but many of the Broadway cast chose to sing in Received Pronunciation – so if you struggle with Irish accents, that is an alternative option.

STYLE OF MUSICAL: Contemporary musical (legit-based).

VOCAL SET-UP/MUSICAL TIPS

1. The two verses should be delivered in a breathy Speech quality, as Block demonstrates on the suggested recording. To create this sound, use a conventional Speech quality – with a horizontal thyroid cartilage, a neutral larynx and a neutral tongue position – but mix in aspirate onsets to give your singing a sense of urgency.

2. Towards the end of the first verse, you ask why you should deny yourself. Try lifting your larynx, thinning your vocal folds and singing this lyric very quietly in a Cry quality, as Block chooses to do in her own performance. This gives that particular moment a feeling of introspection that is entirely appropriate.

3. In the choruses your sound should be based around a conventional Speech quality. However, some of the higher notes will not sound or feel comfortable in that set-up. On these phrases you should tilt your thyroid, thin your vocal folds and tighten your AES to progress into a Twang quality. You can hear Block use this set-up when she sings about being damned to hell. Work to blend the Speech and Twang qualities as much as possible so your choices sound like 'one voice'.

4. Twice you sing the word 'I' on a sustained high note: in the middle of the song and on the last note. Both of these moments should be delivered in a Belt quality. Remember to tilt your cricoid cartilage, lift your larynx, raise your chin slightly and add some torso anchoring at these points.

5. In the section that leads up to the final belt, there are several of the highest notes in the song. These can either be delivered in an Advanced Speech quality, as Block does on the word 'beckoned', or in a Twang quality, which she uses when singing about staying below. The set-up for Twang has been previously described. If you employ an Advanced Speech quality you should anchor your torso, stay in a thick vocal-fold set-up, but add a little thyroid tilt and lift your chin slightly.

6. Block employs a pop style in elements of her performance, by gliding between notes on occasion. If this is not to your taste, you could deliver a performance that avoids pop-glides.

Sheet Music

The correct sheet music for this song is available at www.musicnotes.com.

'Astonishing'
from *Little Women*

Music by Jason Howland, lyrics by Mindi Dickstein

Choose this song if: you enjoy playing driven, intelligent, single-minded, dynamic women. This song gives you the opportunity to showcase a powerhouse contemporary musical-theatre voice.

Given Circumstances

WHO ARE YOU: Josephine (Jo) March, a nineteen-year-old would-be writer. You are an optimistic, self-motivated, independent and inspiring feminist – though you can be prone to moments of self-doubt.

WHERE ARE YOU: The attic of the March family home in Concord, Massachusetts, USA.

WHEN IS IT: 3.00 p.m., a weekday afternoon, May 1865.

WHAT HAS HAPPENED BEFORE: Two years ago on Christmas Eve 1863, in the midst the American Civil War, you were in the attic of your family home. You were trying to convince your sisters Meg, Beth and Amy to help you put on a show you had written: an 'operatic tragedy'. You hoped this would brighten the mood in the household – particularly for your mother Marmee, as she was very worried about your father, who was away working as a chaplain in the Union army.

In the New Year you went to visit your wealthy Great-Aunt March. Whilst you were there, she reprimanded you for spending your time writing what she considered to be frivolous stories. She told that you should instead be focusing on finding yourself a husband, a suggestion that you did not welcome, as you said you would never marry. You were tempted by her promise that if you changed your tomboy-like manner – and learned to behave like a proper lady – then she would take you to Europe. You had always felt that visiting Europe would help your development as an author.

When February came you were invited to Annie Moffat's Valentine's Day Ball where you met Laurie, the grandson of your neighbour, Mr Laurence. Laurie was attracted to you, and after some initial resistance on your part he managed to charm you into dancing with him. You very much enjoyed his company, but after you returned home, you discovered that your youngest sister Amy had burned the manuscript of a story you had written. She had done so because she was jealous that you had been invited to the ball and she had not. You immediately rushed up to the attic to rewrite your work.

As the end of winter approached, Laurie came to visit. He hoped to distract you from your writing by taking you skating. When you eventually agreed, Meg encouraged Amy to follow you both. Amy did so as she wanted to make amends for her previous behaviour. Disaster nearly struck when your sister fell through the ice. Fortunately Laurie was on hand to save her – and the aftermath of the averted crisis allowed yourself and Amy the opportunity to clear the air.

In the March of 1865 your mother left for Washington because your father had been struck down with pneumonia. With money very short, you'd been forced to sell your hair in order to pay for the train ticket. When your great-aunt found out what you'd done, she voiced her disapproval, and said that now she would no longer take you to Europe.

Two months have now passed and, with the war ended, Laurie has just come to visit from Boston. He told you that his father had enrolled him in college, but that he didn't want to go because he'd prefer to stay in Concord with you. Then he proposcd. You reacted very badly to this, reminding him that you had said you would never marry. As you felt that you had always been clear about this, and with you now feeling that Laurie doesn't really understand you, you have just ordered him to leave.

WHO ELSE IS THERE: You are alone.

CONTEMPORARY UP–TEMPO

WHO SHOULD YOU SING TO: Yourself, though in an audition you can share many of your thoughts with the panel as though they are your inner-consciousness.

Textual Analysis

The driving staccato introduction reflects your mood at the beginning of the song: you are furious. As a committed feminist, you had sworn that you would never compromise your aspirations by marrying a man. You felt that Laurie understood and respected that choice, so you are fuming about his proposal. Your objective in the first section is: to vent your anger. The second, third and fourth stanzas form a new unit. Your objective in this section is: to work out how this eventuality transpired. Actions such as: I cross-examine, interrogate and grill myself are good choices at this point. With you feeling very much alone, during the second verse you then play a clear and painful objective: to wish that your sisters were here with you. This is the lowest point of your life, and more than anything you want them here to offer their support.

The music slows significantly for the next section and you enter a moment of deep contemplation and self-examination. Your objective in this unit is: to work out what your next step should be. You don't yet know where life's path will lead you, but you are aware that you have a burning desire to make an exceptional mark on the world. You want to be astonishing.

You begin the next section by asserting your belief that there is a life that you are meant to lead. Your objective at this point is: to galvanise yourself into action. You are ambitious, and by voicing your ambitions out loud you try to ensure that you will act on those instincts. Useful actions to try in this section include: I encourage, uplift, spark and invigorate myself. After the event of the song (see point 4 below), you then play a joyful objective till the end of the song: to envision yourself being successful in the future. You pursue this intention in order to banish all self-doubt and give yourself the courage you need to face the difficult challenges that undoubtedly lie ahead.

KEY MOMENTS/TOP TIPS

1. A significant factor when performing the song is to consider the external stresses that Jo is under. Her father is very sick, her mother has left her alone for the first time in her life, and she has just had to sell her hair through poverty. These pressures undoubtedly make her quick of temper.

2. An important aspect of the song is its setting. The attic is a place where you nurtured your dreams as a writer and shared many happy times with your sisters. When you refer to your surroundings in the song, picture them clearly and imbue them with the quality of memory – this is where your sisters laughed with you, shared their secrets or rehearsed one of your plays.

3. The title of the song, as is often the case, is key to its interpretation. Jo wants to be 'astonishing', not simply average. Ensure you play a character with an extraordinary amount of self-belief and energy, who has a firm sense of her own destiny.

4. An event happens on the word 'today'. In this instant you decide that the time for talking has ended – you must now take positive action if you are to fulfil your dreams.

Vocal and Musical Analysis

WHO TO LISTEN TO: Sutton Foster on the original Broadway cast recording (1998).

VOCAL RANGE: G♯3 to E♭5.

ORIGINAL KEY: B major.

ACCENT: General American.

STYLE OF MUSICAL: Contemporary musical (pop-based).

CONTEMPORARY UP-TEMPO

VOCAL SET-UP/MUSICAL TIPS

1. The frenetic opening section should be delivered in a Speech quality. On the slightly higher phrases, add a tiny bit of twang to the set-up by tightening the AES, as you can hear Foster demonstrate when she asks herself: What did I miss? This will give the higher phrases a little extra 'ping' to the sound.

2. In the second section, where you reminisce about home, you should sing much more quietly. Use a Cry quality with a raised larynx, and keep the AES relaxed to avoid adding twang (you can go further with this set-up than Foster chooses to). Keep the quality clear and simple: particularly the first time you say the word 'astonishing'.

3. In the next section, where you state that you believe there is a life that you have to lead, slip back into a Speech quality – but this time make use of aspirate onsets to give your sound an excited, breathy quality.

4. When you sing the words 'even now', transition into a bright, strident Twang quality, as you can hear Foster clearly demonstrate.

5. On the lyric when you sing about finding your life in your own way, release your thyroid tilt and relax your AES to transition into a Speech Quality. You should then slightly raise your chin, anchor your torso and tilt your cricoid cartilage to allow you to belt the word 'today'.

6. The whole of the next section is delivered in a mixed belt. Maintain the torso anchoring and physical engagement you employed on the word 'today', but add a little thyroid tilt (with the sensation of a moaning sound) on the higher pitches – for example, on the word 'shine'.

7. When you sing about the fact that you will blaze, your vocal colour should be momentarily a little quieter. Trying using an aspirate Speech quality at this point. You should then return to either a strident Twang, or a mixed belt for the remainder of the song – depending on which you find

more comfortable (Foster uses Twang except on the final consonant of the word 'astonishing' where she modifies the vowel sound in order to access a belt).

8. The last note is difficult because it sits a little lower than is ideal for a belt. Try to avoid pushing your sound and driving your breath at this point.

Sheet Music

The correct sheet music for this song is available at www.musicnotes.com.

'Everything Else'
from *Next to Normal*

Music by Tom Kitt, lyrics by Brian Yorkey

Choose this song if: you have a contemporary musical-theatre voice, and enjoy exploring sensitive, emotionally complex, angst-ridden, teenage roles. The song was originally written to be sung whilst playing the piano – though this is not necessary, or appropriate, in most auditions.

Given Circumstances

WHO ARE YOU: Natalie Goodman, an intense, workaholic final-year high-school student. You are a pianist with an ambition to study music at Yale, and are prone to be defensive and sarcastic.

WHERE ARE YOU: In a music-practice room at a your high school, in a run-of-the-mill suburban town, USA.

WHEN IS IT: 8.30 a.m., a rainy Monday, September, during the autumn semester, present day. (At the time of writing it is still appropriate to set the song in the present day – but as the musical ages it may become appropriate to set it in the year it was written, which is 2008.)

WHAT HAS HAPPENED BEFORE: At four o'clock this morning, you discovered your mother, Diana, downstairs in the kitchen. Unbeknown to you, she had just been snorting cocaine and having an imaginary conversation with your brother Gabe (who died sixteen years ago). You had yet to go to bed, as you had stayed up late doing your schoolwork. When you told your mother about the tasks you still needed to complete, she criticised you for working too hard. She then somewhat inappropriately told you that she was heading back upstairs to have sex with your father, Dan. This type of behaviour, which you find very wearing and frustrating, is typical of your mother – and is a result of her bipolar disorder.

This morning at breakfast, during the usual early-morning chaos, you asked your mother if she and your father would be attending your school's winter music recital. You had been practising very hard for this event as it means a great deal to you. Without even asking for the date, your mother dismissively said that she would put it on the calendar – despite the fact it had been left open, untouched, on April for five months. She then proceeded to behave in a strange and manic fashion: first by wishing you a happy Easter and then by making sandwiches on the floor – after which you left to catch the bus.

You arrived at school thirty minutes ago. Upon arrival you headed straight to the music department, and have since been practising a Mozart piano sonata.

WHO ELSE IS THERE: You are alone.

WHO SHOULD YOU SING TO: The audience, which in this scenario is the audition panel.

Textual Analysis

When the introduction begins you are busy making notes on your sheet music (see point 1 below). Your objective here is: to complete your work on the sonata. The piece of music is very difficult and complicated, and so on the final two piano chords that occur just before you start singing you might try slamming your pencil down as though frustrated with how problematic you are finding the practice. In the opening few lines your objective is then: to protest about how difficult Mozart is to play. You do this in a sarcastic manner – by blaming this on the composer's madness. When you say the word 'but' there is a change in the text and a new unit begins. At this point your objective becomes: to convince the audience that Mozart's music is wonderful. You explain that you love it because it is ordered and rational – and each chord seems to flow logically from the next. In this section try exploring such actions as: I awaken, inspire and enkindle the audience.

When you sing about everything else going away, you are referring to your troubled family life – and, in particular, your mother. Your objective at this point is: to escape from reality. Your desire for escapism is brief, and in the bridge you return to the here-and-now of your piano practice. But this quickly leads you into another flight of fancy. You daydream about how succeeding in your recital might set off a chain of events that would lead to you being accepted into Yale, and escaping from your home-life. Your objective in the bridge is: to imagine how your life might change for the better. Actions you could explore in this unit include: I galvanise, invigorate, spur and vitalise myself. At the end of the bridge you realise that none of your ambitions can be achieved unless you play the sonata well in the recital – and that can only happen if you rehearse. Your objective in the last section is therefore: to make yourself practise harder (see point 3).

KEY MOMENTS/TOP TIPS

1. In a performance of this song in the musical you would be playing the piano, but in most auditions this is not advisable, and of course is not feasible if you don't play the instrument. Even so, the activity of practising is important when acting the song. It is therefore suggested that you begin the song kneeling on the floor with a few pages of sheet music for a Mozart sonata scattered around you. You can then make notes on the music – perhaps by marking the fingering, phrasing or dynamics you would use – as an alternative activity to playing the piano.

2. Each time you sing the title lyric, we should appreciate that Natalie is a very unhappy, lonely teenager, who simply wants the love of her mother. In these moments try playing such actions as: I comfort, protect and cushion myself.

3. The event of the song occurs when you talk about your paranoid parents. At this moment you express, perhaps for the first time, your true feelings about your mother: you have a great deal of repressed anger towards her. Explore

slowly getting to your feet during the bridge so you are standing defiantly in time for this event. You can also try using a brief pause after the word 'say' before you go into the final section – almost as though you have shocked yourself with your emotional outburst.

4. During the final section you should return to your practice. Try going back to your starting position of kneeling on the floor, and making further notes on your music. This helps convey Natalie's ruthless determination to rehearse and to succeed in her recital.

5. A key to Natalie's psyche is that she feels ignored and unloved by her mother, who she wrongly believes only cares about Gabe. Natalie describes herself as the invisible girl, in comparison to her dead brother, whom she calls 'superboy'. Try playing her as emotionally fragile.

Vocal and Musical Analysis

WHO TO LISTEN TO: Jennifer Damiano on the original Broadway cast recording (2009).

VOCAL RANGE: G3 to C5.

ORIGINAL KEY: C major.

ACCENT: General American.

STYLE OF MUSICAL: Book musical.

VOCAL SET-UP/MUSICAL TIPS

1. The introduction contains a difficult run in the right hand of the piano part. To make it easier for the pianist to sight-read, and ensure you get a clean introduction, it is suggested you cut the seventh and eighth bars.

2. The majority of the song should be delivered in a Speech quality, but with some twang added to the set-up by slightly tightening the AES.

3. During the bridge, to help convey Natalie's growing determination, try using glottal and aspirate onsets to add emphasis, as Damiano does so successfully on the suggested recording. Your sound should also be louder than previously, so use thicker vocal folds in this section.

4. When you sing the line about your paranoid parents, you should move into an Advanced Speech quality. Add some torso anchoring and thyroid tilt at this point. This will add a 'moaning' quality to the sound, as you can hear in Damiano's performance.

8. Each time you sing a line containing the title lyric, trying making your sound much sweeter. Explore singing with simultaneous onsets, raising your larynx and using legato phrasing.

Sheet Music

The correct sheet music for this song is available at www.musicnotes.com.

'Just One Step'
from *Songs for a New World*

Music and lyrics by Jason Robert Brown

Choose this song if: you have a contemporary pop voice and can belt to a B. This role suits actresses who enjoy playing comedic, neurotic and histrionic roles.

Given Circumstances

Note: *Songs for a New World* is a revue show, rather than a musical with a through-narrative. The given circumstances below, though derived from the lyric, are therefore invented and could be altered to suit your needs.

WHO ARE YOU: Diane Goldstein, a rich, self-absorbed, melodramatic Jewish-American socialite in your mid-thirties. You have always been taken care of financially by your rich husband, Murray, and as a consequence you have become spoilt, selfish and demanding. As someone who has got on in life through your good looks, you are struggling with the fact that you are ageing and have recently put on a little weight.

WHERE ARE YOU: On the balcony of a luxurious penthouse apartment on the fifty-seventh floor of a skyscraper on Fifth Avenue, Manhattan, New York City, USA.

WHEN IS IT: 3.10 p.m., a bright spring afternoon, 1997.

WHAT HAS HAPPENED BEFORE: A decade ago you married an investment banker named Murray Goldstein. You were at the height of your attractiveness and Murray, who was twenty years older than you, saw you as something of a trophy girlfriend. Despite the age difference, for a long time you were happy to be treated in this manner, as Murray constantly lavished expensive gifts on you, providing you with a fabulous lifestyle. You subsequently had three children together.

However, in the last eighteenth months your relationship began to sour. By constantly spoiling you, Murray had encouraged your selfish nature – and eventually he started to grow tired of your constant demands. He started spending more and more evenings away from home and you began to feel neglected. Your husband told you that his absence was because he was busy with work, but in fact he was having an affair with his twenty-year-old secretary. You discovered this deception several weeks ago when you saw a text message on his phone, though you did not say anything at the time for fear that he would throw you out and you would lose your privileged lifestyle.

As a way of getting back at Murray, you have recently become ever more demanding in terms of the gifts you expect him to buy for you. The other day you asked him to purchase a ludicrously expensive beach house, and then requested a dog – which you knew would aggravate him, as he hates pets. When he refused to buy you either of these gifts, it led to some awful rows, though you still didn't reveal what you knew about Madeline.

This morning you insisted that Murray take you shopping at Macy's department store. After having a blazing row in the shop, he refused to purchase an expensive black sable coat. You then both returned to your penthouse apartment where the fight continued. With the shouting between you reaching a crescendo, and Murray refusing to listen any more, you have just stormed out onto the balcony and threatened to kill yourself by jumping off the ledge.

WHO ELSE IS THERE: You are alone on the balcony, though a small crowd has gathered in the street below to see if you will jump. Murray is within earshot inside the apartment.

WHO SHOULD YOU SING TO: Murray, who is in the apartment behind you.

Textual Analysis

At the start of the song you have no real intention of committing suicide. You are simply being melodramatic. Your objective in the first verse is: to get Murray's attention. You want him to back down and come out on the balcony, apologise to you, and agree to buy you the fur coat. When you are unsuccessful in this objective, during the second verse you then want to make Murray feel guilty. You seek to take the moral high ground by saying you won't fight over a coat, whilst simultaneously pointing out that he could easily afford to buy you one.

In the first pre-chorus, which starts with you saying that you know you are not wanted, your objective is: to play the martyr. You want Murray to take pity on you. This then leads you to threaten during the first chorus to take a step off the balcony and by doing so kill yourself. Your objective here is: to force Murray to back down. You are unsuccessful in this aim, as you realise that your husband doesn't believe you will really jump. Your objective at the start of the third verse therefore becomes: to convince Murray that you are serious. You want him to be clear that you are not joking. You then become distracted and excited by the attention of the gathering crowd below. Try playing the following objective at this point: to revel in the attention you are receiving from the street below.

During the second pre-chorus your ire shifts from Murray to his mother. You believe that she has never truly liked you, so your objective in this unit is: to make Murray be honest about his mother's hidden antipathy. You want him to confess that she wasn't happy when the two of you were married, as she viewed you as a gold-digger. The second chorus then begins and you once more threaten to jump off the balcony. As adrenalin pumps through you, and with you feeling high on your own defiance, your objective in this unit is: to make Murray worry that your suicide is imminent. A funky bridge section then begins with you pointing out that it is Murray who makes all of the money in the relationship. The objective at this point is: to accuse Murray of being a cheapskate.

Actions that you might play in this unit include: I ridicule, humiliate and taunt him. The heart of the song then occurs when you reveal you know about the affair (see point 5 below) and the things that your husband says about you behind your back, such as calling you fat. Your objective here is: to expose what Murray has been up to. You are making him realise that you have more knowledge about what has been going on than he thought.

A longer unit then commences at the beginning of the third pre-chorus (which starts with the word 'here's') and continues until you belt the word 'fly' at the end of the third chorus (see point 3 below). During this unit, you imagine how empowered you would feel if you actually did jump from the balcony: you wouldn't feel miserable about the affair any more, you wouldn't have to listen to Murray complaining, and people would finally pay attention to you. Your objective in this lengthier section is: to imagine how everyone would react to your suicide. You indulge yourself by believing that this would finally give you what you want. Just before the final spoken lines, you snap out of this fantasy when you finally realise that Murray is not listening to you – moments before you slip and fall (see point 7 below).

KEY MOMENTS/TOP TIPS

1. It is necessary to establish the idea that you are standing on the edge of a balcony. To make this clear, try drawing an imaginary line on the centre of audition-room floor. Start your audition a metre or so behind that line and then approach it with trepidation during the introduction, peering over it as though the line is the edge of the balcony and you can see the street below. Ensure you picture this in your imagination. Alternatively you might stand on a chair.

2. Sometimes in audition it is advisable to cut any dialogue sections in the song, but with this number you should keep them in. Not only are they entertaining, they are necessary to convey the narrative.

3. A difficulty with staging this song is that much of it is addressed to Murray who is behind you in the apartment. When you speak to him during your performance, try throwing your comments over your shoulder – rather than turning to face where he would be. This will ensure the panel are able to see your entire performance.

4. During the song you mention that Maury Povich and Connie are looking up from the street below. Maury is a real-life American television presenter, and Connie Chung is his wife and co-presenter. They are very much people you would know socially and would want to impress.

5. The main event of the song occurs when you reveal to Murray that you know that he is having an affair. Use this as an opportunity to root what is essentially a comedic song in a more truthful and painful reality.

6. A further event occurs when you confess that perhaps it's true that you have been too demanding and controlling in the relationship. In this moment you realise that you share some responsibility for the breakdown of your marriage.

7. At the end of the number Diane accidentally slips from the balcony. This is hard to convey on a flat floor. Try exploring ways to make this clear. You might take a sharp, panicked intake of breath on the last note of the piano accompaniment (as Mulaskey does on the suggested recording), perhaps accompanied by a movement of your feet and arms that suggest you have suddenly slipped. If you feel that you cannot make this moment clear and convincing, then it is suggested that you cut the moment where Diana falls. It is not suggested you fall off a chair, as this can both be dangerous and look unconvincing.

Vocal and Musical Analysis

WHO TO LISTEN TO: Jessica Mulaskey on the original cast recording (1997).

VOCAL RANGE: F♯3 to C♯5.

ORIGINAL KEY: B major.

ACCENT: The song is written to be delivered in a New York Jewish accent.

STYLE OF MUSICAL: Contemporary musical (pop-based).

VOCAL SET-UP/MUSICAL TIPS

1. The predominant vocal set-up for the song is Speech. When performing this song it is particularly important to marry the spoken and sung voices, so that they seem like a continuation of the same sound. To achieve this make the sung sections as conversational as possible. This can be achieved by avoiding excessive vibrato and by keeping the note-lengths short. You should also add a little twang to this Speech set-up by narrowing the AES a little.

2. Try delivering the song with the soft palate in mid-position. This will give a hint of nasality that is appropriate for the accent. You can hear this position clearly demonstrated by Mulaskey on the suggested recording.

3. The extended note on the word 'fly' near the end of the song should be belted.

Sheet Music

The correct sheet music for this song is available at www.musicnotes.com.

'The Life I Never Led'
from *Sister Act*

Music by Alan Menken, lyrics by Glenn Slater

Choose this song if: you enjoy playing slightly awkward,
introverted characters who can be wide-eyed and excitable.
The song allows you to showcase a belt to a C.

Given Circumstances

WHO ARE YOU: Sister Mary Robert, a naive, sheltered, but
perky young novice who dreams of living of a more
adventurous life outside of the convent.

WHERE ARE YOU: In the room of Deloris Van Cartier in St
Catherine's Convent in Philadelphia, USA.

WHEN IS IT: Early evening, spring, 1978.

WHAT HAS HAPPENED BEFORE: On Christmas Eve last year,
Deloris Van Cartier, a flamboyant nightclub singer, witnessed
a shooting by her gangster boyfriend, Shank. With her life in
danger she was forced to take shelter in St Catherine's as part
of a witness-protection programme. Once inside the convent,
with only the Mother Superior knowing her true identity,
Deloris disguised herself as a nun, Sister Mary Clarence.

In this new guise, Deloris was given leadership of the convent
choir by the Mother Superior – and transformed it into a
musical and financial success. She helped the nuns – and
particularly you – to find their voice, both literally and
metaphorically. Through singing, you discovered qualities in
yourself that you never knew you had.

In the short term, the proceeds from the choir's new activities
were helping to save the convent from closure, as it had been
struggling financially. This culminated in the choir being
invited to perform at a concert that will take place tomorrow,
a concert that will be attended by the Pope. The proceeds

from the concert have the potential to secure the future of the convent for the long term, but unfortunately the publicity surrounding it has helped Shank track Deloris to St Catherine's. A few minutes ago, Deloris was warned of her ex-boyfriend's imminent arrival by the Mother Superior. You overheard, and so discovered her true identity.

With Deloris needing to leave immediately she has just returned to her room to collect her belongings. You followed her there. When you asked her how she could abandon the choir on the eve of the concert, Deloris retorted that she now needed to think about herself. You have just told her that you are worried that becoming a nun is not what you are meant to do with your life, and asked her whether she thinks you should leave the convent.

WHO ELSE IS THERE: Deloris is present at the beginning of the song, but leaves halfway through.

WHO SHOULD YOU SING TO: Deloris. After she leaves, the song becomes a soliloquy and you should then sing to yourself – before finally addressing the universe.

Textual Analysis

At the beginning of the song your objective is: to decide whether you want to leave the convent, or remain and complete your novitiate (training as a nun). In order to try and make this life-changing decision, during the first verse you list all of the behaviours and adventures, large and small, that you have never tried. In doing so you begin to realise how much of your life you have been missing out on. When you then start dreaming of going surfing and dancing on tables at the start of the second verse, you have a new objective. This is: to inspire yourself with new possibilities. Actions you might play at this point include: I enthuse, animate, vitalise, rouse, thrill and embolden myself.

After becoming enthused by the prospect of life outside the convent walls, in the bridge of the song you try to get Deloris to understand how much she has inspired you. Your objective in this section becomes: to get Deloris to give you a push out the door. You are so close to taking the decision to leave, but you feel you need a final piece of encouragement in order to finally make that choice.

In the musical, a short section of dialogue then occurs where Deloris tells you that she cannot tell you what to do. She says that the decision must be yours alone, and then leaves. In an audition, of course, this dialogue will not take place, so you need to make it clear that Deloris leaves at this point (see point 3 below) – and you must therefore make up your own mind.

In the last verse you slowly begin to gather yourself. Your objective in this section is: to build up the courage to leave the convent. Explore playing some of these actions at this point: I boost, calm, toughen, fortify, strengthen and encourage myself. After the key change, you then begin to vividly picture a bright new future. Try playing the following objective at this juncture: to obliterate any doubt. You are completely successful in this objective, so that in the last two lines you announce emphatically your decision to the universe: that you are going to begin a new life outside of the convent walls.

KEY MOMENTS/TOP TIPS

1. The song is directed mainly to Deloris. You can either choose to deliver the sections that are sung to her towards a fixed point behind the audition table, or you can sing to the panel, as if they are all Deloris.

2. One of the challenges when acting this song is the speed in which the thoughts arrive. Mary Robert's imagination is running ahead of her as she thinks of the many possibilities of a life outside of the convent. For each new adventure you list, you need to see a clear image – whether that be Paris's Eiffel Tower, or a vision of you swimming naked. Carefully prepare these images as part of your rehearsal process, so that you can see them at the speed demanded by the tempo of the music.

3. An event occurs when Deloris leaves, which happens during the repetition of the words 'let go'. To make this clear, try

letting your eyeline move slowly across the wall behind the panel whilst you sing those lyrics, as if you are watching Deloris head out the door. Perhaps stifle an impulse to follow her, and then bring your focus back to yourself, to convey that you have been left alone in the room.

4. Explore how the journey of the song affects your physicality. Your movements might change from being awkward and self-conscious at the beginning, to being bold, open and adventurous in the space as the song progresses.

5. As an audition panel, we particularly enjoy the song if the actress playing Mary Robert becomes completely absorbed by the visions of her possible future life. Let your playfulness, youthfulness and enthusiasm come out through the material.

6. You can have fun after you have belted the word 'dead' (see point 7 below) by quickly covering your mouth in shock after singing the note, as though this is the first time you have ever made such a loud noise, and you have surprised yourself.

Vocal and Musical Analysis

WHO TO LISTEN TO: Katie Rowley Jones on the original London cast recording (2009).

VOCAL RANGE: A3 to D5.

ORIGINAL KEY: D major.

ACCENT: General American.

STYLE OF MUSICAL: Contemporary musical (pop-based).

VOCAL SET-UP/MUSICAL TIPS

1. In the first verse, try using a Speech quality, as the lyrics should sound very conversational. You can make use of aspirate onsets and half-speak some words, as Rowley Jones clearly demonstrates.

2. As you progress towards the first chorus, and the piano part becomes busier, the material wants to sound more 'sung' – so it is useful to add a little more thyroid tilt and twang to your sound by tightening your AES. You can also make the phrasing more legato.

3. The sound you want for the second verse, second chorus and bridge is an archetypal Alan Menken set-up (think Disney or *Glee*). This involves you tightening your AES to arrive in a Twang quality. Try not to sound too classical on one hand, or too poppy, on the other.

4. When you repeatedly ask Deloris to help you let go, slowly relax your AES to take the twang out of your voice and end up in a vulnerable Cry quality, as Rowley Jones chooses to do.

5. Return to a Speech quality at the start of third verse, with a heavy use of aspirate onsets. This breathiness can help portray Mary Robert's inner turmoil at this point.

6. After the key change you should once more use a Twang quality. Particularly tighten the AES on the higher notes to give them some extra 'ping'. You can hear Rowley Jones demonstrate this on the words 'new' and 'through'.

7. The word 'dead' should be belted. Remember to anchor your torso and lift your chin slightly as you approach this moment. You then need to tilt your cricoid cartilage.

8. The available sheet music is written to conclude on a lower note (as in the suggested recording), but if you wish to show off your belt register, you could finish by belting the word 'lead' on a C (as Marla Mindelle did in the original Broadway production). If you do so, try inserting a tiny pause before you sing the last note, so the word falls on the second beat of the bar. This will help build the sense of musical climax.

Sheet Music

The correct sheet music for this song is available at www.musicnotes.com.

CONTEMPORARY UP-TEMPO

'Pulled'
from *The Addams Family*

Music and lyrics by Andrew Lippa

Choose this song if: you enjoy playing rebellious, quirky teenage roles. The song enables you to showcase a belt to C, and suits a contemporary musical-theatre voice with a pop/rock edge.

Given Circumstances

WHO ARE YOU: Wednesday Addams, a teenage girl who is a member of the strange, spooky, macabre Addams family. You can be stubborn, and have always had strange and sadistic tendencies – though this has begun to change recently since you have fallen in love.

WHERE ARE YOU: In the playroom of your family house, the Addams Family mansion, Central Park, New York City, USA.

WHEN IS IT: 4.30 p.m., late November (the end of autumn), present day.

WHAT HAS HAPPENED BEFORE: Yesterday you visited the Addams family graveyard with your ghoulish relatives to celebrate the great cycle of life and death. As part of this annual ritual you all danced on the graves of your ancestors to summon up their spirits. When your Uncle Fester was left alone with the dead members of your family, he then raised what he considered to be a significant problem: you had fallen in love with a normal man from Ohio by the name of Lucas Beineke. As Fester was concerned about the relationship, he asked the ancestors to spy on Lucas – to decide if he was worthy of your love.

This afternoon your mother Morticia received a bouquet of flowers from Lucas's parents, and the entire Beineke family are due to attend a dinner this evening at your house. After discussing your romantic life with his wife, your father Gomez became worried that you were growing up too soon. When you came into your mother's boudoir shortly after – and expressed a longing for flowers and bunny rabbits – your parents were both astonished at your changed personality. A more usual behaviour for you would be to squeeze the guts out of a frog.

For the last few minutes you have been hanging out in the playroom, where you have been stretching your younger brother Pugsley over a rack – which he finds incredibly pleasurable as he enjoys torture. Whilst doing so, you confided to him that you were confused about whether the dinner with the Beinekes was good idea. When Pugsley kindly offered (or so he thought) to blow Lucas up, you then told him that he had completely misunderstood how you feel. You have just decided to tell your brother your true feelings about your new boyfriend.

WHO ELSE IS THERE: Pugsley.

WHO SHOULD YOU SING TO: Pugsley is in the room strapped to a rack (an instrument of torture), but this is impossible to convey in an audition. So for audition purposes you should deliver the song to the panel as if you are alone and they are all your secret confidantes.

Textual Analysis

At the top of the song you are trying to convey a sullen demeanour. Like many teenagers, you are trying to give off an aura of indifference. Your objective in this section is: to convince the audience that you are in complete control of your emotions. You want to appear 'too cool for school'. In this section, try such actions as: I exclude, spurn and disregard the audience. After the word 'suddenly', you drop this hard external exterior (see point 1 below). In the remainder of the first verse, your objective becomes: to get the audience's advice. You want them to confirm whether your suspicions about why you've changed are true – and tell you how to act if they are. In the first chorus, you then confide to the audience the new feelings of warmth and tenderness you have experienced lately. Try playing the following objective at this point: to intrigue them about your new secret life. Actions such as: I fascinate, captivate and spellbind the audience can be interesting to explore.

In the second verse your mind turns towards your mother. Your objective becomes: to gauge how she will react to you falling in love. Concluding that she will be displeased gives rise to a feeling not uncommon amongst teenagers: rebellion. Try the following objective in this section: to defy the will of your mother. You are daring yourself to break the rules she has set for you. Appropriate actions for this unit might be: I bolster, encourage and sustain myself.

During the next section, you make a long list of things that now make you happy. In making this list, your objective is: to indulge your girly side. Having suppressed your femininity for years – in the way you dress and behave – you are now learning to embrace it. You can have a lot of fun with this section playing actions such as: I amuse, excite, thrill, intoxicate and tickle yourself.

After singing about Liberace, you then play one final joyful objective in the last section: to celebrate falling in love. You resolve to stop fighting your feelings, and embrace your new view of the world. This is the event of the song.

KEY MOMENTS/TOP TIPS

1. The opening section, up to the word 'suddenly', should be delivered as deadpan as possible. When performing these opening lines, try to stand completely still, don't smile at all, and look to communicate with a minimum of expression. After this section, infectious excitement should gradually take you over as the song progresses – until eventually you are metaphorically swinging from the chandeliers.

2. Imagine the audience are other teenagers of the same age as you. At first you want to impress them with your moody exterior. Later you want to confide in them about your true feelings.

3. A real–life parallel for a girl like Wednesday are teenagers who dress as Goths – who stereotypically wear all-black clothes and wear white make-up. It can be argued that their distinctive fashion is a way for them to express individuality, yet it can also be viewed as a mask for them to hide behind. During this song, Wednesday finally removes the teenage mask she has been skulking behind.

4. Your use of your body in the space should mirror Wednesday's emotional journey during the song: she is like a caterpillar emerging from a chrysalis. While you should start physically very still, by the time you start talking about puppy dogs, you can, and should, be moving excitedly in the space.

Vocal and Musical Analysis

WHO TO LISTEN TO: Krysta Rodriguez on the original Broadway cast recording (2010).

VOCAL RANGE: C4 to E5.

ORIGINAL KEY: D minor.

ACCENT: General American.

STYLE OF MUSICAL: Contemporary musical (pop-based).

VOCAL SET–UP/MUSICAL TIPS

1. You should aim for your vocal quality at the beginning of the song to be as unfussy as possible, as if you are singing with a metaphorical vocal straitjacket on. To achieve this staid performance, sing in a Speech quality with absolutely no thyroid tilt or vibrato. Make the delivery a little staccato, and cut the ends of phrases short.

2. To reflect the change in Wednesday's mood, make a vocal shift on the word 'suddenly' halfway through the first verse. From this point, whilst remaining in a Speech quality, start to use simultaneous onsets to make your sound more legato

CONTEMPORARY UP-TEMPO

before adding some thyroid tilt on the last few words of the verse to let a little sweetness into your voice.

3. Deliver the first chorus in a quiet Twang quality. Use thin vocal folds and a raised laryngeal position. Only tighten your AES a small amount, however, as you don't want your sound to become too loud or strident at this stage.

4. Remove your thyroid tilt gradually when you ask the question: What will I do? This will allow you to crescendo and access a thick vocal-fold set-up and Speech quality – which is appropriate for the second verse and chorus.

5. The word 'boy' should be delivered in a Belt quality, as should the word 'pulled' when you sing it on the last occasion when you repeat the word three times in a row.

6. When you begin to list the things that make you happy, starting with puppy dogs, you want your vocal performance to have a hushed, enthusiastic quality. To achieve this, use a breathy Speech quality produced by using lots of aspirate onsets. Some words in the list can also be spoken and shouted excitedly, as Rodriguez does on the suggested recording.

7. At the end of list, when you sing about Liberace's greatest hits, you should progress into a Twang quality. You should then remain in this set-up until the end of song. Tighten the AES a little more on the highest notes to give them extra volume. You can hear Rodriguez demonstrate this effectively on the suggested recording, for example on the word 'taboo'.

Sheet Music

The correct sheet music for this song is available at www.musicnotes.com.

'The Spark of Creation'
from *Children of Eden*

Music and lyrics by Stephen Schwartz

Choose this song if: you have contemporary pop voice and can belt to a D. This role suits actresses who enjoy playing wilful, passionate and ambitious characters.

Given Circumstances

WHO ARE YOU: Eve, based on the biblical figure of the same name, wife of Adam. You are inquisitive, curious and restless, and have a yearning for independence fuelled by a rebellious instinct. Although the passage of time is not clearly indicated in the script, it is useful to suppose at this point you are about seventeen years old, as you are on the verge of becoming a woman.

WHERE ARE YOU: In an unspecified location in the Garden of Eden. The exact surroundings are for you to imagine, but undoubtedly this is a place of astonishing beauty.

WHEN IS IT: 10.03 a.m., a beautiful late-summer morning, in the time of the Book of Genesis, seventeen years after the Creation.

WHAT HAS HAPPENED BEFORE: At the dawn of time God (called Father in the musical) created the universe. In six days, and six nights, he made the Heavens and the Earth, populating it with all living creatures. On the seventh day he made Adam – the first man – in his own image, and he created you to be his wife. Father loved you both greatly as his children and you wanted for nothing in the perfect paradise that he had made for you.

Adam was very content with his life in the Garden, and in particular took great pleasure in naming and listing all of the animals of Creation. At first you felt the same, but as you grew older you started to become bored with the repetitive nature of your life.

One day you questioned Father about a strange, glistening tree that grew on a hilltop beyond a distant waterfall. When Father became defensive at your persistent questioning, Adam warned you to stop, but still you continued to ask. Eventually Father revealed that the tree was called the Tree of Knowledge, but warned you both that you were forbidden from eating the fruit that grew in its branches. He made you promise that you would never do so. Adam immediately agreed, but you remained curious and wanted to know why you could not eat the forbidden fruit. Father did not answer your questions, instead telling you to trust that what he said was in your best interest. Finding this response unsatisfactory, you reluctantly promised not to eat the fruit, or even go near it.

This morning you disobeyed Father and went to see the Tree of Knowledge for yourself. Whilst you were there you made an amazing discovery that you immediately wanted to share with Adam. Bringing him to the forbidden place, you showed him how, whenever you stepped near the tree, the daylight temporarily disappeared – turning the day into night – and the fruit glowed with an eerie light. Although Adam was reluctant, you encouraged him to step close to the tree. A few moments ago, somewhat worried by this strange new phenomenon, he described it as a mystery. You responded by saying that the knowledge contained within the tree suggested that a wealth of possibilities existed beyond your current range of understanding. There was a great delight for you in the use of these new words: 'mystery' and 'beyond'. They seemed to hint at an undiscovered potential within you both. Adam did not want to displease Father by being near the forbidden tree, and so he has just left to continue listing the animals – leaving you busy in your own thoughts.

WHO ELSE IS THERE: You are alone.

WHO SHOULD YOU SING TO: Yourself. In audition, though, it is useful to address some of the thoughts to the panel, as if they are your inner-consciousness.

Textual Analysis

Note: There is an introductory section where you sing of your feelings about the word 'beyond'. As it doesn't have the same sense of drive and purpose as the rest of the song, it is suggested that this section be cut, and that you instead start your performance with the first verse after a four-bar introduction – as is the case on the recommended sheet music. The analysis below assumes this cut has been made.

When the driving musical introduction begins, you are very excited. You are fired up by the future possibilities hinted at in your conversation with Adam: that much may exist beyond the boundaries of your current knowledge and understanding. That anticipation takes physical expression in your body – in your fingertips and in the back of your brain. In the first half of the verse, your objective is therefore: to acknowledge the new sensations you are feeling. This leads to an awakening in you – that these feelings cannot be suppressed. Your sense of discovery continues in the second half of the opening verse. You realise that the desire for action that you now possess was inherited from your father. In this unit your objective is: to convince yourself that you and Father are one and the same. You pursue this objective in order to justify your actions in breaking your promise to him.

During the chorus, for the first time, you give a name to feelings of ambition that are now running through you: they are the 'spark of creation'. Your objective in this section is therefore: to define the cause of the strange new feelings you are experiencing.

The possibilities provided by the world around you then grab your attention during the second verse – in the mountains, the rivers, and the tools that are yet to be invented. You begin to see the world in a way you never have before: it offers endless possibilities for discovery and exploration. In this verse, your objective is: to revel in what the world has to offer. At this point try playing such actions as: I inspire, electrify, invigorate, impassion and stir myself.

In the second chorus you begin to comprehend that your desire to explore the world cannot now be quelled, as there is a sense of destiny growing inside of you. Your objective in this unit is: to convince yourself that you must take action. A great shift in the song then occurs. During the third chorus your pace of thought slows significantly and you begin to realise your own potential to create life. Your objective in this section is: to cherish the possibility that you can be a mother. Try playing such actions as: I analyse, comfort and nurture myself at this point. Having made this momentous discovery, you conclude that you cannot abide by Father's restrictive rules any longer. Your objective to the end of the song thus becomes: to celebrate your future potential.

KEY MOMENTS/TOP TIPS

1. The opening few lyrics are not metaphorical – you can literally feel restlessness in your fingertips and thoughts rushing through your brain. You don't need to demonstrate this, but you should imagine that these sensations are occurring in your body, and respond to them.

2. Allow yourself to move dynamically in the space when that feels appropriate. For example, it might be that when Eve sees the mountain in the distance she instinctually rushes a few paces towards it.

3. An event occurs when you celebrate that you are an echo of Father's own words: 'let there be'. You discover in this moment that you are exactly the same as your father – you have an unstoppable need to create.

4. The most important event of the song occurs when you state that you are the keeper of the flame. At this moment Eve recognises that she has the ability to make life, to have a child. She understands that the spark of creation has been passed on to her. During this section you may want to become aware of the centre of your body – that it contains a womb.

Vocal and Musical Analysis

WHO TO LISTEN TO: Stephanie Mills on the American premiere cast recording (1998).

VOCAL RANGE: A3 to D5.

ACCENT: The song is written to be sung in General American, and it is undoubtedly easier to deliver in that accent due to the higher tongue position prevalent in the dialect. However, if you are performing the song in a UK audition, there is a strong argument for delivering it in Standard English, which will sound more neutral to British ears. This can be a good choice as the location of the Garden of Eden is so nebulous.

ORIGINAL KEY: The original key is A major with the song modulating in D♭ major after the introductory Pre-chorus, though in this instance I would recommend performing the song in C major – which is the key of the song in the published vocal selections. This key is much easier to read and play for the audition pianists, and sits more comfortably within an alto's belt range. It also cuts out the opening section as suggested above.

STYLE OF MUSICAL: Contemporary musical (pop-based).

VOCAL SET-UP/MUSICAL TIPS

1. Because the song is quite wordy, it can sometimes be difficult to follow all of the lyrics in an audition scenario. So, when you speak to the pianist, ensure you don't set the tempo too fast, and encourage them to keep the piano accompaniment contained and quiet – so it doesn't overpower the words.

2. The verses should be delivered in a Speech quality. To help communicate the urgency of the lyric, make the phrasing a little staccato, and mix in some glottal and aspirate onsets.

3. The choruses, which begin with the title lyric, should be more legato than the verses. At these points make a greater

use of simultaneous onsets and try to run the vowels together.

4. It is appropriate to add the occasional pop riff, as Mills demonstrates on the cast recording on the word 'denied'.

5. During the final section you should start quietly and then effect a crescendo to build to the end of the song. On the line when you say it's alright if you're a crustacean, try using aspirate onsets to create a quiet, intense breathy Speech quality. Then in the next phrase, when you sing about having an imagination, shift to using simultaneous onsets. This will add volume and help move you into a pure Speech set-up. Then gradually add some torso anchoring during the next phrase, before lifting your chin on the word 'higher'. This will put you in the correct position to belt.

6. The last syllable of the final word should be belted. There are two options with this final line. You can copy the riffed ending that Mills does on the recording, or sing the melody notated on the sheet music (which is slightly easier to sing).

Sheet Music

The correct sheet music for this song is available at www.musicnotes.com.

'Waiting for Life'
from *Once on This Island*

Music by Stephen Flaherty, lyrics by Lynn Ahrens

Choose this song if: you have an outstanding belt and like to play characters with a restless energy and an adventurous spirit. The song also has moments of emotional vulnerability, and was originally written for an actress of Caribbean descent.

Given Circumstances

WHO ARE YOU: Ti Moune, a teenage peasant girl. Raised as an orphan, you dream of a life of adventures away from your monotonous day-to-day existence.

WHERE ARE YOU: A small fishing village on an island in the French Antilles. You are outside in a communal area – perhaps near the beach – as you can see the coastal road and mention other villagers working on fishing nets.

WHEN IS IT: Mid-morning, summer, some time in the 1930s.

WHAT HAS HAPPENED BEFORE: When you were a small girl, you were orphaned by a storm. The storm was sent by Agwe, the god of water. Despite the loss of your parents, you were yourself saved from harm when you were sheltered in a tree by Asaka, the Mother of the Earth. After the storm had subsided, the next morning Mama Euralie and Tonton Julian, an elderly peasant couple, found you stranded high amongst the branches. They rescued you, and with your parents nowhere to be seen they decided to raise you as their own.

When you started to grow older, you became curious about why the gods had chosen to spare you from the storm. Mama Euralie told you it was because they had saved you for something special. Now that you've become a teenager, this impression that your life has a larger purpose has developed into feelings of restlessness. You long to leave the village and have an adventure.

This morning, whilst the adults in the village have been working on the mundane chores necessary in a fishing community, you have been feeling particularly bored and impatient.

WHO ELSE IS THERE: At the beginning of the song you can see a Beauxhomme (a member of the wealthy mixed-race ruling class) dressed in white racing down the coast road in his car. Other villagers, including Mama Euralie and Tonton Julian, are also within sight – though they are far enough away to not be able to hear you. In other words, you may be affected by what you see them doing, but you are not inhibited by them.

WHO SHOULD YOU SING TO: To yourself and to the gods.

Textual Analysis

Before the song begins, you are lounging around, bored by the dull routine of the working day in the village – so you may want to start your performance sitting on the floor. The moment the piano begins playing you should spot a car racing down the coast road – and the excitement of this should drive you immediately to your feet. In the opening lines your objective is then: to hold sight of the car for as long as possible. You manage this for a short time until the vehicle finally disappears from view at the end of the word 'far'.

Inspired by what you have just seen, in the next section your objective becomes: to imagine what it would feel like to be free. Try playing such actions as: I gratify, pleasure, intoxicate and exhilarate myself in this unit. After this brief moment of daydreaming, your attention then turns squarely to the gods. Your objective at this point is: to get them to look down at you. Try using an extensive and playful range of actions to get their attention, as this will reflect Ti Moune's infectious and persuasive personality. Choices you might try include: I charm, flatter, challenge, irritate, harass, hustle and urge the gods.

Unfortunately, you are unsuccessful in getting the gods to take notice, so in the second verse your attention is drawn to Mama Euralie, Tonton Julian and the other villagers. They are slowly and happily going about the day's work – which involves tedious tasks, such as fixing the fishing nets. Try playing the following objective at this point: to criticise their lack of ambition. When you then dismiss them from your mind, and talk about the stranger in the car for the second time, your objective at this point is: to indulge your fantasy of escaping the village.

For the rest of the song you once more talk directly to the gods. In the slower section that immediately follows, your tone should feel more intimate. Your objective in this section is: to get the gods to speak back to you. They have not made any intervention in your life since you were a little girl, and so you now feel that they have abandoned you – just like your parents (see point 2 below). Actions that you might play at this point include: I implore, petition, urge and press the gods. After the key change you then make a more passionate plea to these all-powerful deities. Your objective at this juncture is: to get the gods to press the start button on your life. You feel that you have now been waiting more than long enough – you are ready – and so you want them to send you off on an adventure.

KEY MOMENTS/TOP TIPS

1. It is important to understand that spotting a motor vehicle would be rare for Ti Moune. Seeing a man driving down the coast road is an unusual and exciting event in her life.

2. Central to Ti Moune's personality is that she was orphaned whilst she was very young. The death of her parents has left her with a sense of abandonment. During the song she transfers some of these feelings onto the gods, who she also feels have forsaken her.

3. In your portrayal of the song, take into account that Ti Moune is a teenager. As is not uncommon amongst children of that age, she can be sullen, moody and attention-seeking at times, as well as being full of restless energy.

CONTEMPORARY UP-TEMPO

4. When you envisage the stranger returning in his car to collect you, it reveals another aspect of Ti Moune's personality: as a young women passing through adolescence, she is beginning to dream of romantic love, and may even be sexually frustrated, though she is not yet able to fully articulate those desires.

5. There is a short, evocative piece of instrumental music after you ecstatically belt the word 'drive' (see point 4 below). In the lyric that immediately follows the instrumental, you then check that the gods haven't forsaken you. This transition – from a joyful playfulness to a deep sense of melancholy – represents a huge reversal in Ti Moune's emotional state. As a consequence, this short piece of music is a good opportunity to reveal Ti Moune's deep-rooted insecurities.

Vocal and Musical Analysis

WHO TO LISTEN TO: LaChanze on the original Broadway cast recording (1990).

VOCAL RANGE: B3 to D5.

ORIGINAL KEY: B major. (A slightly easier version is also readily available in A major, which corresponds to the 1994 original London version sung by Lorna Brown if you find the key too challenging.)

ACCENT: The most appropriate accent is Haitian. However, for the purpose of a UK audition, any Caribbean accent would be suitable.

STYLE OF MUSICAL: Contemporary musical (pop-based).

VOCAL SET-UP/MUSICAL TIPS

1. The song starts in a Speech quality – a set-up that you should use for the majority of the number. At points you will need to add some thyroid tilt on the higher notes, to

give your sound a 'moaned' quality and make the pitch easier to sustain. You can hear LaChanze demonstrate this on the line when she asks if the gods are there.

2. On the recording the ensemble interjects with backing vocals at various points. You should ignore these and just sing the main melody for audition purposes.

3. In the bridge, when you sing about a stranger racing down the beach, make use of aspirate onsets to produce a hushed, excited quality. When you reach the word 'my', return to using simultaneous and glottal onsets, as this will allow you to shift back into a Speech quality. This change is necessary to help you prepare for the upcoming belt.

4. The second time you sing the word 'drive', it should be belted. Remember to anchor your torso, lift your chin and tilt your cricoid at this point.

5. In section that follows the belt, when you sing directly to the gods, you should use a quiet, vulnerable Cry quality. Lift your larynx, use thin vocal folds, and tilt your thyroid cartilage at this point. You can also employ aspirate onsets to portray a sense of desperation.

6. In the line when you warn the gods about singling you out and then forgetting you, slowly release your thyroid cartilage and gradually thicken your vocal folds. This will enable you to affect a crescendo and arrive back in a Speech quality for the key change, as LaChanze clearly demonstrates.

7. The words 'fly', 'why', 'waiting' and 'begin' (twice) are all belted in the final section.

8. LaChanze chooses to riff on the last syllable. This is not notated in the score, and is therefore optional.

Sheet Music

The correct sheet music for this song is available at www.scribd.com.

'Accident Prone'

Music and lyrics by Kirsten Guenther and Laurence O'Keefe

Choose this song if: you want to explore a piece that offers both comedic and sensitive moments, and the opportunity to belt to a C♯. The number may suit you if you enjoy playing quirky characters.

Given Circumstances

Note: Although 'Accident Prone' is a well-known song in the musical-theatre audition canon, it is not actually from a musical. As it is a stand-alone song, the given circumstances below, although based on the lyric, are invented and may be altered if you wish.

WHO ARE YOU: Sarah, a nervy, clumsy young woman who has a terrible track record with men. This is mainly because of a series of comedic mishaps, but more recently it has involved you being trapped in an abusive relationship.

WHERE ARE YOU: At a party in a large swanky apartment in New York City, USA.

WHEN IS IT: 3.30 a.m., summer, present day.

WHAT HAS HAPPENED BEFORE: Throughout your life you have never had much success with men, which you have always put down to the fact that you are incredibly accident-prone. Your past has been littered with a series of incidents where your clumsiness has led to the breakdown of a romantic affair. These include you dropping the ceramic frog that your first boyfriend had made you in front of your kindergarten class, and biting the tongue of the first boy you kissed at university. You also stepped on the hand of the only one-night stand you have ever hand, tipped another boyfriend out of a canoe on an outdoor adventure holiday, and broke the knee of another when you crashed into him at a roller disco.

As you reached your early twenties this catalogue of failed relationships led you to believe that you would never meet a long-term partner, and that you would grow old alone – a point of view that was exacerbated by a lack of faith on the part of your mother. Six months ago you began a relationship with Gus, a successful hedge-fund manager on Wall Street. At first you were so delighted to be in a settled relationship that you were prepared to ignore Gus's occasional outbursts of temper, but over the last few months his behaviour has grown progressively worse. In that period Gus has been mentally and physically abusive towards you, and has consistently blamed you for any problem in the relationship – even when he is in the wrong. Last week you discovered that he had been having an affair that began shortly after you met. When you tried to confront him about it, he openly taunted you with the details of the affair – yet still you could not summon up the willpower to leave.

This evening you were invited to a party held by one of Gus's high-flying friends. You were initially reluctant to attend, not only because you didn't know anyone at the party, but more importantly because Gus shouted at you for half an hour before you left – saying that the dress you had chosen to wear made you look fat. Since you arrived, he has continued to be abusive. At times during the party he has completely ignored you and flirted with other women. At one stage he took you out onto the balcony to bawl at you again, because he erroneously believed that you had been looking at another man.

During the evening you have had a few drinks. Whilst you are not drunk, the alcohol has relaxed you a little and given you courage. With Gus on the other side of the room, you have now found yourself chatting to a group of women you don't know. One of them has just asked you about who you dated before Gus – and you have decided to tell them everything about your romantic history.

WHO ELSE IS THERE: A group of partygoing strangers. Gus is also hovering in the background, apart from the group but still within earshot.

COMEDY/CHARACTER

WHO SHOULD YOU SING TO: The audition panel – you should use them as if they are the strangers at the party. In one section you also address Gus, and in another you to talk to your absent mother.

Textual Analysis

During the first verse you relay the story of Michael Marlowe, your first boyfriend, and why he broke off your relationship. Whilst you tell this story in a light-hearted, comedic way, you should also pursue the following objective: to get the partygoers to agree that Michael treated you unfairly. You want them to take your side. In the first chorus you then remember the conversation that you had with your mother after the break-up. Your memory of this event is so vivid that you almost relive this exchange. You can play the following objective at this point: to get your mother to take pity on you. You want her to reassure you that one day a man will indeed fall in love with you. In this section you might play such actions as: I implore, beseech and twist your mother.

In the second verse you recount how you met a guy called Steve at your freshman mixer (a university fresher's event) and bit the end of his tongue off when you tried to kiss him. You again relive this event quite vividly. Try playing this objective during the section: to make the partygoers believe that what happened wasn't serious. The reason this objective is interesting to play is because in the process of talking about your past, your storytelling has gained an unwanted momentum. You have revealed an embarrassing fact you perhaps didn't really intend to – so you are now trying to make light of the situation. In the second chorus you then mimic the complaints that Steve made at the time. Your objective in this section is: to paint Steve's behaviour as unreasonable. Choices such as: I mimic, parody, satirise and caricature Steve can be interesting to play. You then finish the story by relating what the ambulance driver said to you about biting Steve's tongue. Your objective in this short unit is: to convince the partygoers that the ambulance driver's behaviour was bizarre and unwarranted.

At the start of the third verse, you light-heartedly describe some of your previous romantic failures. Whilst doing so, you inwardly shift your attention towards Gus. Your objective in this section is: to set Gus up for a fall. You are pretending to create a convivial atmosphere, when in reality you are about to turn on him. In the second half of the verse, when you then address Gus directly, try this objective: to expose his cruelty. You want the partygoers to see what a nasty man he really is. You might play actions such as: I criticise, condemn and denounce Gus.

In the third chorus, after the key change, you attack Gus in a very controlled, piercing manner. A good objective might be: to make Gus feel ashamed. You try to achieve this by challenging him about some of the most abusive things he has said to you. In the bridge you recall how in the past you used to habitually take responsibility for all of the problems in your previous relationships. Your objective in this section is: to stop taking the blame for other people. After the most important event of the song has occurred (see point 4 below), your objective becomes: to celebrate your empowerment. You want to make Gus realise that he can't control you any longer. In this section you might play actions such as: I uplift, regenerate, vitalise, boost and empower and elevate yourself.

COMEDY/CHARACTER

KEY MOMENTS/TOP TIPS

1. There are opportunities for physical comedy and storytelling during this song. For example, you can mime the incident of dropping the ceramic frog. You can also have fun with performing your impression of Steve – perhaps by singing with your tongue stuck out.

2. An event occurs when you say that it's now time to talk about Gus. At this point you move from addressing the partygoers to talking directly to Gus. From this moment, until the end of song, address an imaginary Gus, as though he is standing behind the panel. This is a difficult transition, so be very clear in your focus so that the panel are aware you are now talking to your boyfriend.

3. If you perform the first two verses and choruses of the song successfully the panel may laugh, or be amused. To make the song effective you must work hard to change the atmosphere after the event described above, so the panel are aware that the song is no longer supposed to be comedic. You must silence their laughter. Achieving this dramatic shift can help you convey your versatility as an actress.

4. The key event of the song, and perhaps of the character's entire life, occurs at bar 109 when Sarah says that she knows someone will love her. At this point she resolves that she won't be a victim of abuse any more. As an audience we should feel at this point that – yes – one day Sarah will indeed find love.

Vocal and Musical Analysis

WHO TO LISTEN TO: Lauren Blackman in her solo show as part of the *Spotlight Cabaret Series* (2008).

VOCAL RANGE: G3 to E5.

ORIGINAL KEY: E♭ major.

ACCENT: Texan. General American.

STYLE OF MUSICAL: Not applicable.

VOCAL SET-UP/MUSICAL TIPS

1. The fundamental set-up for the song, as employed by Blackman, is Twang quality. Work with a consistently tilted thyroid cartilage, thin vocal folds and a tightened AES.

2. When you sing the words of your mother and the ambulance driver, it can be fun to perform comedic vocal impressions of them. For this to be successful you need to make clear choices – such as dramatically lifting or lowering the larynx, or using a different accent (Southern American or New York can work well),

3. With your impression of Steve you need to sound as if the end of your tongue has been bitten off. To achieve this you should sing entirely without consonants, as indicated by the sheet music and demonstrated by Blackman on the suggested recording.

4. At bars 79–81 the music is marked '*p*', indicating you should suddenly sing very quietly. This reflects Sarah's vulnerability at this moment. To portray this successfully, use a Cry quality – by lifting your larynx, tilting your thyroid cartilage to thin your vocal folds, and relaxing your AES to remove any twang.

5. In the very next phrase you should observe the crescendo indicated on the sheet music. Realise this by gradually removing your thyroid tilt so you arrive at a thick-fold Speech quality on the word 'gone'. At bar 87 then flip back to the Cry position you were in previously to enable you to sing very quietly. You can go much further with this choice than Blackman does on the suggested recording.

6. In the bridge, when you say that you've had guys yell at you in bar 95, you should use a Speech quality. This will help prepare you to belt the word 'stayed' at bar 107. As you approach the belt, slowly engage your torso anchoring and lift your chin slightly to achieve the required physical posture just prior to the note. You can then tilt your cricoid cartilage.

7. The next section, which begins at the key change, should also be delivered in a Speech quality and finish with a belt – this time on the word 'learn' in bar 121.

8. From bar 123 to the end of the song you should use a Twang quality, with a very tight AES to give you a bright resonance. Look to balance your sound – so this section is of a similar volume to the belted moments.

Sheet Music

The correct sheet music for this song is available at www.scribd.com.

'In Short'
from *Edges*

Music and lyrics by Benj Pasek and Justin Paul

Choose this song if: you enjoy playing madcap, zany
characters that are psychologically unhinged. The song will
allow you to showcase your skills as a comedic actress and a
belt to a C♯.

Given Circumstances

Note: *Edges* is a revue show, rather than a musical with a
through-narrative. The given circumstances below, though
derived from the lyric, are therefore invented – and could be
altered to suit your needs.

WHO ARE YOU: Janie, a volatile, emotional, violent woman with
psychotic tendencies. You are in your late twenties and could
stereotypically be described as a 'bunny-boiler'.

WHERE ARE YOU: In the apartment of your ex-boyfriend,
whose name is Danny, in a small town in the USA.

WHEN IS IT: 1.30 p.m., spring, present day.

WHAT HAS HAPPENED BEFORE: You met Danny six months ago at
a local book club. Whereas Danny became a member because
he had a genuine love of reading, you had simply joined for the
purposes of meeting a new boyfriend, as you had been through
a series of dramatic and painful break-ups in the past few
months (all caused by your jealous and possessive nature).

Although Danny was not really looking to meet anyone, you
pursued him single-mindedly and pressurised him into having
a romantic relationship with you. As he was meek by nature,
he found it impossible to stand up to your forceful personality
– and within six weeks he had reluctantly let you move into
his apartment.

Over the next few months you systematically took over every aspect of Danny's life. You stopped him from seeing his friends, or going out on his own, as you wanted him to spend all his spare time with you. The only place Danny was still allowed to go was the book club – which you had now left.

Last week, having grown tired of your abusive behaviour, Danny found the courage to tell you that he wanted to break-up – and that you should move out of his apartment. Your initial response was to trash the flat and throw vases at the wall – though you did eventually leave the next morning.

Two days later you decided to stalk Danny. You began by spying on him from outside the community centre where the book club was held. When the club had finished you caught him walking out holding hands with a shy, mousey, but sweet girl named Clara – whom you knew from when you attended the club yourself. After you greeted them with a tirade of expletives, Danny and Clara ran away, fearing for their safety.

This morning, whilst Clara was at work, you secretly slashed the tyres of her Volkswagen car with a kitchen knife. You then messaged Danny, very politely, asking him if he would meet you at his flat so you could collect the last of your belongings. He agreed, and you arrived fifteen minutes ago to do just that. You then went about your business very quietly and calmly, fooling Danny into thinking that, for once, you might behave reasonably. With him thinking that all was about to pass calmly, you have just turned to him to say your last goodbye.

WHO ELSE IS THERE: Danny.

WHO SHOULD YOU SING TO: Danny.

Textual Analysis

Note: There is spoken section near the end of the song that is written to be delivered at high speed. This should be cut for audition purposes. The analysis below assumes that this cut has been made.

You play a game with Danny at the beginning of the song. As you feel he has betrayed you, you are furious – so you decide to hide these feelings in order to trick him. During the introduction and opening verse, try playing this objective: to lull Danny into a false sense of security. You do this by making him believe this will be a civilised parting. In order to achieve this, you might play actions such as: I warm, charm, soothe and comfort Danny.

After the event of the song (see point 2 below), you reveal how you truly feel about the break-up. Your objective in the first chorus becomes: to mentally and physically intimidate Danny. It can be fun to explore these actions in this unit: I terrify, paralyse, shock and startle him. Your mood then changes abruptly in the first bridge, when you talk about whether it is wrong to consider killing your ex-boyfriend. Try playing the following objective in these four lines: to make a joke out of your previous threats. This perverse behaviour is a way of you lording your power over Danny, who is finding the experience terrifying.

The focus of your ire shifts in the second chorus to Danny's new girlfriend, Clara. An interesting objective to play at this point is: to make Danny fear for her life. Try using actions such as: I spook, unnerve, disconcert and alarm Danny. In the section that follows, when you say that maybe you have gone too far, the lyric then takes another surprising twist. It appears that you abruptly feel some remorse. However, at this point you are once more playing the following objective: to lull Danny into a false sense of security. It soon becomes clear you have simply been toying with him when you start telling Danny repeatedly that you want him to die. The following objective is something you might play in the next section: to enjoy imagining the horrible ways that Danny might die. This leaves you to play the following triumphant objective in the last line: to prove to Danny that you are well and truly over him.

1. In the first section, on the line when you say that the break-up came at quite a cost, there is a moment where a hint of your true resentment comes through. Try playing this section as if your mask of politeness slips for an instant.

2. A clear event occurs when you tell Danny that you want to punch him in the face. In this moment all your pretence should be ripped away. From this point onwards, Danny should be perfectly clear that you are angry with him – and are hell-bent on taking your revenge.

3. After this event, the methods you describe for getting back at Danny and Clara become increasingly psychotic. Try to craft the dramatic trajectory of your performance, so that only by the end of the song does your ex-boyfriend (and the audience) fully comprehend how mentally ill you are.

4. During your performance, picture what Danny's responses to your excessive behaviour might be. It is useful to pretend he is frightened and physically feeble. Picture him cowering, flinching and trying to slip out the door in the face of your threats.

5. The section in which you alternate between singing the word 'die', and naming various diseases that Danny might catch, has a Latin feel. In your eccentricity, you might engage in a silly, celebratory salsa to indulge your pleasure in Danny's imaginary demise – and perhaps hit a comedic still point each time you name a disease.

6. It is worth remembering that this is a comedy song. Whilst you must play the truth of the relationship, make your work heightened and absurd to successfully convey the humour.

Vocal and Musical Analysis

WHO TO LISTEN TO: Whitney Bashore at the Iowa Choral Directors Summer Convention (2014), available on YouTube.

VOCAL RANGE: F♯3 to D5.

ORIGINAL KEY: A major.

ACCENT: General American.

STYLE OF MUSICAL: Revue.

VOCAL SET-UP/MUSICAL TIPS

1. During the opening section you should aim to fool the panel into thinking they are about to hear a conventional pop ballad. To achieve this, start in a sweet Twang quality – with the use of slightly tightened AES, a high larynx, a tilted thyroid cartilage and simultaneous onsets.

2. Having made a very pleasant sound in the opening section, you should switch into a very prosaic Speech quality when you sing about punching Danny in the face. Don't use any thyroid tilt or vibrato – so the vocal colour is very direct and without ornamentation.

3. The title words of the song should be delivered in a clipped, staccato fashion. This helps convey the sarcasm behind them.

4. When you sing the words 'I hope you die' it is fun to make your sound quite childish, as Bashore does on the suggested recording. To achieve this sound, lift your larynx a little, make your sound more staccato and forgo any vibrato.

5. When you sing about the fact you may have gone too far, try singing in a brash Twang quality, with a very tight AES, as Bashore demonstrates on the suggested recording.

6. Bashore makes a lovely vocal choice when she sings in an almost operatic Sob quality about giving the relationship one more try. If you want to copy this set-up, remember to lower the larynx slightly, use plenty of thyroid tilt, and run the vowels together. This makes a pleasing comedic contrast if you then snap back into a Speech quality when you tell Danny that 'he sucks'.

7. Try returning to a whiny Twang set-up when singing the Latin section.

8. The build-up that begins with you saying that you want Danny to be beaten should be delivered once again in a Speech quality.

9. The words 'goodbye' and 'die' near the end of the song should be belted. Remember to tilt your cricoid cartilage, lift your larynx, raise your chin slightly and add some torso anchoring at this point.

Sheet Music

The correct sheet music for this song is available at www.musicnotes.com.

'Moments in the Woods'
from *Into the Woods*

Music and lyrics by Stephen Sondheim

Choose this song if: you are an actress who enjoys handling
extremely complex and intricate lyrics. The song is relatively
easy from a vocal perspective, and allows you to explore both
comedic and poignant moments.

Given Circumstances

WHO ARE YOU: A character known only as the Baker's Wife, a
stubborn, brave and wilful peasant woman in your early
thirties.

WHERE ARE YOU: Deep within the woods. Here the natural
order has been disturbed; many of the trees have been
splintered and broken.

WHEN IS IT: 4.30 p.m., autumn. (As *Into the Woods* is set in a
fairytale kingdom, establishing a year that the piece is set is
both problematic and unnecessary. Because of the feudal nature
of the social hierarchy, it is sensible to assume that the story is
set in a world with similarities to the European Middle Ages.)

WHAT HAS HAPPENED BEFORE: Twelve months ago you were
struggling to have a baby. This situation had been causing a
great deal of tension between you and your husband, the
Baker. At that time you were both paid a visit by your next-
door neighbour, the Witch, who revealed that many years ago
she had caught your father-in-law stealing her beloved
vegetables from her garden – including a handful of magic
beans. The Witch told you both that when she caught your
father-in-law she had demanded that he hand over his
daughter in return, whose name was Rapunzel. This news was
a great surprise to your husband, as he never known that he
had a sister.

The Witch went on to reveal that after your father-in-law had handed over Rapunzel, she was still not satisfied in her revenge. So she cast a spell on him that meant that he – and all his future descendants – would be infertile. And so you discovered that this curse was the reason why you had not been able to conceive.

Having told you this tale, the Witch then promised that she would lift the spell if you would help her collect the ingredients she required to make a potion, these being: a white cow, a red cape, a lock of yellow hair and a golden slipper. The Witch needed the potion to reverse a spell of ugliness and old age that had been placed on her by her own mother as a punishment when she'd discovered that the magical beans had been stolen. The Witch wanted your help because she was not able to touch any of the ingredients herself if the potion was to work.

Your husband then set off into the woods to find the necessary ingredients. At first he refused your assistance, as he said that the spell had been placed on his house, and so it was his responsibility alone to undo. This left you feeling shunned and ignored, so you decided to follow him discreetly.

Once in the woods the Baker realised that if the quest was to succeed you would need to work together as a couple. Your newfound sense of teamwork helped bring you both closer together – and repaired some of the issues you had been having in your relationship. Whilst searching for the ingredients the Baker encountered an enigmatic stranger known as the Mysterious Man. This man, who was secretly his father, was trying to help him undo the spell for which he was responsible.

Eventually, with the help of the Mysterious Man, all of the ingredients were found. Amongst various other complications, this involved you buying the white cow from Jack in exchange for the magic beans. When those beans were subsequently discarded in disgust by Jack's Mother they grew overnight into a huge beanstalk that reached right up into the sky, where there lay a Giant's castle. Once located, the ingredients were turned into a potion that the Witch swiftly drank – restoring her health and beauty, whilst the Mysterious Man promptly died, having played his part in helping lift the curse. You then fell pregnant – and all expected to live happily ever after.

Less than a year later, shortly after you gave birth, your life was thrown into chaos when the Giant's Wife came down the beanstalk looking to take revenge on Jack – who had killed her husband. With one of her footsteps the giantess stood on your house – completely destroying it. This led to yourself and your husband entering the woods once more, this time to escort Little Red Riding Hood, who was on her way to see her grandmother. Little Red's house had also been destroyed by the giantess and her mother was now missing, presumed dead.

In the woods you encountered the Royal Family who were fleeing the kingdom because the Giant's Wife had attacked their castle. Whilst you were all in conversation, the Giant's Wife appeared and demanded that you hand over Jack. In order to fool her, the Royal Family's Steward lied and said that Jack was hiding in a nearby steeple tower – and so the giantess set off to find him. With the Witch threatening to hand over Jack to the Giant's Wife, you and your husband concluded that you must locate him first – and the quickest way to do so was if you split up. An argument then occurred when you decided that you would leave your baby with Little Red, a decision your husband didn't agree with. As a consequence you parted company following cross words.

Soon after parting from your husband you encountered Prince Charming, who last year was married to Cinderella, and who now was out to slay the Giant. Prince Charming was extremely attractive and this made you giddy in his presence. Taking advantage of the fact you were alone, Prince Charming overcame your flimsy protestations and seduced you into having sex with him in the bushes. With the intercourse concluded you have just asked him if you will meet again. However, having been fully sated, and with no intention of ever seeing you again, Cinderella's Prince has just made his excuses and disappeared down the path to find the giantess.

WHO ELSE IS THERE: You are alone.

WHO SHOULD YOU SING TO: Yourself, though in audition you can share many of your thoughts with the panel as though they are your inner-consciousness.

Textual Analysis

When the introduction begins you are completely stupefied. You have just finished having amazing and satisfying sex with a man who is handsome, rich and powerful – a man you might usually only dream of. Your objective when you first begin singing is therefore: to work out whether your encounter with Prince Charming really happened. You are in this dreamlike state until you realise that you returned the prince's kiss – and have committed adultery. In the second stanza your objective then becomes: to work out what the consequences of your actions will be.

Indulging yourself in this contemplative manner is most unlike you, as you are normally incredibly realistic and practical. So you quickly become impatient with yourself for this self-indulgent behaviour, when you comprehend that these daydreams will never amount to anything. In the section after you've told yourself to wake up, and during the first chorus, your objective thus becomes: to get back to reality. Try playing actions such as: I discipline, instruct, chastise, correct and censure myself at this point.

Despite your best efforts to pull yourself together, you begin to daydream again in the next stanza – when you ask yourself if you might be able to have both Prince Charming and your husband. Your objective here is: to work out if a secret affair might be possible. Just when you are close to surrendering to these adulterous temptations you cry 'Never!' and try to push them from your mind. In the second verse your objective therefore becomes: to get yourself back on task. You tell yourself that it is not realistic to have relationship with a member of the Royal Family, and that you should instead concentrate on finding Jack and stopping the Giant.

COMEDY/CHARACTER

After trying to reset your mind you then take a brief moment to reflect on your encounter with Prince Charming; you lament that it was only a passing moment and it will never happen again. Your objective in this unit is: to work out why life always proves to be a disappointment. By asking yourself this philosophical question you come up with an interesting conclusion: if life was full of special, stand-out moments then they would stop being exciting and unique – and so would lose their significance. You continue to philosophise during the third verse when you list everything that has happened to you recently. Try playing the following objective in this unit: to find the irony in the hard times you have endured. You want to make yourself smile.

In the penultimate stanza you firmly tell yourself to let go of what just happened with Prince Charming, but also to never forget it. Your objective in this section is: to learn the lessons of your adultery. You are completely successful in this objective and make a fundamental discovery, which is the event of the song: that by sleeping with Prince Charming – and finding it ultimately unsatisfying – you have discovered how much you truly love your husband.

KEY MOMENTS/TOP TIPS

1. An interesting reading of this song is that the Baker's Wife has just experienced her first ever orgasm. This is why she is in a state of disbelief as the song begins, as this has never occurred in all of the years that she has slept with her husband.

2. Throughout the entire show the lyrics of the songs are occasionally punctuated by heavily accented chords. Sondheim uses this musical device to highlight where the characters have moments of realisation or self-discovery. One such moment occurs in this song after the Baker's Wife talks about kissing Prince Charming back – it is at this precise moment that she wakes up to the fact that she has just committed adultery. Try marking this moment of epiphany, perhaps with a physical still point.

3. At a couple of points in the song you speak about how life forces you to choose between an 'or' and an 'and'. Here you are debating about why you have to choose between the Baker and Prince Charming. It needs to be very clear who you are talking about in these moments. Whenever you are talking about 'or' you are referring to your husband; each time you speak about 'and' you are referencing Prince Charming.

4. Immediately after this song the Baker's Wife is killed by the Giant. It adds a greater sense of poignancy in that she only realises what her husband truly really means to her at the moment of her death.

Vocal and Musical Analysis

WHO TO LISTEN TO: Imelda Staunton on the original London cast recording (1990).

VOCAL RANGE: F3 to D5.

ORIGINAL KEY: E♭ major.

ACCENT: When performed in the UK, *Into the Woods* is usually delivered with British accents. As the Baker's Wife is a peasant, and from a village in the countryside, it makes sense to use a regional, rural accent when you play her. For example, Yorkshire, Lancashire, West Country, Irish, Welsh and Scottish accents work well. If your native accent is a rural one, then I would advise you to use your own voice when singing this song – but try turning up the strength a little. This is generally good practice when singing to ensure the choice is clearly perceived by the audience. Accents that stereotypically denote upper class (i.e. Received Pronunciation) and city accents (such as Cockney, Liverpool, Mancunian) are not appropriate.

STYLE OF MUSICAL: Concept musical.

VOCAL SET–UP/MUSICAL TIPS

1. The song starts with a line of spoken dialogue that is not on the suggested recording. This should be included for audition purposes.

2. Try delivering the opening of the song in a quiet, dreamy Cry quality, as Staunton clearly demonstrates. Tilt your thyroid cartilage, thin your vocal folds, raise your larynx and make use of legato phrasing. You can add some aspirate onsets for emphasis, as Staunton does repeatedly on the word 'kiss'.

3. When you tell yourself to wake up, you should suddenly shift into a thick-fold Speech quality, as Staunton chooses to do. The choruses of the song should be delivered entirely in this set-up. Because of the density of Sondheim's writing in these sections, with the Baker's Wife listing her rapidly changing thoughts and opinions, it can sometimes be hard for the audience to keep up with some of the complex ideas. By minimising the amount of thyroid tilt you use, and staying in a horizontal position, you fill find that the sense of the lyric is clearer for the audience.

4. There are sections of the song in which the Baker's Wife is reflective and begins to daydream. These should be delivered in a Cry quality. Sondheim helpfully sets these sections at slightly higher pitches, so the transitions into using thyroid tilt comes easily and naturally. The sections that should be sung in Cry are as follows: A) when you consider whether you might be able to have both the Baker and the prince; B) in the section when you tell yourself that the encounter with the prince was just a moment; and C) when you long for your life to be made entirely of moments. You can hear Staunton demonstrate all of these shifts with great skill.

5. The word 'never' should be half-spoken. This helps you to get back into a Speech quality in time for the second verse.

6. After the word 'grand', Sondheim indicates the next line should be sung very quietly. By following this instruction,

and suddenly changing the dynamic, it helps portray that this thought has taken the Baker's Wife by surprise.

7. There is a moment of discovery halfway through the song when you realise what woods are for: they are a place to have experiences that are out of the ordinary, like sleeping with a prince. In order to highlight this moment of revelation you should insert a pause before you sing this lyric, and then deliver it in a thoughtful Cry quality. The same approach should be used for the final event of the song when you realise how much the Baker (your 'or') means to you.

8. The last line of the song should be delivered in an Advanced Speech quality. You will need to modify the set-up you have used earlier in the song by adding some torso anchoring and lifting your chin a little at this point. Avoid using too much thyroid tilt – this should feel like a moment that is shared bravely with the universe, rather than being too pretty or refined.

9. Sondheim, more than any other musical-theatre composer (with the possible exception of Bernstein), provides great detail in terms of dynamics. Search the score for all of the changes in volume, the crescendos, etc. These provide great clues to aid your interpretation.

Sheet Music

The correct sheet music for this song is available at www.musicnotes.com.

COMEDY/CHARACTER

'Notice Me, Horton'
from *Seussical*

Music by Stephen Flaherty, lyrics by Lynn Ahrens

Choose this song if: you have a bright, contemporary musical-theatre voice and enjoy playing offbeat, comedic characters who can be a little stroppy. The song also offers the opportunity to reveal moments of sensitivity and vulnerability.

Given Circumstances

WHO ARE YOU: Gertrude McFuzz, a 'girl-bird'. You are very under-confident as your self-esteem has been diminished by the fact that you only have one feather in your tail. You can be demanding and greedy and are prone to throwing tantrums.

WHERE ARE YOU: In a clover field, far from the Jungle of Nool.

WHEN IS IT: Late afternoon, near the end of a long day, in a fantastical time.

WHAT HAS HAPPENED BEFORE: You are the next-door neighbour of Horton the Elephant. A few days ago Horton was bathing in the jungle when he heard a noise coming from a speck of dust. Upon investigation he concluded that there must be a minute person sat upon the speck, so he placed it on a cloverleaf for safekeeping. The other animals in the jungle mocked him for his behaviour, but you did not. You admired Horton's compassion and began to fall in love with him. Soon Horton discovered that the speck was, in fact, a planet inhabited by microscopic creatures called the Whos. When they told him of their plight – that their planet was on the brink of war and all of their beloved Truffula Trees have been cut down – Horton resolved to guard the clover even more fiercely.

Meanwhile, with your feelings towards Horton growing ever stronger, you had grown despondent at the meagreness of your tail. After taking advice from Mayzie La Bird, who has a fabulous tail, you decided to visit Doctor Dake by the Lake. The doctor prescribed you pills that would make your feathers grow. Upon taking your first tablet you were ecstatic with the initial results – and so proceeded to overdose on them. As a result your tail grew to such an impractical size that you could no longer fly. In fact, you could barely walk.

Soon after you had acquired your unusually large tail, Horton was ambushed by a bunch of monkeys known as the Wickersham Brothers. They stole his precious clover and ran off with it. Horton gave chase, but the monkeys passed the clover on to an eagle named Vlad Vladikoff, who promptly flew away. Horton followed the bird until eventually Vlad dropped the stolen item into a field of identical clovers one hundred miles wide.

Since then Horton has been desperately searching for his clover, hoping the Whos are still alive. Despite the huge distance he had travelled, and your restricted mobility, you managed to track Horton all this way. With him completely absorbed in his search of the field, you have just arrived to show him your magnificent new tail, in the hope that it might win his affections.

WHO ELSE IS THERE: Horton.

WHO SHOULD YOU SING TO: Horton.

Textual Analysis

At the start of the song – having finally managed to catch up with Horton – you immediately rush into a conversation with him. Your performance should therefore begin like an avalanche of semi-garbled speech; the words should pour out of you. In the first half of this opening section your objective is: to make Horton understand how difficult it was to track him down. You want him to pity you, and to acknowledge the great effort you have made. He remains totally unresponsive, so after the word 'deserts' you change tack and a new unit begins. In the second half of the opening section your objective becomes: to prepare Horton for some important news. That news is that you love him. Your sensitive demeanour proves to be of little interest to Horton, and with his head still buried in the clover field, your objective in the first verse then becomes: to get him to look up and admire your tail. You attempt to do this in a very self-deprecating manner, by first prefacing the revelation of your tail with a list of what you perceive to be your physical faults: your small eyes, your large feet and your pitiful tweet. As you are completely unsuccessful in trying to make Horton notice your wonderful new appendage, your objective in the first and second choruses thus becomes: to get Horton to notice you. In order to achieve this you might try out such actions as: I awaken, shake, disrupt and annoy Horton.

During the bridge section, which starts when you say you were just a no one yesterday, you begin to speak with direct emotional honesty. Your objective in this unit is: to make Horton see that he has changed you for the better. You feel that by falling for him you have now found a reason to exist. Try strong, dynamic actions at this point such as: I invigorate, rejuvenate, uplift and energise you. You think you may have finally got through to Horton, but he becomes ever more absorbed in his search for the Whos. Your objective in the last section, when you briefly talk to yourself, then becomes: to renew your determination to make Horton your boyfriend. Having given yourself this brief pep talk, in the final lines you then return to the objective inherent in the title lyric: to get Horton to notice you.

KEY MOMENTS/TOP TIPS

1. As Gertrude has been on a long chase, burdened by her enormous new tail, it can be fun to play the opening section as if you are out of breath. You might run into the space during the introduction and then use aspirate onsets to portray your breathlessness. You might also take a comedic, lung-fillingly large breath after the word 'deserts'.

2. Although Gertrude is a bird, it is not necessary or appropriate to undertake a birdlike transformation in an audition context. You might want to inhabit the physicality of someone who is awkward and nerdy – and find a moment to shake your imaginary tail feather at the panel!

3. The key motivator for Gertrude during the song is, of course, that Horton completely ignores her. To act the song well, you need to imagine Horton's absorbed behaviour throughout. At different moments he might turn his back, walk over to a new clover, or become lost in his own thoughts.

4. There is a lovely moment to be found in the second chorus when you directly order Horton to put down the clover. Try doing this in a very bossy, frustrated manner, as you losing your temper over something so silly can be amusing for the audience.

Vocal and Musical Analysis

WHO TO LISTEN TO: Janine LaManna on the original Broadway cast recording (2000).

VOCAL RANGE: F♯3 to G5.

ORIGINAL KEY: C major.

ACCENT: General American.

STYLE OF MUSICAL: Contemporary musical (pop-based).

VOCAL SET-UP/MUSICAL TIPS

1. The beginning of the song should be delivered in a Speech quality, with a little twang added to make the sound appropriate for contemporary American musical theatre. This is the set-up LaManna demonstrates on the suggested recording.

2. The first verse should be quieter, sweeter and delivered in a legato fashion. At this point raise your larynx, employ

simultaneous onsets, a tilted thyroid quality, and run the vowels together. Also tighten the AES slightly to maintain some twang.

3. The two choruses should be delivered in a bright Twang quality – which needs to be louder and brighter than the verse. You should therefore tighten the AES a little more, particularly on the top notes, so they really 'ping'.

4. During the broadest musical section (that is sung in harmony with Horton in the musical) you have two options. You can either move into a Speech quality, and then use a mixed belt for the higher notes (by adding some torso anchoring, lifting your chin slightly and adding some thyroid and cricoid tilt), or if you find this position difficult you can remain in a Twang quality throughout. The former choice is probably more dynamic.

5. Ignore the harmony line sung by Horton in the aforementioned section and sing the melody at all times. You also don't need to sing Horton's interjections that come later in the song. Score out the words he sings on your sheet music with a ruler, but don't delete the piano accompaniment that plays underneath. The only bars that should be cut are bars 52 and 53, when Horton sings the words 'over' and 'clover'. Leave bar 54 as single-bar pick-up into big musical release that follows.

6. Try singing the last line in a sweet and vulnerable Cry quality.

Sheet Music

The correct sheet music for this song is available at www.scribd.com.

'Times Like This'
from *Lucky Stiff*

Music by Stephen Flaherty, lyrics by Lynn Ahrens

Choose this song if: you would like to sing a love song that is
suitable for a idiosyncratic, unconventional character actress.
The song offers the opportunity for comedic moments and
contains a belt to a C♯.

Given Circumstances

WHO ARE YOU: Annabel Glick, a thirty-year-old representative
of the Universal Dogs' Home of Brooklyn. You dedicate your
life to the good cause of helping animals. This is a task you
take incredibly seriously, and leads you to put your work
before your personal life, even if this means denying yourself
the opportunity for love and happiness. In a sense, this is a
sort of self-defence mechanism, as you are frightened to be
romantically vulnerable.

WHERE ARE YOU: The Club Continentale, Monte Carlo, France.

WHEN IS IT: 8.20 p.m., a Saturday, some time in the early
1990s.

WHAT HAS HAPPENED BEFORE: Yesterday Harry Witherspoon, a
poor shoe salesman from London, discovered that he had
been willed six million dollars by Tony Hendon – a rich
American uncle whom he had never met. (Harry later learns
that this is not, in fact, true.) The real story is that Tony
Hendon was the manager of a casino in Atlantic City and had
been having an affair with Rita La Porta – the wife of the
casino's owner, Nicky. Tony and Rita had embezzled six
million dollars in diamonds from Nicky and were planning to
elope to Europe. However, the previous night Rita had gone to
visit Tony at his house and seen a woman leaving in the early
hours of the morning. In a jealous temper she went into the

house to confront Tony. The house was dark, and Rita – who is legally blind and who was not wearing her glasses – accidently shot dead a man whom she believed to be Tony. (Later in the show we find out she actually shot Luigi Gaudi, a friend of Tony's, and that the whole scheme since then has been an elaborate plot by Tony to escape with the diamonds – he is actually alive and well.)

Back in London, when Harry was told about the will by Hendon's solicitor, he learned that in order to receive his 'inheritance' he must first complete a very bizarre request. He would have to take his uncle's embalmed corpse (it is really Luigi's corpse) on one last holiday to Monte Carlo (Hendon has set this up as a tribute to his dead friend Luigi). Harry agreed to this unusual demand and set off for Southern France with the corpse, pretending his 'uncle' was actually still alive.

Since Harry has set off you have been secretly following him, as you have discovered an important loophole in Hendon's will (it is really Luigi's will). The loophole suggests that if Harry does not adhere to every detail of the legal document – which contains a detailed schedule for the holiday that involves taking the corpse to certain places at exact times – then he will be in default and the entire inheritance will instead go to the Universal Dogs' Home of Brooklyn, rather than to Harry. This is because the dogs' home was Hendon's (in reality Luigi's) favourite charity.

All day you have been trailing Harry – and the corpse – around Monte Carlo, trying to catch him making a mistake and not accurately following the schedule. After an exhausting day, twenty minutes ago you both arrived at the club, exactly on time. Since then Harry has been receiving the romantic attentions of a beautiful and glamorous showgirl, Dominique, whilst you have been sat alone in the corner doing some knitting for the dogs' home. Dominique has just had the whole club on their feet dancing, leaving you feeling embarrassed and isolated, as you were left alone on the periphery whilst she continued to flirt with Harry (to whom you are secretly attracted).

WHO ELSE IS THERE: At this point in the show the club is full of partying guests, but they are all frozen – so for the purposes of audition you should behave as if you are alone.

WHO SHOULD YOU SING TO: Yourself, though in an audition you can share many of your thoughts with the panel as though they are your inner-consciousness.

Textual Analysis

During the introduction you are feeling tetchy. The whole of the club has just been partying and enjoying themselves, and you feel socially excluded. Your objective in the opening section is: to convince yourself that you are happy being on your own.

In the first verse, to try and suppress your unhappy feelings, you begin to remember the kind face of one of your canine friends. Your objective at this point is: to cheer yourself up by thinking about a dog. Try playing actions such as I warm, comfort, and protect myself at this point. During the second verse you then contrast the way that a dog treats you with how the rest of the world does, and most notably Harry. At this point your objective becomes: to persuade yourself that you are better off with a dog.

When you reach the bridge you begin to pass judgement on the flamboyant and fun-seeking behaviour of Harry, Dominique and the rest of the club. Your objective here is: to dismiss the frivolous conduct of the others. In doing so you are trying to validate your own workaholic existence. Then in the final verse, after you have belted (see point 4 below), your objective becomes: to imagine your own idea of a perfect evening. You try to wrap yourself up in this fantasy, like a warm blanket, so that you don't feel so lonely. The twist is that, now you have been to Monte Carlo and met Harry, you no longer want your companion on such an evening to be a dog. You want it to be Harry.

KEY MOMENTS/TOP TIPS

1. It is useful to remember that *Lucky Stiff* is a musical farce. This song should therefore be delivered in a manner that is heightened and comedic, whilst still being emotionally honest.

2. When you sing about not barking up a stranger's tree this is a reference to Harry. Use this moment to direct your annoyance at him, a frustration that masks your true feelings of attraction and longing.

3. There is a small pause after the words 'give me', before Annabel says that she would like a quiet night in alone. Try playing in this moment that Annabel was on the verge of saying what she really wants – which is to be taken out on a romantic date with a man, rather than sit at home on her own with a canine companion.

4. In the past Annabel has used her relationship with animals to protect herself from heartbreak, as she knows a dog will never let her down. In the very last words of the song, for the very first time, she discovers that a relationship with a pet will never bring her true fulfilment – she wants to have a proper relationship with a man, and she would like that man to be Harry. This is the event of the song.

Vocal and Musical Analysis

WHO TO LISTEN TO: Janet Metz on the York Theatre Company cast recording (2004).

VOCAL RANGE: F♯3 to C♯5.

ORIGINAL KEY: E major.

ACCENT: New York.

STYLE OF MUSICAL: Contemporary musical (pop-based).

VOCAL SET–UP/MUSICAL TIPS

1. The opening of the song should be delivered in a Speech quality. Try added some glottal onsets in this section to help up put across Annabel's annoyance and frustration at this point.

2. When you get to the main melody, sing in long legato phrases, to imitate and parody a conventional musical-theatre love song. Use a Twang quality in this main portion of the number.

3. The musical rests before you sing the words 'a dog' are important. They allow you to find a comedic moment, by undercutting the audience's expectations of a typical musical-theatre ballad. You can hear Metz demonstrate this on the suggested recording.

4. The word 'ground' should be belted. Remember to tilt your cricoid cartilage, lift your larynx, raise your chin slightly and add some torso anchoring at this point.

5. After the belt, the final section is best delivered in a sweet, quiet Cry quality to show Annabel's true vulnerability and loneliness.

Sheet Music

The correct sheet music for this song is available at www.musicnotes.com.

COMEDY/CHARACTER

www.nickhernbooks.co.uk

facebook.com/nickhernbooks

twitter.com/nickhernbooks